Multiple Multisensory | Busting the Ma

Multisensory rooms are widely used across the coun..y in schools, care settings, hospitals and homes. Even settings such as football stadiums and airports are installing multisensory environments. Nevertheless, a significant lack of effective research has led to a sense of unease around sensory rooms. This crucial book explores the use of multisensory rooms in order to ease that anxiety, taking the mystery out of multisensory rooms and supporting the reader to reflect and make the most out of their space.

Key features include:

- Guidance on creating sensory spaces on any budget, to suit any level of need.

- An overview of the history of multisensory rooms, and a detailed exploration of the actual way in which the rooms are used today.

- A framework for evaluating existing practices and equipment, in order to maximise the potential of the room.

- A focus on the practitioner as the most important piece of "equipment" in any sensory room.

Written by a leading sensory specialist in a fully accessible way, this book is an invaluable tool for anybody who uses, or is considering using, a multisensory room.

Joanna Grace is a Sensory Engagement and Inclusion Specialist, author, trainer, TEDx speaker and founder of The Sensory Projects. Through her work at The Sensory Projects she seeks to contribute to a future where people are understood in spite of their differences, doing this by sharing the knowledge and creativity required to turn inexpensive items into effective sensory tools for inclusion.

Joanna is an outstanding teacher who has worked supporting students of all abilities in mainstream and special school settings. Her work at The Sensory Projects extends beyond this to include adults and babies. Joanna has been a registered foster carer for children with additional needs. She is an avid consumer of research. When not on tour Joanna spends her time writing from her home in Cornwall in a tiny village with no road names or house numbers.

Multiple Multisensory Rooms: Myth Busting the Magic

Joanna Grace

Routledge
Taylor & Francis Group

LONDON AND NEW YORK

First published 2020
by Routledge
2 Park Square, Milton Park, Abingdon, Oxon OX14 4RN

and by Routledge
52 Vanderbilt Avenue, New York, NY 10017

Routledge is an imprint of the Taylor & Francis Group, an informa business

British Library Cataloguing-in-Publication Data
A catalogue record for this book is available from the British Library

Library of Congress Cataloging-in-Publication Data
A catalog record for this book has been requested

ISBN: 978-0-367-34185-5 (pbk)
ISBN: 978-0-429-32436-9 (ebk)

Typeset in Sabon
by Apex CoVantage, LLC

This book is dedicated to the man whose desire for change held my nose to the grindstone as I wrote.

My sincere thanks to all the people who helped me with my research through their advice and insight, and by giving up their precious time to be interviewed; without you this book would not have been made possible.

And thank you to Spike for seeing me through.

Contents

Foreword   xiii
Peter Imray
Foreword   xv
Richard Hirstwood
Introduction   1
   Orientation   2
   Your part in this conversation   4
   Address to parents   4
   Address to professionals   5
   Address to parents and professionals   7

Section 1   9
   Now back to the story. . . . Where did
   multisensory rooms begin?   9
   Orientation   9
      The institutions of the past   9
      The practices of the past   10
      A past touching distance away   11
      The structures of the past scaffold the present   13
   Overview   14
   F.I.S.H. (Find Idea Starters Here)   14
   The terms and conditions   15
   Orientation   15
      Language, labels, prejudice and understanding   15
      Let us do away with language   17
      We can do it without words   18
      With: new times – new terms   19
      The days of profound and multiple learning
      disabilities are numbered   20
      What name would you like?   21
      #flipthenarrative   22

Contents

Overview   23
F.I.S.H.   24
The dawning of Snoezelen   24
Orientation   24
    A tent pitched on history's barren grounds   24
    Change is defined by ideas, not spaces and objects 27
    It is not about the room, it is about the heart   28
Overview   30
One little F.I.S.H.   30
Five big F.I.S.H.   31
The beginning of multisensory rooms   33
Orientation   33
    The ownership of Snoezelen turns a philosophy into a room   33
    The branding of multisensory rooms changes how
information is shared and provokes the evolution of
a new philosophy   36
    Debating approaches   36
Overview   38
F.I.S.H.   38
Rooms multiply like rabbits   38
Orientation   38
    The proliferation of multisensory rooms and their use   39
    Massive overclaims about the efficacy of multisensory rooms
grow the multisensory room industry   40
    The proliferation of multisensory rooms is about more
than money   41
    Dangers arise from the misunderstandings   42
Further drivers of the proliferation of multisensory rooms   43
    Better than nothing   43
    Attractive   44
    A lack of research   45
Overview   46
F.I.S.H.   46

Section 2   47
Orientation   47
Why is there a lack of research?   47
Anti-research   48
So bad it could be funny   49
A stand-up routine of research fails   50
    Fibre optics and bubble tubes hold magical healing properties   50
    One person with an additional need represents all people with
that need, and two people with additional needs represent
anyone and everyone with any kind of additional need   50

The voice of staff is the voice of everyone   51
The love of multisensory rooms is universal and
knows no bounds   51
Control groups are not necessary, as one type of
additional need is the same as any other   51
The magic vanishes at the door   51
Overview   52
F.I.S.H.   52
What does it all mean?   52
Orientation   52
   Unpicking the dark humour   53
   The lack of research leaves us vulnerable   54
   Are claims that multisensory rooms do no harm valid?   55
   Funding is not available for other resources   55
Overview   56
F.I.S.H.   57
What does the research that is out there tell us about the
effectiveness of multisensory rooms?   57
Orientation   57
   Mixed and mild   58
   Mixed results   58
   Positive effects observed may be caused by other factors   58
   Mild findings   58
   It is not all positive   59
   We just do not have the proof . . . and that is scary   60
   Research is needed   60
   Do we really need it?   61
Overview   63
F.I.S.H.   63

Section 3   64
   Orientation   64
Without research advertising may take the place
of knowledge   64
The new era of multisensory rooms looks set to repeat
the mistakes of the past   67
No one is immune from bias   68
Overview   70
F.I.S.H.   70
Orientation   71
Is there another way?   71
Nature   72
Behaviour   73
Even if they work, are they worth it?   74

Contents

Overview   74

F.I.S.H.   75

Orientation   75

Alternative spaces   75

    Big spaces   76

        A tremendous tent   76

        A yomping yurt   77

        An improvised tent   77

        A hygge home   77

        A gorgeous garden   77

        A withy wonder   78

        Beautiful blackout   78

        Simply space   78

        Superb shadows   79

        Glorious gazebos   80

        Water worlds   80

    Small spaces   81

        Brilliant brollies   81

        Lovely "Little Rooms"   81

        Activity arches   82

        Sequence strings   82

        Happy Hula-Hoops and stupendous shower curtains   83

    Affordable   84

    Considerations   84

        A sense assessment   84

    Why would they want to go into the space?   85

    What do I want to explore in this space?   86

Overview   87

F.I.S.H.   87

Section 4   88

    Orientation   88

    Report from research: how are multisensory rooms

    currently being used?   88

    Results   90

    Overview of themes identified from the interviews   92

        Next to no one receives training on how to use a multisensory room, but pretty much everyone gets taught how to turn the equipment in a multisensory room on and off   92

        Non-directive users of multisensory rooms were more likely to see long-lasting effects from using the rooms   92

        Multisensory rooms are used with the intention of furthering engagement or promoting relaxation   93

    Questions prompted by these findings   93

Further findings relating to room accessibility	95
Multisensory rooms can be surprisingly inaccessible – design	95
Multisensory rooms can be surprisingly inaccessible – usage	96
Overview	98
F.I.S.H.	98
A detailed look at limiting factors influencing multisensory rooms	98
Orientation	98
Trigger-happy facilitators	98
Broken items	100
Difficult journeys to the multisensory rooms	101
Timetabling	102
Parked	104
Cinemas	105
Tech fear	106
Set up time	107
Containment zones	107
Overview	108
F.I.S.H.	108
The limitations of my research and the positive findings	109
Orientation	109
The limitations of my research	109
Positive findings	110
Control	110
Darkness	111
Uninterrupted	111
Focused	112
Wowness	112
Overview	114
F.I.S.H.	114
Section 5	**115**
Orientation	115
The most important piece of the kit	115
It is innate	117
Wheat from chaff	118
A dozen clues	119
Four characteristics of people who do not get it	119
Toughened	119
Power	120
Ended up here	121
Short thinking	122
Characteristics of people who do get it that are lacking from people who do not get it	123

Contents

Reflective   123

They see personhood as separate from functionality   124

Empathetic   130

Confident   131

Strategies to enable someone who does not get it to get it   133

Feedback   133

Teach in the way they learn   134

Generate awareness: experience, micro-steps and acceptance of difference   135

Develop their view of their role: moving people on from being stunned or stagnant in their practice   136

The wow space   137

Reflecting on the question   138

Why employing only those who get it does not exempt you from needing to provide ongoing support   139

Overview/F.I.S.H.   140

Focus on the positive   142

Orientation   142

The sensory story   143

Developing sensory awareness and ability   145

Hugh learning to see   146

Finding rest   148

Multisensory room with preschool-aged children   149

Making connections and gaining independence   149

Learning to reach   150

Learning to look   151

Ready, steady, go!   151

Barry's story (Hirstwood and Smith 1995, pp. 86–88)   153

Overview   154

F.I.S.H.   155

What about the people?   155

Orientation   155

Flo   155

Mo   157

In our weakness we find our strength   157

Use according to strengths   158

F.I.S.H.   159

Discussion   160

Conclusion   166

References   168

Index   173

Foreword

There are a number of reasons why you should read this book, not least of which are that Jo Grace has very interesting things to say and is a very talented writer. She has the uncanny knack of making us look again at what we have always looked at but never properly seen. In this book, as in her previous works, she is shouting at shibboleths, those secret passwords that everyone who works within special educational needs knows, and especially within the very specialist world of profound and multiple learning difficulties (PMLD) and severe learning difficulties (SLD). Indeed, even these terms are shibboleths for her to shout at.

But the main topic of this book is, as you've already gathered from the title, the Multisensory Room. Everyone knows (don't they?) that every special school and every adult care establishment for those with complex needs must have a sensory room, and that every child with complex needs must have access to a sensory room. Everyone knows (don't they?) that the sensory room has to have lots of specialist stuff in it, so that we can make connections with the very complex learners who occupy them. In a recent English educational tribunal appeal, the defence case of the mainstream school (that was objecting to a judgement that they should listen to the parental choice and take a pupil with complex needs) was built around the fact that they did not have a sensory room and therefore could not fulfil the Education, Health and Care Plan that noted its requirement. Everyone knows (don't they?) that sensory rooms for learners with complex needs are the equivalent of state of the art computer banks, one of the key means by which they can achieve parity and inclusion.

But the fact that everyone knows something does not make it the truth and this is the central point of Jo's book. When working with people who are the most vulnerable, who are so easy to dominate, for whom who it is so easy to assume that this is for the best or that is the answer, who need to be listened to but who struggle to be heard, we must always question. Question, question, question. Why am I doing what I'm doing? What am I trying to achieve? Am I making a difference? But we can't really answer these questions unless we have knowledge of profound and multiple learning difficulties; the deeper the knowledge we have the likelier we are to be able to answer these questions. However, as Jo is quick to point out, knowledge itself is not enough.

There is in education, a four letter word which is unspoken, viewed with deep suspicion, often regarded as the antithesis of teaching, of denoting weakness, spoken of occasionally but whispered not shouted, and with a certain embarrassment that the word should be mentioned at all. The word is used occasionally with very small children in early years, but it is soon abandoned and never mentioned at all at secondary level. We must, after all, be professional! If you haven't guessed it already, the word is love. This is something that Jo is not embarrassed about and perhaps indicates that Jo is taking on the mantle of other writers on profound learning difficulties who have gone before, and for whom love is also a central plank of education, notably Flo Longhorn, whose work I would also guide you towards should you not know it.

In the run up to the 1992 US presidential election, Bill Clinton's campaign team were discussing what the key issues might be, to which James Carville, a Clinton aide, replied *"The economy, stupid!"* In a variation on this, we might be reminded to look at our own schools and other places of education and care and in response to the apparently perplexing problem of what the key issues might be, answer succinctly *"The staff, stupid!"* And here's the central point of Jo's writings: we have to ensure that staff (all staff, not just teachers) are enabled and encouraged to gain knowledge and that this becomes a key element of budgeting, and equally importantly, we have to ensure that that all staff, including teachers, are allowed, enabled, encouraged, to love. With knowledge and love, we can move mountains.

Peter Imray

Foreword

It is with great pleasure that I contribute a foreword to this book written by Joanna Grace, a lady with great passion for her work.

Throughout this text, Joanna takes us on a roller coaster ride of the positives, negatives and challenges of the multisensory rooms in existence today.

This book made me angry and happy in equal parts. Not because what is written, but that as Joanna points out, the path that the multisensory room has followed is so different from the way it was supposed to be! Having being involved in the very early days of multisensory rooms here in the UK, with great designers, our aim was to design and develop spaces which would offer a new and exciting place for learning and exploration for anyone with a learning disability. What was intended as an addition to services available at the time appeared to become too commercialised.

Joanna takes us on a journey from the very early development of Snoezelen and its relevance to the thinking and ethos of special education at that time, through the rapid increase in numbers of these spaces, along with the commercialisation of multisensory rooms and the apparent lack of validation of this approach by relevant and rigorous research.

From the Dutch philosophy of Snoezelen first described by Hulsegge and Verhheul, which greatly inspired me when I first visited them in Holland, multisensory rooms have changed beyond all recognition from these early spaces. No longer is the multisensory room seen as a place for investigation, mindfulness and joy, but somewhere for achievement and progress to be measured and validated.

Joanna focuses on the issue of good design for a multisensory room – a subject very close to my heart. A well-designed multisensory room is a magical place for children and adults, young and old. But when a company simply sells a package of equipment to a buyer and when that buyer has limited knowledge of what they want or need, then the result will be a space that does not work effectively; and this theme is highlighted to great effect in the book.

Joanna's research for this book included a review of readily available articles pertinent to multisensory rooms and interviews with key stakeholders within the multisensory room field, including companies with a commercial interest and those who deliver training in the use of multisensory rooms (myself included), but most importantly, teachers and practitioners who use these spaces on a daily basis.

This research begins a conversation about how you, the practitioner, can maximise the effectiveness of your sensory space. Joanna reminds us that it is the skill of the practitioner, and not the cost of the multisensory room and its equipment within, which will have the most impact on efficacy of the space.

She rightly highlights the paucity of research into this area – that some of this has been commercially led research and that what research there is, some may feel offers little guidance to practitioners and potential buyers of these spaces. Joanna challenges you into action – what can you, the practitioner, offer to address this deficit in research?

Ultimately Joanna's text highlights a need for further research, questions the viability of a multisensory room today, asks about the practitioner's part in the process of its use, but most importantly, provides a framework to reflect upon maximising the effectiveness of your multisensory room or space. Joanna has drawn her conclusion, and this book will help you draw your own conclusions – is your multisensory room a valuable resource, when used to its maximum potential, or an expensive mistake?

If you are thinking that this book is going to paint a negative picture of multisensory rooms, fear not, because Joanna offers hope, ideas and observations and challenges you to make your multisensory room function well for you and the individuals with whom you are working. If you would like to reflect upon your own practice in your multisensory room or space, read on.

Richard Hirstwood

Introduction

Sensory rooms are multiple and multiplying. Conversations about them get confused as vastly different spaces are referred to by the same name. Their massive proliferation is, perhaps, driven more by our misunderstandings than it is by sales or successful outcomes. Yet in spite of these misunderstandings and a paucity of research into their effectiveness the government requires all special schools to have one in order to be considered to be adequately providing for their students (DFE 2015, p. 51).

It is likely that you, as someone who has picked up this book, currently feel a sense of unease around the use of multisensory rooms. Perhaps you have access to a wonderful room but do not feel you get the most out of it. Perhaps you want to create a room but are unsure what should be in it. Perhaps you have seen a brilliant room but doubt the benefits claimed by its proponents. Perhaps you have seen amazing things happen in a multisensory room but wonder if even they justify the extraordinary price tag on the room. Perhaps a great many things.

What you want is for someone to explain the rooms to you and sort the wheat from the chaff, explaining what about current practice and ideology is right and what is wrong.

I have seen the inside of many a multisensory room and supported some marvellous people to access the wonders within. In writing this book I conducted an extensive literature review reading every piece of research published on the use of multisensory rooms that I could find, along with many of the great books on multisensory rooms. I also conducted my own research, speaking to parents, practitioners, experts and installers of multisensory rooms across the UK to find out how the rooms are used today and to ask them difficult questions about the rooms' most important piece of the kit. I have been a special school teacher supporting children with complex disabilities within multisensory rooms and a foster carer for children with complex disabilities who enjoyed using multisensory rooms. I hold a master's degree in special education. I have friends and family members who also benefit from using multisensory rooms. Suffice to say I have a professional, personal and academic background that *could* enable me to claim authority. I *could* write what you are looking for, but it would be *my* view, and it would not be "right." It might be right in my eyes, but it would not be right across all cases and all circumstances.

No matter how well informed, or how experienced, no one person is in a position to tell you what is right for *your* multisensory room. Each room is, and should be, different. The needs placed on a room are different depending upon who enters the room and who supports their access. With so many permutations there is no one right way.

What we need is to have an informed way of thinking about multisensory rooms that enables us to clearly discern what we need, and do not need, in our rooms and how we should, or should not, use them.

I fear we are facing a case of that old adage: Give a man a fish and you will feed him for a day. Teach a man to fish and you will feed him and his family for life.

The trouble is that when you go about explaining to the hungry man that you will teach him to fish you risk being bashed over the head with the fishing rod so he can grab the fish currently in your hands.

So whilst I hope to teach you to fish I will also share with you some examples of great practice I have seen in multisensory rooms so that you can use them as inspiration now to sate your appetite.

The foolish teacher refuses to give out fish and insists on trying to teach a hungry student.

The foolish student takes a fish and does not stay for the lesson.

The only trouble is. . .

. . . I do not know how to fish!

But I do know how to tell stories. So what you will find in this book are stories, created from truth in one form or another, adapted from real life, compiled from several experiences, demonstrating a research finding, or created to highlight an aspect of practice. And by sharing these stories perhaps we can figure out how to fish together.

ORIENTATION

You picked up this book because you are a reflective individual and, whilst this book may not contain within its pages what you thought it would when you first picked it up, here you will find the history and insight you need to further hone your reflective nature and enable you to generate practice relevant to the people you support, whether that be within a multisensory room or within another sensory space.

Section 1 explores the foundations upon which our current multisensory rooms are built, foundations in history dating back to the old institutions, and foundations in practice with the early Snoezelen rooms and the later multisensory rooms. We look at the language that has described these rooms and the people who use them and how this has influenced thinking and practice. We recognise that the rooms have proliferated at an amazing rate and consider, in the light of their history, how this came about.

Section 2 looks at the knowledge foundations upon which multisensory room practice is based. We note the lack of methodologically sound research into the use of the rooms and unpick the reasons behind this deficit. Without firm guidance from evidenced based practice, we rely on information from advertisers to inform us about the rooms, and understandably this has many limitations. There are, of course, alternative ways to provide multisensory environments and in Section 3 you will find a bundle of ideas for alternative sensory spaces, big and small, together with advice on things to consider when enabling access to a sensory space and when resourcing that space with equipment.

Section 4 reports findings from a novel piece of research looking into how multisensory rooms are used within the UK, conducted specifically to inform the writing of this book. This research gives insight into the factors that can limit the effectiveness of the rooms, including those that make the rooms inaccessible, either by design or through poor usage. Knowledge of these potential limiting factors can help reflective practitioners to maximise the effectiveness of their sensory spaces, be they professionally installed multisensory rooms or small improvised multisensory environments. Interviewees questioned for the research were asked to identify the power behind the rooms and, beyond the controlled nature of the space, highlighted three key factors that they felt gave the rooms their power. These are all factors that can be actioned in improvised spaces as well as in professionally installed multisensory rooms and understanding their importance will help practitioners to get maximal benefit from their sensory-spaces.

Section 5 looks at the most important piece of the kit in a multisensory room: the people. The facilitator has long been recognised as the most important resource within a multisensory room but until now writers on the subject have shied away from inspecting this particular piece of equipment in any detail. Section 4 starts a conversation intended to tackle that taboo. With insight from the interviewees questioned during the research interviews we identify twelve factors that can influence the effectiveness of a person facilitating in a multisensory room and consider how we best support these people in order to ensure best practice within the space. We hear stories of incredible practice within multisensory spaces, big and small, that will help you to further reflect on what you want to do in your multisensory room or improvised sensory space.

The book ends with a discussion of what has been reflected on through its pages and the author's conclusion. You are of course free to draw your own conclusions. What you have in your hands is not a how-to guide; it is a tool for reflective practice. Although being told what to do is simple, being reflective is powerful. This book will empower you to enhance practice in your multisensory room or alternative sensory space.

Your part in this conversation

Before we begin, I want to remind you of who you are in this conversation. As someone reading this book you are likely to fall into one of two categories: 1) a parent to someone with a profound disability; or 2) a professional supporting people with profound disabilities. I acknowledge that among the readers there will be people without jobs but with a professional or simply compassionate interest, and people who are in a profession where they do not directly support people with profound disabilities but who have a curiosity or a desire to do so. Likewise there will be family members who are not parents, or primary carers who are not birth parents, and maybe you fall into both categories, but for simplicities sake forgive me, for now I am going with simply parents or professionals.

Address to parents

You are the people who know best what your child's life means, you feel their life with every beat of your heart. Your life and their life are so closely linked you would struggle to separate one from the other, or imagine one without the other. Before they were born you were other, you had your own life and interests and things you thought were important, but those things changed as they were born – as they do with the birth of any child, but for you they have changed more.

It is likely that you have had experiences that have left you traumatised. The love that connects you so powerfully to your child is like a giant elastic band and when catastrophes happen and threaten to break that connection the band twangs back from the blow and you feel the reverberations through the years. You lose sight of who you were, of who you are, even sometimes of who they are, as you shudder with the shock of the challenges thrown your way.

You look around at the people who seem to know more than you do. At people who seem more stable than you feel. You look around for people who hold answers for you. For people to help you. To help your child. You imagine they might know more than you do.

These people, myself among them, do not know more than you do.

No one knows more about your child than you do.

You are the expert.

You are the top professional when it comes to provision for your child.

You know best.

That you do not know about a particular practice, or how to operate a piece of machinery, or that you have not been trained in a particular medication or whatever it is, does not matter, for these are things you can learn; what you know is who they are. In all the chaos of the provision, and the lack of provision, that surrounds them, knowing who they are is the most important thing.

That love that threatens to break you, that flings you about, that keeps you awake at night, which is the source of all your fear and all your hope – that love is powerful. You know that better than most because your love has been tested and it remains.

Do not be frightened of its movement and do not doubt yourself because of it. You are powerful. You see them. You know who they are. Tell us, who they are, because the world is a better place for them being here, and we all stand to gain from knowing them better.

Address to professionals

In the workaday world it is easy to lose sight of why we do what we do. I remember this point being brought home to me so very clearly by a mother speaking at a conference about her deceased child. She described his life, one so extraordinarily precious to her. She told us of the trauma of his birth, she had been expecting a "normal" healthy child but the birth had become an emergency for both herself and the child and together they fought for their lives.

For the first hours, days, weeks and months of this child's life no one could say whether he would live or die. Over the first few years of his life the medical team around him became more adept at meeting his needs and managing his condition and he became more stable. He was several years old before he was able to leave hospital, and even then he was only able to leave because his mother and father had themselves pretty much trained to become medical professionals in the intervening years, learning to carry out all the complex procedures required to keep their son alive and to save his life if his condition threatened it.

Taking her son home had been a cause for celebration and terror, the celebration of a milestone reached, and the terror of all the "what ifs" that mounted up as they wondered if they would cope at home. It took an enormous effort to cope, now sleep deprived and weary from years of trauma with their old lives no more than a smudge on the window of their minds.

Through his early childhood he had many emergency admissions to hospital. Once again the teams were called to rally about him and save his life. Once again the family rang around their well-established support network calling for people to bring them clothes, to collect their other children from school, to let people know. The dark terror of nearly losing him was as dark four years on as it had ever been, the only difference was that now they were used to it, it had become their normal.

Time and again he would come home from hospital and they would celebrate anew his return home. But the celebrations were fragile and always at the forefront of their mind was the thought of what would be next, would the next time be the time they lost him?

The mother showed us photographs of him at this time, a pale sad-faced child surrounded by adults with fear in their eyes, prematurely grey and aged by the stress of the years. She stopped on a particular image of a birthday party. The room full of medical equipment, boxes, and the trappings of disability – wedges, wheelchairs, hoists, pumps, monitors – looked more like a hospital ward than a home. In front of the child sat a cake with candles burning on it. Candles he would not be able to blow out. And his mother stood in front of us at that conference looking into the photo, into a past where her son was still alive.

"We wondered if we had done the right thing in keeping him alive." She said aloud, "We had made such extraordinary efforts but for what? He was in so much pain, we did not go out for fear of infection. There was no joy in his life."

"When we keep people alive we make a promise to them, and we should match that promise by giving them equal support to live the life that we have held onto for them."

"My family and I did everything we could for our child, but we did not help him to live."

"And then he went to school."

She clicked over to the next slide on her presentation and there was a photo of that same child but his face had colour in it and he was laughing.

"School is where he lived."

We, as an audience, watched relieved and elated as she clicked through a multitude of slides that showed her son engaged and happy taking part in all sorts of activities at his school. There were enough memories in those pictures to outweigh the terror of those early years, to give her a memory of a life lived to grieve, not the guilt of a death prolonged over many years.

Seeing him take part in activities at school had in time given the family confidence to have fun at home. They began to see him as a child who could play and have fun, not purely a medical emergency to be managed. His siblings came forward in the pictures; they were the experts in play and now that their brother was allowed to be a part of games they clearly relished taking the lead and including him in their mischief. At times silliness overwhelmed the seriousness for a moment or two and he was seen for the boy he was, not the disabilities he had.

We all get used to our normal with surprising speed. The lady I am remembering had had a life before her son was born, a life that vanished and her new life of parenting a medically fragile child began and rapidly became her normal.

We who support children like her son get used to the normal of our day-to-day routines. A child reaches for a toy for the first time, someone vocalises, we wipe another bottom, hoist another body. We have seen a seizure before, we have seen vomit and blood before, and we are familiar with the cry of the ambulances sirens. We get up on a Monday and think "work today"; we go home on Friday and think "weekend."

That our day-to-day actions have the capacity to be life changing is far from our minds, and even on days when we see something truly remarkable, like someone's first steps, the brightness of such moments is still dulled by the fug of it being everyday.

This is just what we do and we do not count ourselves as remarkable, so what we do must be ordinary, must it not?

What you do not only has the power to be life changing every day, it is life giving. Enabling people with complex disabilities to engage with the world and access sensation and communication enables them to live the life they have. Your job can be the difference between someone being simply alive and someone living the life they have. As everyday as it may be to you, it is far from ordinary.

Address to parents and professionals

When I think about how quickly extraordinary circumstances become ordinary to us I am reminded of a quote from Marianne Williamson (1992), often misattributed to Nelson Mandela:

> Our deepest fear is not that we are inadequate. Our deepest fear is that we are powerful beyond measure. It is our light, not our darkness that most frightens us. We ask ourselves, Who am I to be brilliant, gorgeous, talented, fabulous? Actually, who are you not to be? . . . as we let our own light shine, we unconsciously give other people permission to do the same. As we are liberated from our own fear, our presence automatically liberates others.

When you support people who lead foreshortened lives, or people whose lives are impinged upon by the disabilities they have, it is worth remembering just what you do. Remember that although it is normal to you, it is not in any way normal: it is extraordinary.

Earlier, I described a young man's life as being extraordinarily precious to his mother. That is misleading. What happens when life is threatened, or hampered by disability, is that it brings to the fore how precious life is; not extraordinarily precious but ordinarily so.

All life is precious. One life is no more or less precious than the next one, the life of a medically fragile individual is no more precious than the life of a non-disabled child, no more so than your own life. In daily facing what might be lost, or what has been lost, we are reminded of how brightly life can shine and we may seek to bring that brightness to those we feel need it more. But all lives should shine so brightly, should be lived so brilliantly, yours included.

I want you to remember that your everyday normal is not so everyday. It is not a grey wash of one week blending into the next, it is your today and it is their today. Live it viscerally, for yourself as well as for the people you support. Now is all we have.

These sentiments are all well and good, but I acknowledge some people tend towards a more nihilist attitude. For example one of my interviewee's said: "no one asks to be

7

born, we all die anyway, there is no point. There is nothing after death and life is just hard, why bother?"

For the nihilists out there, I have spoken to a few of you in writing this book and on occasion count myself among you: take the nothingness as an invitation towards creativity, as a means of liberating yourself.

Leaving aside debates about the afterlife, there is truth in what was said: birth is something that happens to us, life throws many challenges our way and we do all die in the end. Inspect anything closely enough, take it apart, understand its component parts for meaning until they become transparent to your mind and you are left with nothing.

But nothingness need not be cause for gloom. In fact nothingness, in its nothingness, can be whatever you choose it to be; you can act on it with your will and make of life whatever you want from it. We are a movement across that empty canvas, rather than a mark upon it. You can dance, you can fight, you can flee, you can race; there are many ways to move. My advice would be to live with love; let that be your movement, and you will not regret it.

(I know there are people who will write me off for my use of the word love, and presume this book to be a work of nonsense not something grounded in the cold hard realities of daily life, but there is a growing body of evidence to show that love has a powerful effect on the developing brain, and we who support people with complex brains should not turn our noses up at anything that could have power to affect them in the positive, however fluffy it may sound. See Gerhardt [2004] for an overview of the latest findings from neuroscience, psychology, psychoanalysis and biochemistry with regards to love and its impact on the developing brain.)

Section

Now back to the story. . . . Where did multisensory rooms begin?

ORIENTATION

The value of looking back into a history where multisensory rooms did not exist might not be immediately apparent. However understanding the past helps us to appreciate the circumstances under which multisensory rooms originally emerged. The practices we currently follow, and the understanding we currently have, has grown out of this history.

Reflecting on the practices of the past and the drivers of changing attitudes enables us to better evaluate our own position today. We are not separate from the history of provision for people with profound disabilities; we are a part of it.

The coming four sections offer the briefest of sketches of how people with learning disabilities were provided for in the past and of how people's attitudes towards them have changed, shaped by the cultural understanding of their day, just as our own attitudes now are shaped by the cultural understanding of our day. We are the people of tomorrow's past. What will people looking back on us think of what we do now?

The institutions of the past

Think back to the days of the institutions: big buildings constructed on the outskirts of town where shamed mothers hounded by their families to do the right thing brought their children and left them there. Mothers giving birth to a child with a disability were told that it was for the best that they should let the child die, "poor little mite, what kind of life would it have anyway?" These places seem far away in the depths of time but actually they are really quite recent.

The reasons for the abandonment of children changed through time: the child was sick, or subhuman – not really a child at all. The child was a danger, polluting an otherwise pure bloodstream, the child was a burden on the family and the society. The child was the problem and if the mother were to do the right thing then the child should go. Children were left outside to perish. If the child lived the mother was told to discard it; "take it to the institution and forget about it, never speak of it, you can have another baby."

People with certain disabilities, for example epilepsy, were considered cursed, with seizures commonly being understood as the devil working within someone. The community as a whole would reject the child who experienced a seizure and place enormous social pressure on the mother to dispatch the child to the institution for fear of the consequences having the child live among them could reap.

These responses to children with disabilities were not the individual prejudices of uneducated or overly religious sections of society – they were enshrined in law. The 1913 Mental Capacity Act in the UK demanded that the feeble minded of society be identified, rounded up and locked up. Teachers were asked to identify imbeciles in their classes so that they could be institutionalised. The act saw close to 40,000 individuals locked up.

Although reading about the 1913 Mental Capacity Act now seems horrific, it was actually a part of the progress of the time; it used terms like idiot and imbecile to distinguish people from one another, which was a step on from what had happened previously. In 1886 the Idiots Act had distinguished people with mental illness from people with a learning disability. Further steps in identification were movements closer to a recognition of individual identity.

In 1902 one of the first institutions for people with learning disabilities was set up: the Sandlebridge Colony (later known as the Mary Dendy Hospital, closing finally in 1986) for the permanent care of the feeble minded. The Sandlebridge Colony was considered progressive, for now the community had a place for their rejects.

The practices of the past

In institutions through the 1920s to the 1950s you would expect to see staff treating the people living within their walls with distain, contempt and cruelty. Were the people working in these places somehow uniquely unpleasant, or if we had lived at that time would it have been us?

We all operate against the backdrop of a wider social understanding. At a time when people with learning disabilities were not considered human it is no surprise to find they were treated as unhuman. Think how you treat a fly, or an ant crawling over your picnic – animals you consider to be less than human. This is how you treat something "subhuman" and they did the same as you do for those living things whom they met who were "subhuman."

In old photographs it is common to see people tied to pillars and posts by their bed-sheets. We see people chained to their beds, or simply with their arms bound behind their back by sheets or straightjackets. Staff deployed binding as a means to prevent people from injuring themselves or one another, or from taking part in activities staff considered wrong. If you work supporting people with learning disabilities now you can probably recognise who those bound people would have been.

We recoil in horror that any human could have been so callous to another human being. In our minds we attack these torturers of a bygone age. But perhaps our mental energies would be better spent wondering about which of our current practices will be looked back upon by people forty years on from us and condemn as being inhumane. For we are not so naive to think that progress has finished with us, are we?

1890 saw the rise of eugenics, and with it came the notion that we should keep our bloodlines clean – dispensing of people who contaminate them in any way through sterilisation or segregation. Eugenics is now commonly associated with the Nazis; however it was popular in all countries at the time, and its philosophies only really began to fall out of fashion in the 1940s when the full horror of their conclusions began to be revealed to the world.

People with disabilities were one of the first populations the Nazis sought to exterminate in death camps. Indeed much of the technology used in the death camps was trialled and developed through experimentation on people with learning disabilities. The infamous T4 programme began with the killing of people with disabilities in 1939.

Whilst other groups at the time were not so blatant or organised in their application of eugenics as the Nazis were, they were still operating with a similar understanding. Medical practices sought to fix the brains of the mentally deficient, and people in institutions could expect to be subjected to horrific medical procedures. As they were "subhuman," it was acceptable to test new ideas in medicine upon them, from exposing them to new drugs to performing experimental surgery on them which could lead to further disability, excruciating pain, and of course death.

Knocking someone out with medication was considered to be a way of resetting their brains. Teeth were pulled out because they were considered to harbour dirt. Electrocution was common place as a "treatment." People with disabilities were routinely sterilised. To this day we still consider it radical to "allow" people with learning disabilities to have children. These times were not so long ago; they are the soil out of which our current practice grows.

A past touching distance away

The 1886 Idiots Act might sound a long way off in history, but the 1940s and the 1950s are still in touching distance from us. In 1946 just as the notions of needing to purify the bloodline were petering out, a group of parents came together to form the National Association of Parents of Backward Children, an organisation which later became known as Mencap. "Backward" was the progressive label of the time. These parents wanted better institutions for their children.

The image that came to your mind when I first mentioned institution, of a long room with metal framed beds and white sheets, is probably one from this time. That room you imagined has no toys in it. The children in the photo stare out at you with empty eyes. These children are put outside for "fresh air" at six in the morning and not allowed back inside until nightfall. At night they are not permitted blankets as they were not considered to be safe for them.

If you inspect the image of that room in your mind closely you will notice a grated drain runs down the middle of the room: this is their toilet. Were you to be able to step into that photo, you would be hit by the stench coming from that drain and from the urine-soaked bedding and the generalised neglect.

You are not looking into a dim and distant past; the image you saw in your mind's eye was in black and white, but there are colour photos from this time too. The last people to be sent away to institutions against their will, locked up because of their disability, were sent in the early 1980s. This is the very recent past.[1] And it is from this past that our current understanding and practices spring.

The children in your imagined photo are disciplined with pain. Still considered subhuman or severely subhuman, administering pain is thought to be the best way to educate them. Again, rather than gasp in horror at the actions of people operating during a different era, consider your own life. Might you slap the dog or the cat if it peed on the carpet? Do you know a friend who would? Pain as discipline is acceptable for animals. Treatment of things not human has different moral boundaries in our minds. What moral boundaries do we have in place now that separate "us" from "them"?

If the children did not eat their dinner staff held their noses to force them to open their mouths and then pressed the food inside. If they were sick staff forced them to eat their own vomit. Again these barbaric practices of the past are perhaps not so far away. In my time as a teacher in a special school and as a consultant working within special education I have met many staff who in response to certain actions or "behaviours" adopt a "make them do it" approach, forcing the "naughty" individual to tidy a mess they have made or perform a movement or act they clearly do not want to perform. Early in my career I was involved in the force-feeding of a child, informed by staff senior to me that it was in the child's best interests. Grimly, as I was editing the manuscript for this book, Birrell (2019) reported staff of a residential care setting who had forced a resident of that setting to eat their own vomit. These staff members escaped without criminal prosecution and the service as a whole, which constitutes a big business enterprise, was fined just 4,000 pounds as a penalty for the cruelty inflicted by its "care" staff. The barbarism of the past is with us in our present.

Forcing of compliance is viewed by the members of staff as a strategy for healthy, robust discipline. Many believe we need more of it, not less, attributing a perceived increase of behaviours they find challenging to a lack of strong discipline. If you operate a task-based framework in your mind then forced compliance counts as success. After all, those people pinching the noses of children did achieve the task of feeding the child, just as forcing a child to perform an act achieves the performing of that act. But at what cost?

The structures of the past scaffold the present

It is not only our ideas that reflect the history of provision for people with learning disabilities; the structures around us do too. In the 1960s buildings designed to house people with learning disabilities reflected the medical model of disability held in high regard at the time. They were designed to be sterile medical environments with easy-to-clean surfaces and bathrooms without toilet stalls to make monitoring residents easier. The classroom in which I taught in 2009 had adjoining it a stall-less bathroom with a windowed door so that I could easily observe my students going to the toilet. The set up is the same today in 2019.

Staff in the institutions separated themselves from the people who lived there by wearing uniforms and displaying name badges bearing their professional roles. Many education and care settings today require their staff to wear clothing or lanyards or badges that clearly distinguish them from the people they support. The them-and-us-ness of our outward presentation can be justified in a multitude of ways, as was the wearing of white coats in the 1960s institutions.

The institutions we look down upon were, in their day, heralded as developments in provision for people with learning disabilities by stalwart campaigners of the day, such as Dorothea Dix, who as early as 1850 campaigned for better treatment for people with disabilities and believed that the institutions would offer that through training and medication.

We need to know where our ideas come from. To be reflective of our current position we need to understand in what it is founded. There is no dividing line separating us from the past; we are a movement from it. To look back and think of those historical practices as different from our own, as opposite to us, is to lie to ourselves. We are an extension of all that they did.

The past, as with the present, contains both good and bad. Here is a positive reflection from the past: Dr Edouard Seguin, who lived his life within the 1800s (and who under a pen name wrote about Victor the Wild Boy of Averyon), argued that developing the muscles and the senses would enable people, regardless of their intellectual deficiency, to obtain more control over their central nervous systems and wills (Seguin 1866). We can hear his words echoing in our own justification for using a multisensory room today.

The institutions of the past are the backdrop against which multisensory rooms first emerged. Those institutions are not consigned to history. There are still people living today in the institutions they were sent to as children. In the Seismic Sensory Project[2]

I worked with one such individual who has lived over 80 years of her life within the boundaries of an institution. Of course her institution no longer has the same name, but what does a name change mean to her? The walls are the same walls she has lived her whole life within, stained with the memories of her childhood.

The Winterbourne View Scandal in 2011 brought into the public's consciousness the continued existence of abusive practices within "care" settings, and a succession of subsequent scandals have demonstrated that the problem is far from being solved. A recent example is @JeremyH09406687, known as Bethany's Dad, who took to Twitter in October 2018, successfully using social media to highlight the plight of people, including his own daughter, who are deprived of their freedom in assessment and treatment units.

Globally we continue to witness provision reminiscent of that we experienced decades ago. Many cultures continue to deem it the right thing to do to kill a disabled child at birth. Many countries hold institutions within them to contain disabled people. I provide advice to people working within institutions in Europe where people with profound and multiple learning disabilities are kept in the basement, deemed not to need access to the outside world or light through windows because they are not physically able to respond to it and who live out their lives unvisited by family members who consider their presence in their family as a source of shame.

The institutions are very much still a thing of today, as are the thought patterns of the people who worked in them. Both may have changed dress slightly – the walls may be painted a different colour, the thoughts worded with more contemporary language – but both are still very much here.

OVERVIEW

The lives of people with disabilities have been massively shaped by the institutions, attitudes and social understanding of the day. We are part of the lineage of this evolving understanding, not its end point. As we reflect on the horrors of practices now viewed as outdated, we must remember that we need to change now as much as they needed to change then.

F.I.S.H. (FIND IDEA STARTERS HERE)

What aspect of your current practice might future generations look back on as being outdated?

What are your beliefs about the right way of interacting with a person who has a learning disability based upon?

The terms and conditions

ORIENTATION

This is a book about multisensory rooms, so why are you now facing a section about terminology? To understand the backdrop to the creation of the rooms, presented in the previous section, makes sense as an orientation to their coming about. But of what relevance is language?

Quite clearly we cannot discuss a topic without language to identify its content. And the language of the past, like the provision of the past, is very much a part of our current practice. The terms we use today are a link in a chain connecting the past to the future. Understanding our position in that chain helps us to orientate ourselves towards the forward progress we might wish to see, and this section will help you to do this. The words we use are as much a part of our practice in multisensory rooms as fibre optics, bubble tubes and projectors are.

Language, labels, prejudice and understanding

In 1920 Dr Helen MacMurchy published "The almosts: a study of the feebleminded." The "almost" of the title referred to people she was writing about being considered *almost* human. By the 1950s people with learning disabilities were beginning to be considered human. In 1959, common terms of demarcation were "subhuman" and "severally subhuman." You were expected to be grateful for the use of the word human in relation to you.

In the 1960s phrases like mentally retarded, now commonly used in abusive contexts only, were progressive. You were considered fully human, but with mental retardation. That President John F. Kennedy had a sister who was mentally retarded saw provision for the learning-disabled population pushed up the political agenda in the states.

In 1958 the Brooklands experiment wondered whether people might be better off in home-like environments rather than institutions. Through the 1970s the idea of "normalisation" grew in popularity, the aim being not to make the person normal but to provide for them the things you would expect in a normal life. This idea is admirable, but we may question whether what we define as a normal life is dictated by biases imposed by our own experience of life.

The 1970 Education Act springs out of this cultural background of an understanding that the normal things of life should rightfully be provided for a person with learning disabilities. The passing of the act made education a universal right and for the first time people with a learning disability were entitled to go to school.

Much energy now is expended on campaigning against terms used to describe people with physical or mental differences to the considered norm. Whilst such campaigns

15

can raise awareness of outdated attitudes if they positively teach awareness within them and propose new terms, they can also harm progress if their sole message is one of "do not say _____."

Creating a set up where people feel threatened by the presence of people with disabilities is counterproductive. People made to fear saying the wrong thing quickly get fed up of feeling like they are being policed; they do not intentionally attribute this feeling of fed-up-ness to people with disabilities but subconsciously associate the scolding with the presence of people with disabilities and then seek to defuse their own unease it through offensive humour. Telling people off for the language they use often backfires.

If we look back through the history we can see that language has consistently changed to reflect the developing understanding of the day. Some of the early campaigners for inclusion used terms like "retard" or "subhuman" which we would consider offensive, but used them to push forwards the boundaries of inclusion. The terms we are using today will also become dated.

The 1981 Education Act referred to people with learning disabilities as having "special needs," a term considerably more positive than those that had gone before it, but a term that in today's climate sounds patronising. On March 21, 2017, World Down Syndrome Day, the marvellous #Notspecialneeds campaign hit social media featuring people with Down syndrome clearly pointing out that their needs are no different from the next person's and so should not be considered "special." Campaigns such as this are brilliant at positively challenging the way we think and encouraging people to reflect.

It is a dangerous misunderstanding to think that succeeding in changing a label will change attitudes. The important component of the #Notspecialneeds campaign is its reflective nature, not the wording. An example which clearly demonstrates how ineffective simple language change can be is the rebranding of the "Spastics Society" to "Scope."

In the 1980s "Spaz" was a common playground taunt, used abusively to tease other children, implying that they were like people with spastic cerebral palsy. Today the term of choice is "gay" and it too is imbued with all the pointless prejudice "spaz" was imbued with back then. I was a child in the 1980s playground; I remember people jutting their tongue into their lower lip and making an "urre" sound before yelling "Spaz" at me. Aware that the name Spastic Society had become tarnished, it was changed to Scope in 1994. When I entered teaching in 2004 I met children in the playground calling each other "Scopies." The name had changed but the understanding and awareness around it had not. Label change alone is pointless.

Words are important, but we must not automatically discredit the views of people using the wrong words. I know family members who lovingly refer to their "retarded" sibling – these are not people without ambitions for their family member, they are not people who do not care. These are people who love their family member with the devotion you would expect and want the best for them. They campaign for change and advocate for their family member. Should we tell them off for using the word "retard" and if we did what would be the consequence, might we find them less willing to come forward in the future?

People forget that the acquiring of descriptive terms was in itself an act of progression. Where once people with learning disabilities were grouped with people with mental health difficulties and lumped together as one subhuman lot, the acquisition of a term that related to you and not to someone else was a step towards identity.

Consider the terms you might use to describe yourself. You might use a term that described a particular faith group or political leaning, terms that describe character traits, interests, passions and so on. Would you feel liberated if I took these terms away from you and told you that we are all the same? We pride ourselves on our own individual identities, and if we have a neurological or physical difference these things form part of our identity; to have them named is not inherently insulting.

It remains an act of progress to be correctly identified by a descriptive term within some of the care settings in the UK today. Recently in talking to a large provider of adult care about the Core and Essential Service Standards for Supporting People with Profound and Multiple Learning Disabilities (Doukas et al. 2017), a document which sets out what best practice should look like when providing for people with profound and multiple learning disabilities, the provider was unable to answer the question "How many people with profound disabilities do you care for?" When people are not identified within services as having particular needs, they are lost from provision and those needs go unmet.

Let us do away with language

Occasionally I meet people who say we should do away with labels. Their sentiment comes from a good place but it is ultimately meaningless. "Labels" is a term we use to refer to words that have some form of prejudice associated with them. When labels have no prejudice they are simply words. I do not think these people are seriously suggesting we should do away with language. Labels are only dangerous when they are mistaken for identity.

To describe a person is not an act of prejudice. Description is useful; it is communication. To not be able to denote the people we are talking about makes it hard to move forward. Indeed for the community of people I work on behalf of, one of the major barriers to inclusion they currently face is a lack of terminology. They fall under an umbrella definition of need that is too vague and encompasses too many different needs.

The #TeachUsToo campaign launched by Jonathan Bryan in 2017 highlights the plight of people grouped under a heading that does not accurately describe them. People with profound physical disabilities that inhibit their access to education are currently grouped under the heading "profound and multiple learning difficulties."

There is a clear difference between someone who faces a barrier to learning because of their physicality, for example, someone whose mind functions perfectly but who is unable to move or speak to let anyone know, and someone who has both profound physical disabilities and profound cognitive impairments.

We currently do not have terminology to distinguish between those whose profound disabilities mask their abilities to learn and those who have both profound physical and cognitive disabilities. Although recently I have seen one begin to emerge, as people separate the two groups by referring to people with profound and multiple learning disabilities (PMLD) and people with profound and multiple barriers to learning (PMBL).

Finding a new term would help both people with profound and multiple learning disabilities and people with profound and multiple barriers to learning get their needs better met. People with profound physical disabilities that mask their mental abilities should not be forced to sit through lessons that offer no intellectual challenge. People with profound physical and mental disabilities should not be parked in lessons that offer content out of reach to both their bodies and their minds.

Distinguishing the two groups through our use of language enables the tailoring of provision to suit each according to their need. Imray and Colley (2017, p. 2) point out that "The philosophy and practice of teaching those on the SLD (Severe Learning Disabilities) and PMLD (Profound and Multiple Learning Disabilities) spectrums is not just a matter of differentiation, it is fundamentally different." The same is true for people with profound and multiple learning disabilities and profound and multiple barriers to learning; fundamentally different provision is needed.

We can do it without words

You might think it possible to provide for each according to their need regardless of the terminology is used to describe people. Sadly the reality of the situation is that pots of money are ascribed to particular groups, acts of parliament use words to define who gets what, and people are grouped according to the labels they have. It is very difficult to meaningfully provide for two different groups alongside each other, and it is as hard to provide for people with profound and multiple barriers to learning alongside people with profound and multiple learning disabilities alongside each other, as it would be to teach college students alongside preschool children. Currently though, because of the lack of distinction between the two groups, this is what happens. Words are a tool of our society and we need to use them in order to use the powers of society effectively.

You will note that the terminology we use today of profound and multiple learning difficulties, or complex learning difficulties and disabilities, has a plain language quality to it. Consider this plain language quality set against the negative implications of the terminology of the past such as "severely subhuman," which is the term that would have been used to denote these people, when people such as Longhorn (1988) referred to them as "very special."

In 1988 it was revolutionary to make that bold choice of language change: these people are not severely subhuman, they are very special. Longhorn (1988) used language change in the positive, creating a new term to prompt people to think in new ways. She did not persecute the using of outdated terms. The plain language of our current terms is set against the – what now seems – overly positive or cutesy language of the "special" variety. The current terminology of profound and multiple learning disability is, as with all the terms that have gone before it, from a place in time, and as I write that time is passing, we can feel the language we are using dating on our tongues.

With: new times – new terms

Recent decades have seen advocacy groups push for person first language. I am not a Down syndrome person, I am a person *with* Down syndrome. The person comes first, the condition or disability is secondary. That word order changes its association in our heads. "I am a disabled person" makes the disability the whole of the person, whereas "I am a person with a disability" makes the disability an accessory to the person.

Currently person-first language is considered best practice. However some communities reject it, as they reject the notion of their conditions as being an inherently negative thing. Consider your nationality: it is unlikely that you consider this a negative aspect of yourself. If I were to describe you as an English person you are unlikely to turn around to me and say "No, I am a person with Englishness." You would not, because you do not consider being English to be an insult and you consider it a part of your identity. The separation of person from condition, for some, implies a wish to distance the self from the condition. Many people from the autistic community or the deaf community campaign for condition-first language. I am autistic, not I am a person with autism. I am deaf, not a person with deafness.

Of course I am a part of all this, tangled in the semantic conundrum with the rest of you. In my time I have used person-first language "a child with learning disabilities" and still do, although my current usage is more of a holding pattern waiting to see what the next change will be.

As an autistic person I denote myself as autistic, not as a person with autism. I could no more point to a part of me that is not autistic than could a neurotypical person be able to point to a part of them that was not neurotypical. My whole self is autistic. I am autistic. I am not a person with autism, and my friend is not a person with neurotypicism.

I personally struggle with the word neurotypcial, commonly used by the autistic community to denote people who do not have a condition that qualifies them as neurodiverse, because I feel the use of typicism, implying typical, implying normal, suggests that being neurodiverse is somehow not normal. When in fact it is perfectly normal; it just might not be as statistically common as other brain types.

With relation to the specific group of people my life has focused upon I first strictly used "people with" ahead of the terminology of the time, "profound and multiple learning disabilities." I come from a relatively inclusive background. Within my family are people with neurodiverse conditions and people with physical disabilities. My mother was an early inclusionist and her mother was too, in her own way in her own time. Differently abled people have always been a part of my life. I had to learn about prejudice through my career. I did not start out thinking it was there and needed tackling, because in my life it had mostly not been there.

As I gained experience I realised that there were people who thought that a particular term meant everyone to whom that term applied was the same. I honestly had not thought (prior to meeting these people) that it would be possible to grow into adulthood and still think something so foolish. Statements such as "autistics have no emotions" or "Downs children are all so loving" divested me of my naivety. It is indeed possible to maintain high levels of ignorance well beyond your teenage years!

I switched from saying "people with" to saying "individuals with," wanting to point out with my words the uniqueness of each person. I would not need to do this for people without a disability as their uniqueness is presumed by society already. In a society that presumes homogeneity, there is a need to clearly demark individuality. Yet as I write I am watching the first signs that this, too, is a term whose time has passed. On December 19, 2018, Openfuturelearning.org posted a photo on social media of a young man with Down syndrome beside which was written the words "client, individual, service user," all of which had been crossed out and replaced with a single word, "human." I found it jarring to see a term I considered appropriate placed alongside two I have never used. Within 48 hours it had been shared by close to 2,000 people. The times, and the terms, they are a-changing.

The days of profound and multiple learning disabilities are numbered

However prefixed, the term profound and multiple learning disabilities is dating fast and its sister term of complex learning disabilities and difficulties is of a similar ilk. I have struggled with it for numerous reasons: the inability to distinguish between the two clearly different groups of people currently caught up beneath its umbrella and its relation to the medical model of disability are two of my biggest difficulties with the term. But a third issue with the term stands out to me, and this time it's personal: As someone who wants for myself condition first language, if I am to look for a new term to use to denote the people I work on behalf of, choosing something that begins with a "with," with an adjunct, is to deny to them the respect that I give myself. I am not saying that using person first language about people with profound and multiple learning disabilities is dis-respectful, just that it would be disrespectful for *me* to do that. I wanted a term that defined in the positive and defined by ability not deficit. I began using "Sensory Beings" in 2016, later defining Sensory Beings as "people whose primary experience of the world, and meaning within it, is sensory" (Grace 2017). I placed a matching definition on us as Linguistic Beings, so as not to define one group against a norm, but instead to recognise differing but equal views of life. My aim is not to turn Sensory Beings into Linguistic Beings, or for that matter to turn Linguistic Beings into Sensory Beings. My aim is to enable Sensory Beings and Linguistic Beings to each share a little of each other's world so that all might gain through a broadening of their horizons, an idea I spoke about in my 2018 TEDx talk "Inclusion: for pity's sake?"

I confess to not spending a lot of time considering this term, I just reached in my mind for what was present at the time, asking myself what is the positive I first see, and answering "these are people supremely good at being in the moment." It is no surprise that I held this quality in high regard; I am a child of my age just as we all are. In today's society we are seeing an increase in interest in mindfulness practice correlated to a rise in the reporting of anxiety disorders. To be able to be present in the moment, in the present day and age, is a prized skill.

Equally it is no surprise that I hit upon the word sensory. My whole working life has been exploring the sensory world. When I work with people with profound and multiple learning disabilities it is to explore sensation together, so I see them as brilliant at being in the sensory moment: they are Sensory Beings. Of course the term does not encapsulate everything about them – no term could, and much is missed that I would wish to include. But for me it was a pragmatic move at the time. I needed something different to say so that was what I said.

Since I coined the term Sensory Beings in 2015 I have seen it picked up and used by other professionals and parents; often people are delighted by it. "My child is a Sensory Being!" They see it as a celebration. I do not think that this adoption means I have come up with the right thing to say; it is simply the right thing for me to say now. I think the willingness of people to adopt it indicates that we are at a point of change with regards to our current terminology. As we face that change I hope we do it through the positive construction of new language, not the negative persecution of old language, for we are all in this chain and our words will date in time as did the words of those who came before us.

What name would you like?

In nearly all situations, good people will call others what they wish to be called. Someone might prefer a particular abbreviation of their own name or will choose to go by a different moniker altogether; most people will respect this. When it comes to the community of people who have disabilities of one kind or another, it is often advocacy groups that coin the latest terminology, demanding respect in accordance with the age they live in. We see that with the use of the word "backward" by parents in the 1950s pushing against "subhuman" demarcations, and we see it again in the current age with the # Notspecialneeds movement, with self-advocates pushing against the use of "special needs."

Using the preferred terms of the individuals themselves is clearly the right thing to do. Most differently abled people are capable of choosing a term of identification for themselves. Sensory Beings, by definition, are not capable of doing this. Were they capable, they would fall out of the group of people I intend to denote by the term Sensory Beings and into a more cognitively able group.

Without the guidance of the person themselves there is no clear rule for what to call a person. I believe the second-best option after personal identification is that we use terminology that we would be happy using in relation to ourselves. I have demonstrated this in my choice of a term that applies the respect I claim for myself to them; also, however, someone who finds person-first language to be their personal preference may be more respectful of Sensory Beings if they find a person-first way of denoting them.

The idea that there are right and wrong terms, that there is inherently offensive and non-offensive language, is a simplistic misunderstanding. A quick browse of the internet will tell you without doubt that what one person finds offensive another one does not. There is not a clear hierarchy of terms in the here and now and there never will be. The rightness of a term emerges out of an understanding of an age. Whilst we can clearly know what was wrong with terminology of the past, we are too close to the present to yet know which of our terms will come to be accepted and which rejected.

The acceptance and rejection does not come about through the merit of the term itself; words are just letter strings with no inherent value. The acceptance and rejection of a term comes about through its use, through the jostling and the debate around it. Right now as we turn the terms of today over, we cannot know which will last. One person will find a term offensive, and another person will be offended by the competing term, but one person is not right and one is not wrong. Try as we might, the semantic tangle will continue. Only time will tell.

What is clearly offensive and wrong is to presume that a label alone wholly indicates a person. Although I consider myself to be wholly autistic, you do not know me wholly from the term autistic. Labels are dangerous when they are mistaken for identity.

I asked Elly Chapple, founder of CanDoElla, who frequently discusses labels online as she campaigns to #flipthenarrative with regards to how people with disabilities are perceived, to share her thoughts on this matter. Here is what she said.

#flipthenarrative

It's not an easy task to write something about "labels" when I'm fully aware of the larger discussion ongoing, and that we all have our own experiences around this too.

Labels historically have contributed to identity; we all use them. I'm white, female and hearing impaired. I'm still human and deserve the same life chances like anyone else. I received an education like all my differently labelled peers.

If we adopt "global expectations" (Chivers 2019) of an identity without understanding and knowledge about what that identity is as a whole – and often this is crucially through the actual experience of "being with" people rather than "learning about" people as identities in theory only – we are potentially at risk of misusing the identity of that label and therefore the humanness and ability of that person like any other. Learning about others we live amongst in any field is fundamentally rooted in relationships. Taking the time to actually get to know people and how you connect or not. Building trust, consistency, honesty, respect, the ability to say sorry and when we are stuck the ability to ask for help so we do not reach a negative or crisis point.

Language is important in so many ways to transfer how we feel about *who* we are interacting with, **why** we are and **how**. All humans need empathy, kindness, compassion, understanding and respect. If expectations are embedded within a "label only" view, disconnected from the whole human, they risk serving to remove or reduce the identity of a human being and skew the narrative to a negative space. In essence often limits are set, ceilings are lowered and our behaviour towards people lets them know – everyone feels and can sense the pulse of intention we emit. And how we make them feel is important in setting the tone of our expectations and belief in them. What they can do, what they can achieve and whether we see them as equal, as one.

I'm certainly no expert, I'm just finding my way and asking lots of questions and reflecting as I go, focused on my journey to learn about how we can #flipthenarrative together, as one.

OVERVIEW

The terms we use to describe people with learning disabilities have changed and will change again. The changing of terms alone does not create cultural change. The driving force for positive change is increased understanding and awareness.

Historically language change has happened in response to changes in understanding and awareness, as a reflection of it, rather than as a cause of it. Arguments about terminology drain useful time and energy from people who might otherwise spend their time promoting increased understanding and awareness.

Changing language without changing understanding and awareness has little utility. Arguing to do away with language that denotes particular groups within society is counterproductive. Accurate descriptive terms are a powerful tool when championing better provision for minority groups.

We stand currently on the brink of a language change and should consider carefully the terms we use and why we use them.

F.I.S.H.

What are the implications of the terminology you currently use to describe people with learning disabilities? Would you be happy to hear yourself spoken of in such terms?

What terms would you like to see used in the future to denote the people you share your multisensory room with?

How can you contribute to increased understanding and awareness of people with neurological or physical differences, both through your choice of terminology and through your use of language in communicating the strengths and abilities of these people to the broader population?

The dawning of Snoezelen

ORIENTATION

The starting point for multisensory rooms is recognised as being the practice of Jan Hulsegge and Ad Verheul, who worked in a large institution in the Netherlands in the 1970s and 1980s. Their work creating first a multisensory tent in the grounds of this institution, and later a room within it, forms the bedrock of the multisensory rooms we know today. Yet their intentions for that space, and the driving philosophy behind the relationships forged in that space, have largely been lost from current practice. In the coming sections you will read about how the first multisensory room came to be and what the creators of that room thought were its most important features.

I am aware that as I write I am about to imply that particular people had an idea. As with most developments in our thinking, be they philosophical, scientific, psychological and so forth, it tends to be the case that many people have similar ideas at a similar time. The people we remember as the inventor or the originator of a particular idea or practice are rarely the first, nor are they necessarily the ones that were best at it or had the best idea. That a person or persons become the reference point for a particular idea or invention is usually more to do with marketing or recording than primacy or supremacy. As I tell their stories I am using them as examples of their time, not awarding them merit compared with others doing similar things at the same time. And I am human, so no doubt I will miss someone who deserved mention.

A tent pitched on history's barren grounds

I have spent so much time describing the historical backdrop to multisensory rooms both in terms of the concrete reality of the practices and places of the past and in terms of the language and concepts used because there is a very real danger in viewing things purely from our own standpoint in time. When we see things in isolation, disassociated from the history that created them, separate from the philosophies that govern them, we cannot possibly fully understand them. When you meet a person, insight into their history helps you to know them better. It is the same with multisensory rooms.

The biggest danger with regards to multisensory rooms is viewing them as an object or set of objects, when in fact they are a manifestation of thoughts and ideas and attitudes. And those thoughts, ideas and attitudes spring from a particular place in time and cultural understanding and these things are in a state of constant flux. To fix on the room, and the objects within it, is to miss the point entirely.

Ironically, that it is not the room that is important but the thoughts and ideas within it, is precisely what the first advocates of multisensory rooms were at pains to point out. Jan Hulsegge and Ad Verheul created one of the first multisensory rooms against the backdrop of a large institution where people with profound and multiple learning disabilities had less access to relevant stimulation than did other residents.

People saw what Hulsegge and Verheul were doing, saw the room, saw the resources and heralded a new *thing*, and they – the inventors of this *thing* – insisted that it was not the thing, namely, the room, but the philosophy behind it that everyone should adopt. However, shout as they might above the din, the lure of stuff and designated space was too much. No sooner had the rooms been conceived of than they became the distraction from the philosophy they so beautifully evidenced rather than the explanation of it that their inventors hoped they would be.

Seeing the first rooms against the context of the institutions of the time helps us to understand people's response to them and why the stuff of the rooms was so coveted. At the beginning of this section I had you imagine an institution, knowing that your notions of what they looked like probably matched with my own. Before considering the sensory wonders of the first multisensory room, it is worth going back and reminding yourself with actual photographs from settings of the time. I am writing a few days before Christmas and have myself just glanced back through a very particular set of images known as Christmas in Purgatory (Blatt and Kaplan 1974).[3]

The institutions were barren of resources, and gifts given to residents were removed immediately. The people living within their walls were not people in the eyes of those in charge of their lives; they were subhuman or severely subhuman. They were deemed as not needing pleasure or stimulation. They had to be kept in line, disciplined, washed, punished, fed. Hulsegge and Verheul (1986) were writing about a time (in the 1970s – their book was written after the events described within it) when recognising the humanity of a person with a learning disability was a radical act.

The institution that Hulsegge and Verheul worked in had an annual summer fair, and families were invited to attend – itself a bold mark of a wish to include. The inviting in of the families and the public sent a message that the people in the institution should not be forgotten but instead remembered, celebrated and visited. Activities were set up for all to take part in. Hulsegge and Verheul recognised that for a certain group of people living in the institution, none of the activities on offer were accessible. Inspired by their own experiences of nature, they set about creating a tent in which people with profound disabilities might be able to experience some of the pleasurable sensations they had enjoyed.

Hulsegge and Verheul (1986, p. 31) describe the sharing of sensation as "Snoezelen," pronounced snooze-el-len, and give the following example of it:

> Lying in a meadow chewing a stalk of grass we watch the clouds pass overhead. We are very comfortable; the sounds of the traffic are far away; we hear nothing but the croaking of the frogs and the wind rushing in the reeds. We can smell the fresh grass and we feel utterly contented. Nothing changes until the wisps of over-blow dandelions, carried by the wind, attract our attention. We try to catch a few of these little parachutes. Later we pick one of the overblown dandelions and blow off the wisps and watch them drift away until they are out of sight. After all this sniffing at the grass and meadow flowers we doze off a little. It is simply lovely, such an afternoon of "snoezelen"!

It is easy to imagine Hulsegge and Verheul in this situation: their relaxedness was what enabled their perception, and their tiredness increased their curiosity for the natural world around them. As they lay relaxing and delighting in noticing the small things that would have otherwise passed them by they recognised that this sort of relaxation was out of reach for those people they cared for who had sensory impairments that would prevent them from seeing a small thing against a bright sky, out of reach for people who could not comfortably lie on the floor. They thought what a precious thing it was to lie in a sleepy curious state and wondered if they could recreate it for the summer fair.

The term Snoezelen has since been trademarked by the company Rompa. Snoezelen is a contraction of two Dutch words meaning to sniff and to doze, implying the active curiosity of sniffing set against the relaxed state of dozing. Think of Jan and Ad lying in the field entranced by the beauty of nature.

Later writers have asked for more from multisensory rooms than for them to be sleepy curious places (Hirstwood and Gray 1995, p. 3). To want more on top of what you already have is one thing. To lay aside a desire for sleepy curiosity and aim for something else entirely misses the great ambition within such a seemingly low key statement. It is a statement from a particular time.

When the opportunity to lie peacefully and indulge natural curiosity is not there at any point in life, to seek to find it is a huge ambition. If you live a life where you have constant access to such a state, then it is less of an ambition. The worth of the ambition is not measured against the ambition itself – to relax and be curious – but against the context of its stating.

Hulsegge and Verheul (1986) saw multisensory rooms as places for people who could not access the natural world. Later researchers have found the natural world to be better than multisensory rooms at promoting engagement (Cuvo et al. 2001; Fowler 2008; Hill et al. 2012) for those able to access it. Organisations such as the Sensory Trust seek to find ways to make nature more accessible rather than to offer alternatives to it.

We see in our story Hulsegge and Verheul, young and able-bodied, lying back in the grass enjoying the sensory pleasures of a summer day, their curiosity ignited and their creativity burning. They returned from this adventure to set up a series of tents in the grounds of their institution. The tents were to provide the backdrop against which people, with less sensory capabilities than themselves, would be able to perceive natural wonders. They equipped the tents with soft cushions to enable people to be comfortable and placed in them other interesting, stimulating items such as lights and pieces of shiny paper in addition to the many things from nature collected together to be discovered. People were encouraged to come into the tents, relax and explore.

Imagine the decadence of such a provision, so close to a time when people were stripped of all they had. Those same people who had previously had the pleasures of life removed from them were having trinkets brought to them: tin foil, torch light, fresh herbs. It was a flower growing in a desert. A sip of water after a long hot walk. The celebration with which multisensory rooms were heralded is proportionate to the deprivation that preceded them; not a measure of the provision they offer.

Change is defined by ideas, not spaces and objects

What is evident in Hulsegge and Verheul's (1986) writing is their inherent respect and love for the people they work for. To them the tent does not matter; what they want is for others to see these people as they see them and to respect them as they respect them. In what they write you can hear them pushing back against a society which considers the able-bodied, able minded person as automatically superior.

"Mentally able people," they argue, "in seeing the world too rationally, do not make the most of their senses" (p. 11). "We regard the mentally handicapped person as unique, someone who gives his personal, special meaning to people, things and atmospheres" (p. 13). "Most important are the interpersonal contacts. These can never be substituted by machines or effects" (p. 14).

Hulsegge and Verheul (1986) speak up in defence of behavioural responses to situations which others of the time would have deemed requiring of discipline: "When a person still has a spark of independence we ought to respect it, cherish it" (p. 15). These sentences are rich with the vision they had for inclusion and with information about the time they had it in. Consider the word "still" in the sentence quoted: the person "still" displaying their independence, their defiance, after a lifetime within an institution . . . that is a very bright spark indeed. Hulsegge and Verheul (1986) do not stop at saying they should be respected, they go one further with the emotive word: cherished. These people and their responses to the situation they are in, are not subhuman, they are not to be punished, they are to be honoured and revered.

Look at them, Hulsegge and Verheul (1986) say, and consider whether they might not actually be better than you in some way. "We are very much hindered by our rational attitude . . . this impedes a more primary use of our senses and purer experiences" (p. 22) "Our senses often get clotted up, we may lack the ability to react spontaneously to primary stimuli" (p. 35). "Our rational attitude often kills the quiet surprise so that we do not give it a real chance" (p. 35).

Do not assume them to be lesser, say Hulsegge and Verheul. They are themselves and they see the world differently. It is not for them to change, but for us. "Our acceptance of him should be active; we should not reconcile ourselves to his incapabilities but start from his abilities" (p. 21). It is about us changing our minds, us taking part in an active process of enabling the abilities of others to shine through. It was not about the tent and what was in it, or the room that that tent became after it was so popular that they did not want to take it down when the summer fair had ended.

Hulsegge and Verheul (1986) had such success in enriching the lives of the people they worked on behalf of and in changing attitudes because of the way they thought and felt, not because of the equipment they had. The same equipment in the hands of another would have had no effect at all. It was their underpinning philosophy that made the change. It is statements like "Today it is a matter of being equal. In humanity there are no levels" (p. 22) that define them, not the dimensions of a space or the choice of objects within that space.

It is not about the room, it is about the heart

In their book *Another World*, written about their experiences of using multisensory rooms, Hulsegge and Verheul (1986) repeatedly point out that their practice is not about the rooms. They are very clear that they do not want to give instructions as to what to do in a multisensory room, describing themselves as writing with the intention of leaving their reader free to decide how to put their words into action, and urging everyone to adopt a critical attitude and reflect on their practice. This resistance to giving clear instructions runs all the way through their work, even into the definition of Snoezelen itself, which they purposefully avoid defining too closely (p. 31), instead wishing for people to create their own definition.

Hulsegge and Verheul (1986, p. 10) believe that "a theoretical basis is necessary for practice in a multisensory room." But they do not think they should dictate that basis to someone else. Each person should decide on their own rationale. A set of activities or a particular set up of a room is not enough; the people using the room must think and feel. Flo Longhorn (1988, p. 166), who was doing similar things at the same time but in America and the UK, echoes this sentiment, commenting that "it is very easy to smile and say nice words but through touch the child receives the feelings of the partner." She is emphasising how it is not necessarily what is done or said that is important, but the feeling that underpins its doing.

Longhorn (1988, p. 32) suggested school action plan begins with the marvellous instruction to "Look at yourself, now think hard." Contemporaries of the time, now recognised for their innovative practice (for example Lilli Neilsen and Veronica Sherbourne), all founded their practices on relationships, trust and care. The "what" and "how" of the practices they advocated came second to the inherent respect for the people for whom their practices were developed.

"Snoezelen" as used by Hulsegge and Verheul (1986) is not a room; "Snoezelen is not restricted to a particular place" (p. 32); it is a philosophy. "The 'Snozel room' is a place where that philosophy can be easily embodied but other situations such as personal care are ideal for it too" (p. 39).

The most important part of Snoezelen, in Hulsegge and Verheul's eyes, was physical contact. They recommended hugging, caressing and stroking hair, and advised people to lay aside their embarrassment and express warmth and tenderness (p. 29). Longhorn (1988) too states that physical contact is essential and recommends that children with disabilities be allowed to hug and embrace the people supporting them. Again echoing the experiences of Hulsegge and Verheul (p. 37), she reports that the self-consciousness of staff can be problematic when introducing a new multisensory programme. Hewett (2007) highlights that the risks of not offering touch to a person with profound and multiple learning disabilities outweigh the logistical and awareness issues involved in providing that touch. Hewett's work emphasises that it is not just that the personal inhibitions of individual members of staff need to be overcome to provide proper human support to people with profound disabilities, but also that we need to tackle larger issues such as policies and broader attitudes that regard touch as dangerous.

Feelings and thoughts lie at the heart of good multisensory room practice, not equipment and activity suggestions. "Snoezelen is an emotional affair, not requiring years of training" (Hulsegge and Verheul p. 117). Snoezelen is about people: the people being welcomed into the Snoezel room and the people doing the welcoming. Neither the room, the tent, nor the equipment are essential to Snoezelen.

What role do people play in our current conception of multisensory room practice? If asked "What is the most important piece of the kit in your multisensory room?" most people will happily give the standard "right answer" to the question, which is "the person." But if the importance of people in multisensory room practice were so widely recognised, surely that would be reflected in our practice and in the literature surrounding that practice.

If "the person" really were our most important piece of the kit, more attention, time and resources would be poured into ensuring that that particular piece of the kit was functioning at its best. If the person is the most important piece of equipment in a multisensory room, why do writings on the topic not mention them? Surely the most important piece of a kit in a multisensory room would warrant a majority slice of the text on the page about multisensory rooms. In this book you will find the most important piece of the kit popping up everywhere and the fourth section of this book is entirely dedicated to them.

How did we get from a starting point where people were so clear that this was about us, not about equipment and space, to a time when government guidelines specify that that equipment and space must exist in order to adequately provide for children in special schools (DFE 2015, p. 51), and you picked up a book hoping for it to contain information on equipment and space?

What happened?

Think about yourself: why were you hoping for those things from this book? Is it because you do not care? Unlikely . . . you would not bother to read a book if you did not care. Is it because you lack time? Is it because you feel under pressure in some way? Has something been said, or read, that has made you doubt yourself? Do you think that an "expert" might know better than you? Hulsegge and Verheul (1986) may very well know better than us, but they did not want to tell us what to do; they wanted it to be from our hearts and minds. How did this change?

OVERVIEW

Hulsegge and Verheul sought to bring to the people for whom they cared something that was extraordinarily precious to them: a shared connection with nature and the environment. Recognising the physical barriers to accessing experience that the people they supported faced, they created an environment that would better enable those people to perceive the wonders of the natural world. In creating a space to support sensory perception they aimed to enable people to share in Snoezelen, a companionable relaxed state of curiosity and wonder. The aim was not to build a room, nor equip said room with dazzling equipment. Rather, the aim was to connect with another human and to share in wonder. Hulsegge and Verheul were very clear that a room was not a necessary part of Snoezelen. The room was a tool for Snoezelen, but a very minor one when compared with human touch or the essential elements of respect and love that made up Snoezelen.

ONE LITTLE F.I.S.H.

Where is nature in your room? Items sourced from nature were a central feature in the first multisensory rooms. Is nature present in your room? Are natural experiences facilitated in another way? Or has nature been lost to a world of gadgetry?

FIVE BIG F.I.S.H.

You will have noticed, laced none too subtly through the previous sections, the message to think and feel for yourself. I realise that this, to readers who have picked up this book looking for practical guidance on which piece of equipment to switch on first or ideas for activities, could seem rather unhelpful. To some readers it will be liberating. Other readers will be frustrated, thinking "Okay, I understand I picked up this book hoping you would tell me how to use the equipment and now you are saying I need to think about myself, but you are not telling me what thoughts I should be thinking any more than you are telling me how to use the equipment; you have got to give me something!"

To those seeking guidance I offer five big F.I.S.H. You can choose whether to take these on board or not, perhaps recognising what aspects of my advice you agree or disagree with will help you to find your own route. Here goes:

1   **Regard them with love.** Not romantic love, not the saccharine love of greeting cards; plain love. Love is not a fluffy thing; there are mechanics to it. Love involves forgiveness and understanding, and all sorts of other difficult things to attempt. To participate in love is to take part in a process: to *be* in love, rather than to fall into the giddy of infatuation love. None of us master it, but we can still attempt to use it as a foundation for all that we do and if we find ourselves doing something that does not sit well upon that foundation . . . well, then we can stop doing whatever that thing is and consider a different approach. When planning an activity or taking part in a communication, consider whether it fits in love; your gut will provide the answer.

2   **Know that they are good.** If you truly believe that a person is good to their very core, then you will always see the communication in their behaviour. When this good person does something that, were you not to know they were good, would reveal them to you as a bad person you stop and question it. Why is a good person acting in this way? What has happened to them, what are they battling against, what does it mean? Knowing that they are good will start you off on the right track with your attempts to understand them.

3   **Assume they are struggling and treat them with compassion.** By "them" and "they" through all five of these points, I do not mean to denote a particular section of people with a certain level of disability, I mean everyone. Life challenges us all, and whilst it is clear that some people lead far harder lives than others, to line us up in order of the severity of which life afflicts us would be a very hard task indeed. Many people struggle against things unseen, and people with many clearly observable difficulties live in an apparently effortless and joyful way. Out of my five pieces of advice I think this one is the most debatable; perhaps there are people for whom life is not a struggle. My position could simply reflect how much

of a struggle I personally find life. But I think it valid; it forces us to think from a position of compassion and from an assumption that a person is doing their best.

4   **Play and be playful.** We all learn and engage more with play than we do with even the best carefully structured and planned activity. I write as someone who will heartily advocate structured planned activities, such as sensory stories. They are wonderful, but nothing beats play. Find the seed of joy in your heart, weed all the seriousness out and go for it with playful abandon.

5   Finally: **View them as able.** The abilities of some people are not always apparent and you may have to search for them. Find that flicker of ability and do something with it. And at the same time, view yourself as able too. If you find yourself standing in a multisensory room thinking "I do not get on with technology" and then going home to curl up on the sofa and knit, then bring that. Bring your ability. Bring in your knitting, let them twine their fingers through its holes, see the bright threads you stitch with, feel the texture of the wool, hear the steady clack clack clack of your needles, find a way to bring your ability to their ability. And do not feel that you are responsible for it all. You cannot solve the whole of your life; why on earth would you be able to solve the whole of someone else's? Play to your strengths: what part of this can you do? Where do your abilities match theirs? Let that be the start point to your thinking.

My F.I.S.H. apply to the people you work alongside with as well as to the people you work together to support. It is easy to be dismissed once you use the word love. Indeed in the writing of this book many people cautioned me against using the word, advising me to find another way of saying the same thing. I determined to do it when interviewing another hero of mine from the world of inclusion, and someone whose name you would likely know, but to whom I promised anonymity, as they were one of my interviewees for the piece of research reported on in Sections 3 and 4 of this book. They had just explained with enormous compassion and respect the thought processes and feelings they went through when supporting a particular person and were searching for a way to draw their statements to a summation so I offered:

"Are you saying it's about love?"

They appeared a little startled and smiled; indeed they actually looked furtively from side to side in a cartoonish manner. I do not know if this was for effect or if it was a genuine response to my having mentioned the L word.

"Well of course! But you cannot *say* that," they laughed kindly.

Every act of their whole career had been an act of love but they had been careful not to break the taboo of actually saying so. Dropping the taboo and just saying it is love is far more succinct and clear than trying to explain the same concept without being allowed to say the word.

The beginning of multisensory rooms

ORIENTATION

The increasing popularity of the Snoezelen approach brought it to the attention of industry and the term "Snoezelen" became trademarked. The trademarking of the term focused public attention on the rooms, with the philosophy behind the approach taking a background role. Unable to use the term Snoezelen to describe their spaces, people developing new rooms began to use the term multisensory room.

A great many different types of rooms were denoted by the term multisensory room and this in itself leads to confusion. At the same time, open discussion of the approach gave way to advertising. Two differing schools of thought emerged, with some people advocating a directive approach and others championing a non-directive approach to interaction within the multisensory room.

In the coming three sections we will look at these changes in more detail.

The ownership of Snoezelen turns a philosophy into a room

The trademarking of the term "Snoezelen" marked a turning point for the development of practice in multisensory rooms. At this point the idea of Snoezelen as a philosophy got lost.

Rompa, the company responsible for the trademark, and their sister company Flaghouse in the US/Canada, did their best to uphold the original philosophy of Snoezelen. Both clearly stated principles that resembled those of Hulsegge and Verheul's Snoezelen in their marketing material. Indeed Rompa were the publishers of Hulsegge and Verheul's book, *Another World*, which details that philosophy. But despite people's best intentions, as soon as the word "Snoezelen" became trademarked, it became a room and the equipment within that room: not a thought process or philosophy.

Other companies sprang up, marketing their own versions of a Snoezelen space. The term multisensory room was created because these new companies were not allowed to use the trademarked Snoezelen term, even if what they were aiming for was a space which would be ideal for Snoezelen. In the minds of the general public, Snoezelen stopped being a way of supporting people and became a type of room. Some people began to distinguish in their minds a Snoezelen room from a multisensory room; they saw them as different things doing different things.

In writing this book I came across many different terms for multisensory rooms. Pagliano (2008) lists a dozen different types of multisensory environments and it is likely that more than ten years on he could now add to that list. The multiplicity of the rooms and the vagueness of the terms used to denote them leads to a lot of confusion. We speak of multisensory rooms, denoting with the term many different types of rooms: light rooms, dark rooms, rooms with fibre optics and bubble tubes, rooms with 4D immersive projection, soft play rooms and more. Lately I am meeting a lot of people keen to call their multisensory space anything but a multisensory room. Posts on social media ask people for ideas for names for the rooms; one prominent multisensory room manufacturer, in talking to me about plans for their new rooms, said firmly, "Of course we will not call them multisensory rooms." This wish people have to distinguish their space from the spaces that have gone before is partly driven by a desire to separate themselves from the confusion that engulfs the rooms and the practices we share within them and to define their own philosophy – much as Ad and Jan recommended that we do.

Here is how the confusion arises: someone stands up at a conference and says multisensory rooms are good for such and such. Four people in the audience hear this declaration and each take what they have learned home to their multisensory room, yet they work within four vastly different spaces and support dramatically different individuals within those spaces. Maybe it was the right advice for one of them, maybe for none of them. Without clearly separating in our minds the different types of rooms we risk muddling what we learn about them.

As I was writing this book I envisioned this confusion as the graphic of a cube (Figure 1.1). Imagine a cube. The cube represents multisensory rooms; most people think of these as just one thing.

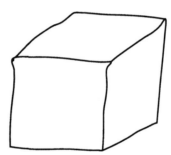

Figure 1.1

Now slice that cube vertically into a dozen pieces to represent the different types of rooms; now you have a dozen pieces, not just a single item (Figure 1.2).

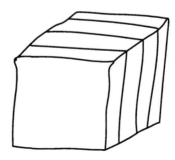

Figure 1.2

Now slice that cube horizontally to represent the different groups of people who might access the room, as you are going to use, for example, a dark room in a very different way with a group of people with profound and multiple learning disabilities than you would with a group of teenagers with autism (Figure 1.3). Now that initial cube is sliced into 144 sticks, each one representing a different circumstance a different approach.

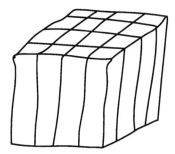

Figure 1.3

Slice the initial cube again; this time your slicing represents the different installers of multisensory rooms. Each company's equipment works in a different way and can do different things. Now you have 1,728 smaller cubes; each one is a different way of working and a different approach (Figure 1.4).

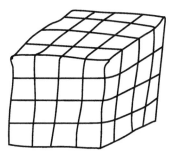

Figure 1.4

We could keep slicing: slicing by your underpinning philosophy, or by the time you have in the room, how often you get to visit, your training or profession, so many things (Figure 1.5). Each one of these makes a big difference to what that expert at the conference who stands up to share their advice would say. Having one term, multisensory room, to denote a great multitude of things is not helpful . . . it's no wonder the message gets confused!

Figure 1.5

The branding of multisensory rooms changes how information is shared and provokes the evolution of a new philosophy

The owning and selling of Snoezelen, and other brands, changed the way information around practices in multisensory rooms was shared. Hulsegge and Verheul and the other developers of sensory spaces (Flo Longhorn and her rumpus room, Lilli Neilsen and her "Little Rooms" and many more besides) were keen to share their practices openly with others. Once a term is owned it gets advertised. Advertising naturally presents only the positive aspects of what is on offer drawing a veil over aspects that work less well.

Together with the new term, those at the time who were aware of the very particular philosophy underpinning Snoezelen felt there was also a need for a new philosophy. They were dismissive of what they saw to be an approach that said just let them relax; if learning happens then it is a bonus, do not direct learning, just let everything flow. They wanted more.

These changes happened as we lingered on the edge of the 1980s and you can see in the changing attitudes thought patterns that reflected the shift in generations, as the hippies of the 1960s and 1970s gave way to the yuppies of the 1980s and 1990s. "Let them go with the flow" is a very 1960s sentiment. "Have an aim, a target, reach for the stars" is much more reflective of the 1980s and 1990s. So we came to a fork in the road with regards to multisensory rooms. One group of people believed that you should enter the room and allow whatever happens to happen. A new group believed that you should have a clear target, a purpose.

Debating approaches

Bozic (1997) describes the two interpretative systems at play within multisensory room practice as being "potentially" (p. 60, quoting Potter and Wetherell 1987, p. 153). Many people understand them to be directly opposed to one another: let them do what they want verses directed targets. Pagliano (2008) identifies five major philosophical approaches underpinning the use of multisensory environments, but for simplicity's sake I will be grouping these broadly into either directive or non-directive approaches.

A more accurate view of the potential contradiction between directive and non-directive approaches within the world of multisensory rooms would be to view them as stacked upon one another. The people wanting targets achieved begin from the assumption that the person they are supporting is relaxed and curious within the room – after all, a stressed individual is not going to get anything out of being pushed towards a particular target. If a person is not relaxed and at ease within a multisensory room, then the first target before you look to any other being achieved is to find a way to help them to relax, or if this cannot be achieved, then to allow them to leave.

The change from a non-directive approach to a directive approach to multisensory room work did not automatically happen as a New Year was heralded and 1979 became 1980. When I first worked in a special school it was clear that among the staff I worked alongside were people who very much believed that children in a multisensory room should be allowed to do as they pleased, and those who felt they should be working towards an end goal. These staff would often come into conflict with one another, but because no one questioned our underpinning beliefs, we did not know what was causing the confusion. Bozic (1997) found that teaching assistants tended to subscribe to the non-directive, child-led view of how a multisensory room should be used, whilst teachers tended to take on a more directive, developmental view of the rooms.

The respect for the humanity of an individual in Hulsegge and Verheul's non-directive approach is enormously appealing. But because an approach was right at one point in time does not mean it is right always. When Hirstwood and Gray (1995) say they want more than sniffing and dozing (p. 3), they are not saying Hulsegge and Verheul are wrong; they are responding with the ambition of the 1980s. They want more! Ultimately our choice of approach needs to be directed by the person with whom we share it. No matter how well thought out and nuanced, any one approach will be right for one person and wrong for another.

Imagine a typically developing, able-bodied child. Suppose their teacher said to you that they were going to put them in a room and just see what happened, that learning might or might not happen, but that what was important was that the child felt relaxed and was in charge of what happened in the room. Would you champion this teacher as a leader amongst educators or would you fear for the educational progress of the child? Would you want to know precisely how the room was going to be set up in order to enable this extraordinary process? Would you doubt any room could truly contain the learning capacity of that child?

In this question we see another split that happened in multisensory room practice: as the rooms grew in popularity, within the education context we saw them being used in a more directive way, whilst in care settings they continued to be used primarily as non-directive recreational spaces.

OVERVIEW

The Snoezelen approach emerged from the genuine desires of a small group of people to enrich the lives of people with learning disabilities about whom they cared an enormous deal. As they sought to do this they shared what they were doing with other motivated parties who used their ideas as inspiration to promote change in their own relationships with people with learning disabilities.

The growing interest in the Snoezelen approach caught the attention of companies who saw an opportunity to provide equipment to, and earn a profit from, these change makers. The trademarking of the Snoezelen approach changed it from something driven by people and informed by shared experience to something driven by products and profit informed by advertising.

The trademarking of Snoezelen also forced those not using equipment provided by the company Rompa, who owned the trademark, to call what they were doing something different. The term "multisensory room" began to be used.

Information sharing around multisensory room practice shifted from open conversation to advertising and was further confused by a great number of different types of rooms being denoted by the catch all term "multisensory room." In a further attempt to differentiate themselves from the Snoezelen movement, proponents of multisensory rooms began to advocate for a more directive approach to interactions within the rooms.

F.I.S.H.

Do your questions about multisensory rooms start with people or products? Are you asking what can we do with this thing, or what can we do with this person?

Rooms multiply like rabbits

ORIENTATION

Through the 1980s and 1990s multisensory rooms multiplied at an extraordinary rate and the claims made by companies about their efficacy rocketed, contributing to their increased uptake. As well as being motivated by a desire to make a profit, companies selling multisensory room equipment wanted to make a difference in the lives of people with disabilities, but they found themselves hampered by a lack of knowledge about the needs and abilities of the people with disabilities in the people supporting them.

Tangible items were easier to gain funding for and many charitable organisations willingly raised the funds to install multisensory rooms in homes, schools and care environments. As provision of the rooms overtook knowledge about them, practice in the rooms worsened. By the mid 1990s we found them being referred to as "holding pens" or "dumping grounds."

People wanted a multisensory room because they were better than nothing and they saw no alternative. They found the technology in the room attractive, and without solid research findings to guide decision-making by those who held the purse strings, advertising became the driving force when deciding to build a multisensory room and choosing resources for inside the room.

The proliferation of multisensory rooms and their use

From a disparate collection of approaches using a disparate collection of equipment, to a position of pre-eminence in almost every centre catering for individuals with learning disabilities, within a decade, the growth of multisensory rooms and their attendant technology can be considered nothing short of amazing. This rise is even more astounding when one takes into account the almost total lack of any official support for the movement.

(Hirstwood and Smith 1995)

At the start of the 1980s there were just a few multisensory rooms in existence and the voices debating their use were all talking about the same sort of space. But as more rooms came into being, each set up in a slightly different way and underpinned by a slightly different rationale, the debate around them became more fractured. People were talking about different things as different types of rooms were used with people with different types of needs, yet they believed themselves to be talking about the same type of room.

Researchers and commentators noted the rapid growth in the number of multisensory rooms and their evident popularity (Hirstwood and Gray 1995; Ayer 1998; Nicodemus 1999; Botts et al. 2008). Many went on to note that not only were the rooms themselves increasing in number, but the populations of people being invited into the rooms were also increasing.

Hulsegge and Verheul (1986) saw multisensory rooms (Snoezel rooms) as being designed specifically for the "severely retarded" (p. 24). Singh et al. (2004, p. 286) noted that multisensory rooms "are increasingly being used for people with mental retardation and mental illness." Other commentators reported them being used with people with dementia, autism, specific brain injury and so on. Longhorn (2018) expressed concern about their growth in the adult care industry, saying "as I am now elderly I think with horror, that perhaps one day I will be parked next to a bubble tube or find myself wrestling with fibre optics!"

As the numbers of multisensory rooms increased so did the populations of people thought to benefit from the rooms, so that from a starting point of one tent for one group of profoundly disabled people we now found ourselves at not so much an end point as a midway point of a great multitude of rooms, claimed to be for a vast assortment of people.

Massive overclaims about the efficacy of multisensory rooms grow the multisensory room industry

As the number of multisensory room sellers increased it becomes increasingly necessary for people selling multisensory rooms to highlight the benefits of their products. Unchecked by insight from research, overclaiming became rife.

Sellers claimed that multisensory rooms were a panacea to cure all ills, for example, this from Flaghouse in 2011:

> there's literally no end to the possibilities of sensory stimulation, which can be brought to people with special needs, young and old. That means that there's also no end to its benefits for mental, emotional and cognitive challenges as well as degenerative conditions such as dementia or Alzheimer's disease in old age and neurological diseases in younger populations.

It would be a very impressive piece of research indeed that drew the conclusion that the benefits of a particular space were endless!

Clearly any company with a product to sell desires to sell that product. If the company is successful in their sales techniques the outcome of this will be an increase in the presence of their product in our lives; this has certainly happened with regards to multisensory rooms. Mount and Cavet (1995) note that multisensory rooms have been widely promoted as associated commercial opportunities have become apparent. Pagliano (2001, p. 4) echoes this sentiment:

> the Snoezelen concept provided the opportunity for the emergence of the MSE (Multi-sensory Environment) industry. The commercial interests of this industry can drive provision more than a genuine desire to achieve valued outcomes for individuals with disabilities.

Hirstwood and Gray (1995) report the findings of an independent study that showed that by and large, most people bought what they were told to buy by the suppliers of multisensory room equipment. Several of the multisensory room suppliers I interviewed in the course of my research echoed this sentiment today, saying that they always asked settings what they wanted in their rooms but that the settings could rarely answer their questions and instead insisted on being told what to buy. Whether it is driven by the sellers or buyers of multisensory rooms, it is clear that rooms are being built based on products, not people.

The proliferation of multisensory rooms is about more than money

To say that the proliferation of multisensory rooms was solely driven by a desire for financial gain from those selling the room would be to adopt an overly simplified version of events, although one leading seller of multisensory resources told me candidly recently that "if a firm sticks the word sensory in front of a piece of equipment it is a license to triple the price." Many of the makers of multisensory rooms I spoke to became involved in the industry because of a genuine desire to see positive change; several pointed out that their qualifications would have enabled them to make more money in other tech based industries had money been their primary motivator.

Overclaims made by the sellers of multisensory rooms do not just come about through a desire to sell; some are motivated by deeply personal experiences. There are heads of big multisensory room companies who have beloved family members for whom they have seen benefit from being in a multisensory room. Their passion for the rooms is one of almost religious conversion; they have seen the truth in their own lives and wish for us all to be enlightened. When they speak about the potential of the rooms for creating change they are not claiming facts, they are declaring faith.

There are heads of multisensory rooms companies motivated by a very genuine desire to provide the best equipment for settings who express great frustration at their inability to do so. This is not through lack or resources or technical understanding but because they are hampered by a lack of insight from the people in the setting they plan on providing for as to what they want or need from their multisensory room.

Hirstwood and Gray (1995) point out that "companies are not necessarily trying to rip you off but they will advise a design based on their marketing angle and their own philosophy which may not be the same as your own" (p. 19). A multisensory room manufacturer cannot sell you a good multisensory room unless you know what you want from it and what philosophy will underpin its use. Lee Bleming (2018b) from the company Sensory Guru emphasises the fundamental nature of design to the success of a multisensory room succinctly, stating "design thinking is critical for anything to work properly."

Other factors come into play as we consider driving factors behind the proliferation of multisensory rooms. Mount and Cavet (1995, p. 54) note that "unfortunately it is easier to obtain funding for the purchase of tangible, novel, specialist equipment (multisensory room) than it is to secure financial support for adequate staffing ratios and appropriate training in order to enable people with profound and multiple learning disabilities to gain the most from their environment." They go on to say that "The electronic wizardry of MSRs (multisensory rooms) create a false impression of quality and luxury, there is a fundamental need to recognise that the quality of staff input is paramount."

Janet Gurney (2019), founder of Us in a Bus, a not-for-profit charity that provides intensive interaction opportunities for people with profound disabilities and complex needs, spoke to me about the trouble she has had over 28 years of being the managing director of Us in a Bus in getting people to fund essential things like staff and buildings, whereas funding for equipment is relatively easy to raise.

Dangers arise from the misunderstandings

You would expect that over a period of using anything, we would get better, more practiced and more skilled at using that thing. The rapid proliferation of the multi-sensory room industry has clouded our understanding of the essentiality of having an underpinning philosophy with regards to the use of a multisensory room. This is compounded by a lack of regulating information from research – we have not had clear guidance from the land of academia categorically sorting out a good claim from a bad and we have been left in a very dangerous situation. You would expect to see provision improve over time. Yet the confusion arising from all I have summarised in the previous section has arguably led, in some settings, to a worsening of provision through the decades.

Hope (1998) reports Savage's (1996, p. 378) suggestion that "the rapid utilisations of multisensory rooms is the vehicle by which professional carers avoid their responsibility towards their patients with dementia." These professionals are not wilfully neglecting their responsibilities; they have been told by companies that the rooms do amazing things, so they view their role to be one of letting the room do its job.

The notion that in purchasing a large piece of specialist equipment we have in some way already done the work is one that is reflected in educational and care settings for individuals with learning disabilities. McKee et al. (2007, p. 305) warned that "multi-sensory rooms might get used over more effective treatments as people believe staff do not need training in order to use them, whereas more effective methods require staff to be trained." Here we see another risk, especially as the cost of multisensory rooms increases and the awareness of the importance of an underpinning philosophy fades as over time: the rooms become more about the equipment and less about the practice within them. An organisation that has just spent tens of thousands of pounds on a piece of equipment that does marvellous things does not see a need to train its staff in how to do marvellous things; they have already spent the money earmarked for the promotion of marvellous things.

People in my study echoed the view that staff felt that their role was to bring people into the room, and that the room would do the work for them. It is easy to see how this view has grown out of a misunderstanding of Hulsegge and Verheul's (1986) original non-directive work in Snoezelen settings, as people wrongly interpret non-directive to mean do nothing.

Hulsegge and Verheul did not do nothing in the room; they let the people they were supporting lead and they did what they were led to do. They did go into the room without a plan, and to staff who see most of their role as being the carrying out of specific plans an activity without a plan is one that does not require any "doing" on their part. This passivity of staff is reflected in research findings from the 1990s: Mount and Cavet (1995) and Hirstwood and Gray (1995) both report staff using multisensory rooms as holding pens or dumping grounds in which to put people when they do not know what to do with them or when they want to get on with other things.

The terms "holding pen" and "dumping ground" sound incredibly cold, but we do not know if the staff acting in this way lacked care or whether they believed themselves to be following best practice. Indeed, Baker et al. (2003, p. 466) speculates that "the popularity of multisensory rooms could be down to staff viewing them as friendly and humane." What better place to take someone than a place that is automatically friendly and humane? Again we see the difficulties that arise when we view the multisensory room approach as being about the room.

Further drivers of the proliferation of multisensory rooms

Better than nothing

Baker et al. (2003) wondered whether the popularity of multisensory rooms could be explained by the limited alternatives available. Hulsegge and Verheul created their Snoezelen space because none of the other activities on offer at the summer fair were accessible to the people they were supporting. Their situation was not an isolated one of a lack of provision, but rather it was reflective of a generalised lack of provision. When you have nothing, something is better than nothing.

As we move out of the 1970s and into the 1980s, occupying a world where people are more interested in providing for the needs of those with complex disabilities, what is on offer to them? If you are a person in 1982 with money in your pocket to spend on resources for people with profound and multiple learning disabilities, aside from a multisensory room and sensory equipment, what could you buy? Now we have all manner of options, from the super high-tech such as eye gaze to the super arty such as immersive sensory theatre, but back then it was pretty much a multisensory room or nothing.

Hogg et al. (2001, p. 354) considers whether "the development of multisensory rooms can be seen in part as a reaction against institutional settings with their concomitant of sensory deprivation." When you are operating in a climate of no provision at all, something, anything, is heralded as wonderful. Of course people were ebullient about the rooms; they were so very much better than anything that had been on offer before. Hirstwood and Gray (1995) reported feedback on one of the first multisensory rooms: "The stressed are relaxing, the silent are speaking, and the withdrawn are coming out of themselves." The rooms, when they were first a part of provision, were amazing, but this ebullience belongs to a time. It is a response to the experience of living as provision changed. It is not evidence of the efficacy of the rooms themselves.

Lancioni et al. (2002, p. 176) report that multisensory rooms have been "readily accepted by staff, probably because of the dearth of interventions and resources available, and the widely held notion that Snoezelen is pleasurable, friendly and humane," and they go on to cite a great many researchers who report similarly. It is easy to see that if you were working in a situation where the alternative to using a multisensory room was nothing at all that a multisensory room would stand as a shining beacon of hope. But is that your current situation? Do you have alternatives? (See page 75 for a list of alternative sensory spaces that are relatively simple and inexpensive to set up.) Other researchers (Challis 2014) have suggested that multisensory rooms belong to a particular period of our development, viewing them as potentially outdated now as accessible technology is available to provide augmented access to experience as well as sensory experiences in and of themselves outside of the sensory environment. They speculate that "there is no real need to take an individual to a dedicated multi-sensory room" (Challis 2014, p. 215). Bleming (2019a) says "Technology has advanced significantly since the development of the first Snoezelen spaces. These bespoke spaces are no longer essential; natural user interfaces make it easy to engage directly with personalised sensory content anywhere."

Attractive

Fowler (2008) describes how multisensory rooms have "caught people's attention and proliferated" around the world despite there being little formal research into their effectiveness. As we continue to update the rooms we continue to turn heads.

I remember my first experience of seeing fibre optics: my grandparents had bought one of those fibre optic Christmas trees that were so popular in the early 1980s and I was entranced by the slow colour change and the startlingly bright light at the tips of the tree's fronds.

Today a fibre optic toy would not turn my head, would not catch my attention; to me they are old news. But on a quick detour via a well-known sensory shop as I changed trains at Birmingham New Street recently, I bought a two-pound fibre optic spray for my 4-year-old son and he was entranced, sitting up in the stillness of his room long past bedtime, hypnotised by the way the little strands bounced and drew wiggling lines of light across the darkness. In his wonder I rediscovered my own.

That capturing of attention is incredibly valuable in making people want something. Currently we want immersive, four dimensional projection rooms. My own head was most certainly turned by an incredible immersive art exhibition that projected the decadent patterns of Gustav Klimt's paintings over the walls, floors and ceilings of an art gallery such that people could step into the landscape of the paintings with the patterns appearing to drip and move about them; gorgeous, utterly gorgeous.

That the spaces are attractive is not in doubt, but that they are attractive does not automatically mean they are effective. And especially that they are attractive to us.

Hulsegge and Verheul started from a wonder at dandelion fluff; for the person who has yet to experience this wonder is there a need to go further?

Les Staves (2018), a man of exceptional wisdom, insight and experience when it comes to supporting children with complex disabilities, recently wrote to me saying:

> Remotely generated effects of lights, or sharks, or thunderstorms sweeping across the ceiling are impressive and exciting but they should not devalue the fun of playing with a torch under a sheet or in a tent where the source of the fun can both be understood and affected.

Our own need to be impressed or wowed will have moved with the times, but the start point for the person we are supporting will be far simpler and we should not devalue it; instead we should use their interest to rekindle our lost wonder.

A lack of research

Botts et al. (2008, p. 145) caution that "interventions often emerge following the supply and demand commercial model, in responses to parents asking for the needs of their children to be fulfilled." They remind us that "we should rely on research evidenced procedures, otherwise we risk money on ineffective fads" and go on to say that in "the absence of proving product efficacy in the form of quality, replicable peer-reviewed research (as is the case for multisensory rooms/Snoezelen), educators should not allocate public funds on unproven, though promising, interventions."

The lack of research underpinning the use of multisensory rooms leaves us at risk of the kinds of misunderstandings exemplified in the previous section. Lack of research into provision for people with complex disabilities is not a problem specific to multisensory rooms. Imray and Colley (2017, p. 1) decry its absence, pointing out that "there is very little research into the learning of those with SLD or PMLD to uphold any views about anything."

The lack of research leaves those of us with limited budgets open to the risk of failing to choose the most beneficial item when making the difficult choice to spend money on one thing over another.

Within education there is a greater move towards evidence-based practice and in some places funding is contingent upon there being a research basis for the proposed intervention, such as in the US Department of Education (2016). Being guided by evidence over advertising would seem like a wise move for anyone with money burning a hole in their pocket.

It seems likely that other organisations, for example adult care organisations, will follow suit and will increasingly demand that funds be spent only on provision that is underpinned by evidence from research. In an era of "fake news" we are increasingly aware of the importance of checking facts, and hopefully we are less likely to believe a sales pitch without questioning the claims within it. We do not want to waste resources, be they resources of time, money, space or whatever, on promises of magic wands; we want what is real.

OVERVIEW

The advent of the multisensory room industry created an environment that allowed multisensory rooms to proliferate. But to believe that this proliferation was driven solely by the desire to turn a profit is to miss a key part of the equation. Many people desire to make a profit from us and yet we do not turn out our pockets to them. What enabled the multisensory industry to drive the proliferation of multisensory rooms, extending both the types of settings installing them and the populations of people invited into them, was the ignorance of the consumer, the attractive nature of the technologies in the room and the lack of desirable alternatives.

A wealth of advertising and a dearth of research led to the disempowerment of people using multisensory rooms and the false belief that the equipment and effects offered by multisensory rooms should be valued over simple interactions between persons.

F.I.S.H.

What provoked wonder in you as a child?

What provokes wonder for the person you support?

Do you go into your multisensory room searching for something you have been promised in advertising, or do you go into your multisensory room because you recognise it as a place where you and the person you support can share in wonder together?

Notes

1   The stories I have created in this section owe particular thanks to *Pride Against Prejudice* by Jenny Morris and *Forgotten Lives* by Dorothy Atkinson, Mark Jackson and Jan Walmsley.
2   The Sensory Projects each seek to demonstrate that inexpensive sensory resources can, with the right knowledge and creativity, be used as effective tools for inclusion. The Seismic Sensory Project is the fourth project run by The Sensory Projects and sought to create long lasting change for individuals or organisations through a year's programme of challenge and support.
3   Accessible here: www.disabilitymuseum.org/dhm/lib/detail.html?id=1782&page=all 21/12/18

Section

ORIENTATION

Initially, multisensory rooms were not the subjects of research because their original proponents, Hulsegge and Verheul, advised against measuring responses to the space. Fifty years have passed since the dawning of Snoezelen and the start of multisensory room practice, and the pile of research we have that relates to practice within the rooms is frighteningly small. When we inspect it and consider the conclusions drawn from it we begin to find ourselves in a situation where the dearth of research and the failings in its conclusions are so bad as to risk becoming funny.

In the coming sections we will look into the causes for the lack of research in this field, examine whether multisensory rooms could ever be a evidence-based practice, and take a glance at some examples of ridiculous conclusions drawn from well-intentioned attempts to inspect multisensory room practice through the lens of research.

Why is there a lack of research?

Initially the lack of research evidence to support the use of multisensory rooms was acceptable, for with such a new resource you would expect it to be the case. But we are pretty much fifty years on from the first use of the rooms and we still have no scientifically rigorous research evidence we can point to that justifies the expense of multisensory rooms. Be clear, it is the expense of the rooms we need to justify, not that they offer stimulation. We know from experience that the rooms engage and delight, but so do torches and pieces of tinfoil. What is it that the rooms are offering that justifies the thousands upon thousands of pounds spent on them?

Some people argue that practices supporting those with profound disabilities or special educational needs do not require research foundations. Arguments such as this are not the bid for freedom from the constraints of academics in their high ivory towers, as their proponents might think. Arguing that a particular group of people do not require researched based practice is to argue for those people to be second class citizens when compared to people considered typically developing. Or it is to argue that their education and emotional wellbeing is of secondary importance in their life. Kossyvaki (2019) asks, "is it ethical to waste money as well as staff and learners' time experimenting with something we have no data for showing that it can be beneficial for learners with profound and multiple learning disabilities?"

You could argue that it is not possible to do scientifically rigorous research on such heterogeneous populations. A lack of research about a population upon which it was not possible to do suitable research would be justified. Challis et al. (2017, p. 2) note that "the special needs educator is typically working at an individual level where the opportunity to generalise rarely arises." Kossyvaki (2019) writes, "Whilst it is true that some research methods fail to capture meaningful results from heterogeneous populations it is not true across the board. Other exceptional heterogeneous populations, for example people with autism, are widely and successfully researched."

Some researchers looking at the lives of people with profound and multiple learning disabilities are starting to move away from traditional scientific approaches (which emphasise distant observer stance) in order to develop methodologies anchored in ethnographic and phenomenological traditions which privilege engagement, participation and "being with others" to develop insights into the meaning of behaviour. Growing uptake and development in research methods such as the ethnographic and phenomenological approaches gives researchers fresh opportunities to meaningfully engage with the lived experiences of a diverse range of people. Integral to ethnographic approaches is "being with" people in their time and space, often talking, participating and observing simultaneously in a process of "participant observation" (Madden 2010, p. 19).

By spending time with and participating in people's lives, it is possible to build an in-depth understanding of their personal modes of communication (e.g. their particular expressions of emotion and reactions in different contexts). This understanding could, in turn, be used to inform more traditional evaluations that aim to understand the influence of interventions such as multisensory rooms. An understanding of people's individual modes of reaction/expression would allow observations to be tailored to each individual rather than relying on homogenised or standardised indicators that may have little relevance for the individuals in question. I am currently collaborating with Dr Sarah Bell at Exeter University to develop a research framework that meaningfully captures the opinions of people with profound and multiple learning disabilities.

Anti-research

Hulsegge and Verheul (1986) did not conduct research about multisensory rooms because to them, what they were doing was not about the room. They also felt that, were staff to be asked to take part in recording of outcomes during a multisensory room/Snoezelen session, this would prevent them from effectively taking part in the session and so would immediately make the research invalid. The research itself would destroy the thing being researched. That thing being the relationship, not the room. You cannot fully be in a relationship when one part of your mind is occupied as an outside observer on that very relationship.

Mount and Cavet (1995) and Hirstwood and Gray (1995), among others, note that this seemingly anti-research approach adopted by Hulsegge and Verheul led to an initially strict adherence to the notion that one should not record responses to a multisensory room. However, in spite of the room/relationship misunderstanding causing research to start out on the back foot, much research has been done into the use of multisensory rooms. Sadly, the conclusions drawn from these noble attempts to apply the lens of science to the conundrum of multisensory rooms have often been so ridiculously interpreted that their interpretations could form the backbone for a particularly niche piece of stand-up comedy, as you can discover in the coming section.

So bad it could be funny

The literature review that underpins this book was conducted by searching Scopus, ERIC (Education Resources Information Centre), Education Source and British Education Index, using terms relating to multisensory rooms, such as Snoezelen, Multisensory Room, Multisensory Environment and so on. Thirty-two papers were drawn from the original review. Over the year of writing this book, more papers came to light or were shared with me by their authors. The influence of these later-found papers is felt within the wider text of this book.

Regarding that initial literature review, some papers that might have been relevant were excluded as they were not accessible to me via the access rights I had to the archives. Further papers were sourced via request from their authors, and books read were either owned by the author or were borrowed from the Scottish Sensory Centre.

That initial haul of thirty-two papers might not sound like a lot but it compares well to other reviewers conducting similar searches; for example, Lotan and Gold (2009) conducted an extensive search of the research archives and found only twenty-eight studies relating to multisensory rooms. Verkaik et al. (2005) searched multiple scientific databases for a year for research linked to the use of multisensory rooms with people with dementia and chose studies that met a certain level of scientific rigour. Of 3,977 studies found, nineteen were selected and of these only three focused on multisensory rooms.

Suffice to say there is very little research out there, which considering we are now nearly fifty years into the use of multisensory rooms is a very poor showing indeed.

A stand-up routine of research fails

Permit me to take you through the dreadful comedy routine of hideous failures in research conclusions; you may provide the classic ch-ching of the high hat cymbal at the relevant points yourself and imagine the groan of the crowd. The humour here is meant lightly; in noting the ridiculousness of the conclusions, I hope to focus attention on the care that needs to be taken when extracting information from research. It is often not the fault of the researcher that ludicrous conclusions have been drawn from their research, however, they are culpable for the failures in methodological design.

In creating this routine I have taken inspiration for my jokes from many studies, and where studies have particular pertinence I have listed them at the end of each section. The studies listed are not all examples of bad research. Rather, many are studies highlighting the failings of studies that have gone before them.

Fibre optics and bubble tubes hold magical healing properties

Have I told you the one about the researchers looking to discover whether a newly installed multisensory room was yielding the benefits they had hoped?

They took Bob, who usually was staffed 1:20 in the living room where there is nothing to do, with a member of staff on duty whose sole purpose is to check no one has died yet, down to the multisensory room where Bob was staffed 1:1 with a member of staff whose job it was to help Bob to do whatever he wanted to do. Lo and behold, Bob did better in the multisensory room! The conclusion drawn: fibre optics are good for Bob (Ba-boom,-ch-ching!) (Mount and Cavet 1995; Hirstwood and Gray 1995; Hope 1998; Houghton et al. 1998; Martin et al. 1998; Cuvo et al. 2001; Lancioni et al. 2002; Baker et al. 2003; Fowler 2008; Fava and Strauss 2010; Hill et al. 2012; Challis et al. 2017).

One person with an additional need represents all people with that need, and two people with additional needs represent anyone and everyone with any kind of additional need

Based on what we learned from Bob and one of his friends who also seemed to enjoy the room, we know that multisensory rooms are an effective intervention for. . .

Drum roll please. . .

Everyone!

Yes, of course, Bob and his mate are just like everyone else and react in an entirely typical way that represents everyone else who has any form of disability or mental difficulty (Mount and Cavet 1995; Houghton et al. 1998; Finnema 2000; Kaplan et al. 2006; McKee et al. 2007; Lotan and Gold 2009; Hill et al. 2012).

The voice of staff is the voice of everyone

Bob and his friend went down to the multisensory room with Megan. Megan is usually rushed off her feet in the day room. In the multisensory room Megan got to sit
down for a moment and get some peace and quiet. She even took a little nap. We know
Bob and his friend enjoyed the multisensory room because Megan said "he had a nice
time." We asked Megan if we could film the "nice time" but she said no, she would
be too embarrassed for us to watch (Hope 1998; Finnema 2000; Lancioni et al. 2002;
Baker et al. 2003; interviewee 12; Fava and Strauss 2010).

The love of multisensory rooms is universal and knows no bounds

Another classic. Inspired by the work done with Bob, a new set of researchers wanted
to find out more about multisensory rooms. They began taking people from Bluebells
nursing home into the new multisensory room one by one.

Over the course of the study some people became distressed when asked to go down
to the multisensory room, so they were allowed to drop out of the research. By the end
of the study everyone apart from Bob and his friend had opted not to go to the multisensory room. Their findings were that "everyone" in their study loved multisensory
rooms. So once again we learn through the research that multisensory rooms are good
for everyone (Hope 1998; Lancioni et al. 2002)!

Control groups are not necessary, as one type of additional need is the same as any other

A group of super able people were sent by researchers into a multisensory room and
another group of less able people were sent off to do a sensory activity. The group
in the multisensory room were observed to be noticeably more active and engaged in
comparison to their less able peers. Once again the conclusion drawn is that multisensory rooms are a wonderful thing (Hope 1998; Finnema et al. 2000).

The magic vanishes at the door

One final punchline in this litany of research disasters is not a disaster of research but a
disaster *reported by* research. Near universally, researchers find that settings that have
spent thousands upon thousands of pounds installing and maintaining multisensory
rooms reap meagre benefits from the rooms themselves whilst people are inside the
room. But worse than the paucity of benefits experienced in the room is that what little
benefit there is evaporates at the door as soon as the room is left.

Consequently, hoping to implement evidence-based practice, Bob's setting is considering whether they should not just keep Bob permanently inside the room to ensure

they do not lose any of the expensive benefits (Finnema et al. 2000; Cuvo et al. 2001; McKee et al. 2007).

OVERVIEW

Without firm guidance from research we are reliant on anecdotal evidence from individuals, or advertising from companies hoping to take money from our pockets, as we consider what is for the best with regards to practice in multisensory rooms. Attitudes of Should-not, Could-not, and Would-not account for the continued lack of research into a practice that costs individuals and settings extraordinary amounts in terms of time, space, money and staffing. It is time we overcame our hesitance to embrace evidence-based practice and worked together to contribute to the field the knowledge and insight currently missing.

F.I.S.H.

How could you contribute to the research field? Could you conduct a small piece of action research, or become involved in a larger study? Sharing your work in a journal, magazine or online publication means that its impact could potentially be felt beyond the walls of the room you work in.

Would you be willing to support a researcher who was curious to find out more about multisensory room practice? Have you considered contacting research facilities near to you to see if they have students interested in studying your practice?

Do you share the good practice that happens within your multisensory rooms beyond the walls of that room, beyond the walls of your setting?

How could you make your current practice in your multisensory room form part of the research archive others draw upon?

What does it all mean?

ORIENTATION

Beyond fundamental errors in the research that has been conducted into multisensory rooms and the overzealous conclusions that have been drawn from such research is a greater misunderstanding: one of correlation and causation. It is possible that through five decades of research we have had our attention on the wrong thing. The original proponents of multisensory rooms were keen to point out that the magic was not to do with the rooms, and many contemporary researchers indicate that they believe their positive findings regarding multisensory rooms have more to do with the relationship between people within the rooms than they do with the rooms themselves.

Without guidance from research we are vulnerable to overestimating the value of multisensory rooms. Can their worth really be considered equal to the great expenditures of time, money, space and staffing that they demand?

In the coming sections we will examine common flaws in the research conducted into multisensory rooms and reflect on some of the misunderstandings at play within the field. We will consider their costs and ask whether alternatives are viable or whether current funding models limit our options to multisensory rooms alone.

Unpicking the dark humour

What my tongue-in-cheek comedy routine in the previous section describes is just a small insight into the "paucity of relevant, rigorous research into the perceived benefits of multisensory rooms," a phrase first used by Mount and Cavet (1995, p. 52). I am writing more than twenty years on from that highlighting of the dearth of research, and yet little has changed. What we see is research conducted without control situations or control groups, conducted on tiny numbers of people, without thought as to the potential effects of staffing or set up of a room and reliant on highly suspect measures of reporting.

Basic secondary school science lessons teach us to control for our variables when conducting research, yet consistently within multisensory room research we see many variables at play, and not only are they not controlled for, they are not even mentioned. We are also taught to acknowledge our own bias; although staff often have the most knowledge about a particular person's responses and methods of communication, the idea that their reporting is free from bias is extremely naive. Researchers should be using the knowledge of the people supporting individuals with profound and multiple learning disabilities to develop frameworks relevant to those individuals which are then used to observe them.

Of course the offer of some provision over no provision is going to yield positive results. When evaluating something over nothing we would expect to see positive responses, but those responses do not mean that the room is having an effect; they mean doing something, anything, has an effect. Just as offering a hungry man bread and him reaching for it does not mean he prefers bread over cake. It simply means he was hungry.

Many researchers indicate that they believe their positive findings are not related to the room but are instead due to the relationship between the person in the room and the person facilitating that experience (Haggar and Hutchinson 1991; Mount and Cavet 1995; Hirstwood and Gray 1995; Martin et al., 1998; Hope 1998; Fowler 2008; Fava and Strauss 2010; Challis et al. 2017). As Hulsegge and Verheul (1986) were at pains to point out: *It is not about the room!*

Findings from studies conducted on one or two people are really only relevant to those one or two people as conclusive evidence; to everyone else they offer insight but not proof. The use of staff reporting as a measure of effectiveness is deeply flawed because whilst staff may well know the person they are supporting better than anyone, their potential for bias in their observations is huge. Good research would ask those insightful staff what we could observe in Bob that would indicate a positive response, and what would indicate a negative response. Then external observers could dispassionately record actual responses without knowing as they were doing so what they indicated.

Please forgive me the sarcasm in the "comedy" routine earlier. The failures of reflective practice when it comes to multisensory rooms are so tragic that they fall into the category of laugh or cry. If I felt the rooms were useless I would not consider the research failures so tragic and this book would simply be a declaration of snake oil found. What makes it so upsetting is that we are collectively spending thousands and thousands of pounds on a resource for people in great need of better provision and yet, due to a collection of misunderstandings, they are not seeing the benefit of that expenditure. Furthermore it is not just money at risk of wasting but also valuable time, space and staffing.

The lack of research leaves us vulnerable

I am certain that some multisensory rooms have tremendous potential, and that others are a complete waste of space and money. But even those with tremendous potential, if not supported by relevant training, risk becoming awful wastes of space and money. In conducting my research I asked people whether they had been trained on how to use a multisensory room, distinguishing "use" from "operate the equipment." Not only did ninety-six percent of the people I interviewed say that they had not had access to any training with regards to how to use a multisensory room, most laughed in my face in response to being asked the question as if it was absurd to even suppose that they might have had training. One of my interviewees summed up the situation succinctly, saying: "We have received training on how to operate the equipment, but absolutely no training on its purpose for useful learning. Honestly, it tends to be a place where pupils get parked while staff chat." Sarah Hall (2018) from Willow's Sensory Services points out that "schools are happy to pay thousands of pounds for equipment but not for training."

Drawing no distinction between parents, family members, carers, practitioners and professionals, we who support people with profound disabilities such that they are reliant on us to be not their voice but their microphone as we advocate for what is best for them are at serious risk of wasting so much. Wasting time, money, space and, worse still, opportunity.

Are claims that multisensory rooms do no harm valid?

I have heard a tepid argument for multisensory rooms based on them doing no harm. This would broadly seem to be the case, although there are research studies that have shown the rooms to have a damaging effect on particular people (McKee et al. 2007) or a detrimental effect to the hoped-for adjustment of skills or behaviours (Hope 1998). But broadly the rooms do no harm. So if they do no harm . . . we might as well have them?

When considering the argument that they do no harm, it helps to bring our thoughts back to the personal. Viewing the debate through the lens of an individual, we can begin to recognise the danger in which the lack of clear evidence-based practice leaves us. Bring to mind one person you care deeply about: a person who has profound disabilities, a person who might rely on you to advocate for their best interests. You have a set amount of time, space and money to support that person, and I am going to take a vast amount of it and use it for something that will have little to no effect for them. Have I *really* not done them any harm? What could you have used that money on if I had not spent it? What could that space have been? What could their time have been spent doing?

Imray and Colley (2017, p. 1) argue that current educational provision for people with special educational needs is not just poor but "it is positively harmful since it directly reduces the opportunities for learners to learn and wastes extraordinarily precious and expensive learning time." Is this an argument we could apply to people with profound and multiple learning disabilities? *Routes for Learning* points out that

> Our learners (with PMLD) are entitled to access a curriculum and assessment framework which is fit for purpose and meets their specific needs – there is little benefit or increase in entitlement if they are included in structures which fail to do this.
>
> *(WAG 2006 p. 46)*

Are our multisensory rooms really the best use of their incredibly precious time? Is the unquestioning use of multisensory rooms as a provision that is presumed to meet their specific needs really doing no harm?

Funding is not available for other resources

People have argued that it is naive to think of pots of money being available for other things if not spent on multisensory rooms. Janet Gurney (2019), founder of the Intensive Interaction provider Us in a Bus, talked to me of the difficulties she had through twenty-eight years of running Us in a Bus persuading people to fund things like staff, buildings and office space. She explained that people prefer to fund a "thing."

Multisensory rooms are a very clear "thing" and your local do-gooding organisation will merrily lead the way with fundraising for a "thing," especially a "thing" they can have their photo taken in afterwards. Local companies similarly will recognise the advertising potential of sponsoring a "thing." Sponsoring training or increased staffing ratios is less photogenic. It is also more morally fraught as quite rightly big funders like the National Lottery do not want to see essential services propped up on the back of one-off funding grants.

Clearly it is true that it is easier to fundraise for a multisensory room than, for example, for staff to develop their relationship skills. But should we accept such truths as permanent or should we challenge them? If our conclusion is to throw our hands up and declare this simply to be the way of the world, then we do not change it.

What if instead of continuing to accept such fundraising models, we sought to educate the communities that support our organisations? What if we found a way of getting people excited about funding a piece of training or an extra hour of staffing to enable a room to be properly set up? Whilst it might be true that people are more likely to respond to a campaign for a particular thing, it is also true that the money you draw upon is in the pockets of a particular group of people and if you use it for one thing it will not be there for another.

This is not me saying do not buy a multisensory room. Think back to that person I asked you to bring to mind earlier: imagine the time and space and money you would need to create a multisensory room for them and to staff it according to their needs. If you had that time and space and money, you could do amazing things, could you not? Hirstwood (2015) says "the design of multisensory rooms should be based on the requirements of their users, not cost or company packages." Pagliano (2001, p. 8) agrees saying that "the multisensory environment should be built from the child out with the goal of making the child's world more meaningful." And that is possible, but it starts with thinking about a person, not browsing a catalogue for resources or even a book for ideas.

OVERVIEW

When multisensory rooms first began being used, spectators noticed amazing effects and collectively we set about studying the rooms. We are dealing with confusion between causation and correlation. Imagine seeing a building burn and noticing the amazing amount of damage done by the flames and then setting about studying how many firefighters attended the blaze in order to find out what had done the damage. You could easily conclude over time that the greater the number of firefighters in attendance at a fire, the worse the damage will be. Of course you'd be wrong!

In the burning building example, both the number of firefighters and the extent of the damage are controlled by a third factor: the fire. With regards to multisensory rooms, the room and its effect are both controlled by a third factor: the relationships within the room, and it is these that we should have been studying all along. The initial proponents of multisensory rooms said that the impact of the rooms was not to do with the rooms themselves, and many researchers since have reported that their positive findings about the rooms are probably due more to the relationships within the rooms than to the rooms themselves. We need to stop counting firefighters and start paying attention to the fire.

Rather than decrying the possibility of successful research into provision for this population, we should set about creating the methods we need to accurately reflect a picture of practice as it stands. Kossyivaki (2019) asks whether it is ethical for us to hold onto knowledge that, were we to share it, could benefit the lives of others. Provision as a whole benefits when we engage with research.

Funding models that only allow the allocation of funds to a particular provision should be challenged. In terms of their costs, multisensory rooms draw on a limited pool of resources (both monetary and otherwise). They are an alternative provision, but an alternative to what? Have we considered what said resources could be utilised for if they were not allocated to multisensory rooms?

F.I.S.H.

If you conducted a piece of research, how could you avoid the pitfalls described in this section?

Are you the recipient of donated items or activities? Are these items or activities what you would choose to spend time and funds on if the power was yours to make that decision? How can you better inform fundraisers of your needs?

What does the research that is out there tell us about the effectiveness of multisensory rooms?

ORIENTATION

In the coming sections we look at what the existing research into multisensory rooms says about the rooms and find that, unlike advertising about the rooms, it makes no bold claims. Some of the positive findings about the rooms indicate further contingent factors, such as the frequency of access to the room as playing a key role in the positive outcomes. Negative and mixed results are also present, "mixed" being people finding positive and negative outcomes as well as people finding outcomes which are themselves mixed; for example, behaviour improving in the room but then deteriorating after being in the room.

At the end of this section we listen to researchers' and commentators' petitions for more research and question whether after fifty years of practice in multisensory rooms we really need research at all.

Mixed and mild

After all my decrying of the paucity of the currently available research into the use of multisensory rooms, let us take some time to find out what has been found out. What *is* the little that is out there?

Mixed results

Research findings into the effectiveness of multisensory rooms have been mixed. Finnema et al. (2000) found that responses to multisensory rooms changed week to week, Lancioni et al. (2002) reviewed studies of the use of Snoezelen and found very mixed results, some studies reporting positive effects, some mixed and others negative. Reviewing six long-term studies, they found only two showing favourable benefits to using multisensory rooms. Botts et al. (2008, p. 144) also found "inconsistent results" when they reviewed the research into multisensory rooms.

Positive effects observed may be caused by other factors

There is much anecdotal evidence to suggest positive outcomes from using multisensory rooms, but it is often not clear whether the research is indicating the rooms had an effect or whether it was the changes in behaviour and ratios of staff that had the effect; for example, Houghton et al. (1998) found modest improvements in skills following the introduction of multisensory room sessions to their school day, but wondered whether this was more down to the novelty of the experience rather than the particular experience itself.

Hope (1998) recorded both positive and negative reactions to multisensory rooms from people with dementia. Staff taking part in this study regarded the multisensory room as the chance to spend "quality time" with the people they were supporting, suggesting that positive reactions could have been due to the increased attention for which the environment was the excuse rather than the cause (p. 382).

Mild findings

Singh et al. (2004) found aggression and self-injury lowered within a multisensory room. Verkaik et al. (2005) found some evidence that multisensory rooms reduced apathy in people in the later stages of dementia.

Fowler (2008) reports that anecdotal research evidence suggests multisensory rooms help people to relax, decrease challenging behaviour, agitation and anxiety, increase interaction between people and the environment and increase concentration.

Fava and Strauss (2010, p. 167) found "Snoezelen decreased disruptive behaviours in individuals with autism but not those with profound mental retardation." However, their findings indicated the use of the multisensory room needed to be intense for it to be successful; participants in their study had three sessions a week for seven weeks, whereas most people accessing a multisensory room in a particular setting get one session per week.

You will note that none of these findings are particularly triumphant, that there is a tentativeness to them all and that no researcher claims a direct effect from the rooms themselves.

It is not all positive

Research findings have not all been tepidly positive; some have been tepidly negative or confused or completely neutral. Baker et al. (2003) conducted a large-scale study over three countries on the use of multisensory rooms to support people with dementia and found no effect. Hope (1998) found a positive change in behaviour for people with dementia in fifteen out of forty-five multisensory room sessions, and although behaviour was deemed to be better within the rooms, they found a rise in negative behaviours once the session had ended. Hope (1998, p. 383) wisely advises that "carte-blanche exposure to multisensory rooms should be avoided, as whilst positive responses would seem to be common it is also clear that for some there are very clear negative responses." Whilst Hope's (1998) work is based in a care setting for people with dementia it is reasonable to presume that this piece of advice could be applied in any setting, especially settings catering to diverse populations where we would not expect a "one-size-fits-all" approach to work.

Hogg et al. (2001) echo Hope's sentiments that, whilst much of the literature points to positive outcomes, a few studies yield entirely negative outcomes. They go further, examining the quality of the studies being considered, and find that the better designed studies reported both positive and negative effects with none showing a substantive demonstration that the effects of a multisensory room are maintained over time.

Pagliano (2001) reports the findings of Hopkins and Willetts (1993, p. 94) who observed that in badly used Snoezelen, children become passive and confused by conflicting stimuli. McKee et al. (2007) assessed the impact of a multisensory room on the disruptive and prosocial behaviour of men with autism, and found that for some, disruptive behaviour was increased.

We just do not have the proof . . . and that is scary

The evidence we have about the effectiveness of multisensory rooms universally lacks the scientific rigour required to be counted as significant. Fava and Strauss (2010, p. 161) sum the situation up when they say: "there is a lot of research to indicate that positive effects may be triggered by MSR (multisensory rooms), but much of this is methodologically weak, whereas stronger studies conclude no effect or even a negative effect." Challis et al. (2017, p. 1) echo this sentiment close to a decade later, indicating that things still are not changing, with the comment that: "the long term benefits of working with multisensory spaces are still to be assessed, where research has been carried out results have tended to be inconclusive."

Researchers and commentators express fears for the misuse of multisensory rooms, including their potential to divert the attention of staff away from recognising the potential of everyday sensory stimulation (Mount and Cavet 1995; Orr 1993), that they might be unstimulating and incomprehensible (Mount and Cavet 1995), that they could be used to bombard the senses and cause "shutdown" rather than relaxation (Hirstwood and Gray 1995), that undue and unfair demands might be placed on people within the rooms (Hirstwood and Gray 1995), that altered sensory stimulation could alter bodily self-consciousness (Noel et al. 2015), leading to confusion and even fear, that the combination of sensory effects and pharmacotherapy, such as antipsychotics, could trigger hallucinations for people that could add to their distress or disorientation (Lancioni et al. 2002), and that with the dawning of immersive multisensory rooms (rooms with multi-walled projections and interactive surfaces) we are about to see a repeat of the research errors of the past with substantive claims being made on the back of little to no actual evidence for their veracity. And they expressed concerns that progress will once again be driven by the available technology (Challis et al. 2017), rather than by the abilities and needs of the users of the rooms.

Research is needed

Researchers and commentators have been clear about the need for research to support the use of multisensory rooms. Mount and Cavet (1995, p. 54) stress the need for a critical evaluation of multisensory environments, warning that

> in the absence of rigorous research the value of multisensory rooms will be overestimated and they may be regarded as active treatment centres when in fact they are being used for containment or as a dumping ground where people with learning difficulties are placed and ignored.

This cry for better research echoes down to us through the decades: Bozic (1997) says the use of multisensory rooms in schools needs evaluation. Ayer (1998) notes a need for rigorous research to assess and evaluate the impact of multisensory rooms on children with profound and multiple learning disabilities. Finnema et al. (2000) note the same with respect to people with dementia. Singh et al. (2004) describe the dearth of research available into the use of multisensory rooms.

Houghton et al. (1998) declare that there is a "real need for empirical research to examine the effectiveness of multi-sensory rooms" (p. 269). They explain that "the proliferation of multi-sensory environments with their financial/time/person/space commitments deserves to be investigated" (p. 268), noting that "to date research done into multi-sensory rooms has been almost entirely descriptive with no empirically based measures of effectiveness" (p. 268). They also point out that it is hard to tell from the research into multisensory rooms whether the positive results claimed are a result of the room or of other factors, e.g. being away from another room or having one to one non directive attention.

Lancioni et al. (2002, p. 180) explain that research needs to be clearer on when and for whom Snoezelen has a positive effect, adding that the research that "is currently out there is not strong enough to draw firm conclusions from." Lotan and Gold (2009) demand that future research be more in depth and more rigorously framed. Verkaik et al. (2005) say that guidelines for care should be based on scientifically proven strategies and that currently there is a lack of rigorous research with regards to the effect of multisensory rooms for them to be considered best practice. Botts et al. (2008) also conclude that multisensory rooms, in research terms, do not meet the standards required for evidence-based practice. Lotan and Gold, writing in 2009, state that "due to an almost complete absence of rigorous research in the field of multisensory rooms confirmation of this approach as an effective therapeutic intervention is needed" (p. 207).

Heagele and Porretta (2014) note alongside the popularity of multisensory rooms the lack of empirical studies to evidence their effectiveness. Challis et al. (2017 p. 1 and 2) describe the long-term benefits of working with multisensory spaces as "still to be assessed," adding that "where research has been carried out results have tended to be inconclusive."

And so six paragraphs down from where we started, after nearly fifty years of work within multisensory rooms and with research spanning over two decades, we find that the research community still has adequate multisensory room research very much on its "to-do" list.

Do we really need it?

Well, of course researchers will say research is needed; the doing of research is their bread and butter and they are predisposed to believe it to be worthwhile. We have all heard tales of research being done, supposedly to underpin practice, but the research set up is so vastly removed from the reality of daily life as to render the findings effectively meaningless. Of course we can see such and such progress if we have a lab and five lab assistants and a specialist piece of equipment with an expert to operate it all, but what do the findings of such a piece of research mean in your average classroom or care setting? Researchers do research to entertain themselves (some people would say).

If we have made it through fifty years of practice without a solid research foundation for what we are doing in multisensory rooms and many great things have been done in the rooms, then do we really need research? Should not we just all get on with it? If it is going well so far, let us keep at it.

But is it going well? How do we know? Can you prove it? What if you are wrong? There are plenty of examples in history when people have merrily thought something was right and beneficial and have believed themselves to have experienced these benefits only for us to find out further down the line that they were mistaken. Many an outdated medical practice springs to mind! It is perfectly possible for us to think something is working and is good and for it not to be. We are all fallible.

You may think that you do not require "good" research to underpin your practice. You are thinking of the person I asked you to call to mind earlier; you know their preferences and abilities, you have a plan for what you will do together and you are able to assess whether it went well or not based on the communications you share during that time together. That is great. And just so long as you can be certain that your views on what is and is not beneficial are not being swayed by beliefs based on outdated, disproven ideas, and that your desire for particular spaces and things within them is not influenced by advertising, and that you are operating alone without being swayed by the crowd of people around you who all eagerly reach for the next promise in the hope of something better . . . now hang on a minute, you are beginning to sound like a dangerous person.

However well intentioned, not one of us exists outside of the influence of our age and the cultural conditioning that comes with it. Research is not perfect, but at least in well-conducted empirical studies we can gain some kind of outside perspective on things. We are not immune from the snake oil sellers. All through history people have succumbed to beliefs from persuasive people. We are no different. We need a measure outside of ourselves to help us judge whether something is a good idea or not, and peer-reviewed research is one of the best measures we have.

McKee et al. (2007) advise that professionals obtain practice information from peer-reviewed empirical studies before spending money on resources such as multisensory rooms over other evidenced-based practices. Botts et al. (2008, p. 145) say that "by promoting interventions that lack a scientific research base, vendors and educational decision makers who purchase and institute unproven products are potentially harming the students whom they desire to help by keeping them away from involvement in clinically proven programs." Are we choosing multisensory rooms over something else that would be better?

OVERVIEW

The research that has been done into multisensory rooms has not produced clear results, with researchers finding negative as well as positive findings and at times finding mixed results within a single study. Researchers are careful to caution people against reading too much into their findings and also highlight that other factors maybe influencing their results.

More research is required but we need to be vigilant that it is on the right thing. Consider the firefighter example from page 56. How much will we learn about the cause of the damage from studying the equipment the firefighters bring to the scene or the uniforms they wear?

F.I.S.H.

Are we choosing multisensory rooms over potentially better alternative provision?

When considering the needs of the person you support, how many alternative provisions have been evaluated alongside the opportunity to spend time in a multisensory room?

Considering the needs you hope to address in a multisensory room, what other options do you have for meeting those needs?

Section

3

ORIENTATION

Without firm guidance from research, advertising can end up as a source of information for people looking to find out more about multisensory rooms. Although we might like to consider ourselves immune from its persuasive nature, we are highly unlikely to be so, and indeed to be immune from social pressures such as the lull of the advertiser's smooth tongue could well be a cause for concern. Oftentimes the division between which statements have a firm evidence base behind them and which have a monetary motive behind them is clouded by misinterpretations of the research that is out there. The following sections explore the roll of advertising in our understanding of multisensory rooms and the limitations of understanding based on the research currently available.

Without research advertising may take the place of knowledge

Without a demand for evidence-based practice there is a risk that we will be exposed to claims about interventions that go unchecked. Mount and Cavet (1995, p. 52) note that "emotive language has been used to support the development of these environments; needs and rights are frequently mentioned; and claims about the therapeutic and educational benefits have been widely publicised." They go on to say that "prospective purchasers of Snoezelen environments may be vulnerable to persuasive marketing strategies," and that "there is a danger that in the absence of rigorous research the value of multi-sensory rooms will be over-estimated." Ayer (1998, p. 96) too warns that "without good research into multi-sensory rooms the value of them maybe grossly over-estimated." In light of evidence from my own study I would argue that there is reason to believe this has happened.

Many researchers and commentators warn of the grandiose claims and the lack of a research basis for the advertising surrounding multisensory rooms (Mount and Cavet

1995; Houghton et al. 1998; Orr 1993; Hope 1998; Ayer 1998; Cuvo et al. 2001). The blame is not to be laid solely on the shoulders of those doing the advertising. For example Messbauer (2012) makes massive claims as to the impact of multisensory rooms in individual transformations. It is clear from her writing that a huge amount of prep work went into creating these transformations and that they happened through the sensitive relationship created within the room, supported by the environment of that room. Someone taking Messbauer's work as evidence in support of their own multisensory room misses a very important point: their room has not got Messbauer within it!

At other times confusion can occur when people use the phrase "research has shown" too lightly. I know myself to be guilty of this when presenting at conferences. I will indicate that something is based in research, but in the half-hour slot I have to talk I do not have the time to go into the sample size of that study, or whether there was a control group, or if it was empirically measured, and so on. I simply say "research says." Of course I hope that you will wonder what quality of research it was, and whether other research says otherwise, but I do not highlight those caveats.

Writers may not be aware of the quality of the research to which they refer, or may face a word-limit problem the same as my time-limit problem, which inhibits their ability to caution their audience sufficiently; for example Nicodemus (1999, p. 19) states that "research has shown" that children are happier, vocalise more and tend to stay on task more in a multisensory environment. Yet we know that reviews of the available literature show that pretty much all the studies out there lack the methodological rigour required to draw firm conclusions. So has research really shown that conclusively?

Research into multisensory rooms has not shown anything clear at all. Different standards of proof are required for different forums; claims can be made in a blog post or magazine article that go unchecked. The benefit of peer reviewed research is that it is underpinned by a clear burden of proof that drives it towards being impartial. We are all more susceptible to what we want to believe; we need clear markers to direct us. Peer reviewed research is not immune from bias, but it is the strongest form of neutral commentary we can hope to have.

McKee et al. (2007) note that many claims have been made about the supposed ameliorative effects of multisensory rooms in relation to a wide range of challenges, including self-injury and challenging behaviour. All of these claims are based on studies with methodological shortcomings that would prevent the drawing of firm conclusions about the impact of multisensory rooms. McKee et al. (2007, p. 305) explain, citing many other researchers as they do so, that

> the result of increased prevalence of multisensory rooms was a proliferation of claims (lacking scientific rigor and going far beyond what data could support) that they have a positive effect on self-injurious behaviour, chronic pain, aggression, and the effects of head injury and dementia.

Flaghouse (2011, p. 48) provides a great example of the "proliferation of claims." In just one article they claim the following: that "Snoezelen works for a broad range of populations in a wide range of facilities." It would be more accurate to say that Snoezelen has been used with a broad range of populations in a wide range of facilities as there is no methodologically sound research pointing to it having "worked." That

> there's literally no end to the possibilities of sensory stimulation, which can be brought to people with special needs, young and old. That means that there's also no end to its benefits for mental, emotional and cognitive challenges as well as degenerative conditions such as dementia or Alzheimer's disease in old age and neurological diseases in younger populations.
>
> *(p. 49)*

Literally no end to possibilities and benefits is essentially a declaration of having found the panacea to all ills! Flaghouse (2012, p. 17) claims that "the Snoezelen environment is non-threatening, allows users to overcome inhibitions, enhance self-esteem and reduce tension." Some studies have had to be abandoned due to people refusing to enter multisensory rooms because they are distressed by the strange environment (Hope 1998).

"Research has shown a multitude of benefits from MSRs" (Flaghouse 2012, p. 17). But the research that claims these benefits has not been conducted in a scientifically rigorous enough way to confirm any of them.

"Research has shown MSRs give participant and caregiver the opportunity to improve communication and enhance their understanding of each other" (Flaghouse 2012, p. 17). Again, no research has been done that is sufficient to prove the validity of that statement; however the word "opportunity" could be the get out; a five-minute sit-down gives an opportunity to communicate. Whether that opportunity is taken or not is another matter and the room in which that opportunity occurs is not a necessary component of that opportunity.

Flaghouse (2012, p. 17) further claims that "the ability to choose or control stimulation within a multi-sensory room enables users to self-regulate." That a multisensory room provides an environment where people can choose and control stimuli means that it enables them to choose and control stimuli. The skill of self-regulation is much harder won; I may crave loud noise or bright lights in the way that I crave chocolate or wine. That I am able to control how much of these things I am exposed to does not mean I am able to self-regulate my intake of these commodities. Indeed, multisensory rooms could provide an environment where those prone to overindulgence could lavish themselves with too much of a good thing. Who is to say? We certainly cannot, as there is not the evidence out there to back Flaghouse's claim or mine.

How do you feel when I tell you that the claims just cited were all made by Barbara McCormack, vice president of the American company Flaghouse, which owns the exclusive rights to use the term Snoezelen in their part of the world, with rights purchased from Rompa, which owns the copyright globally? How do you feel when I tell you that these claims were all made by the mother of a child with Aicardi Syndrome, a rare genetic disorder that affects only girls? The prognosis for her daughter at birth was that she would live a short and pain-filled life impacted by seizures, unable to ever walk or talk, unable to see. For the first years of her life her daughter only cried or screamed, she did not recognise her parents, she knew only pain. It was in a multisensory room that her daughter first wanted to be a part of the world and that she, Barbara, first saw her daughter experience joy (McCormack 2003).

You feel differently. Nothing can be fully understood without looking into its history. One is a claim of evidence, the other of faith. *Declaring* faith is not wrong; it is our *understanding* of a declaration of faith to be a declaration of fact that leads us astray.

The new era of multisensory rooms looks set to repeat the mistakes of the past

With the advent of the new immersive multisensory rooms comprised of multi-walled projection and interactive features, we are beginning to hear matching overclaims about their capabilities. Pavlik (2017, p. 15) writes that "experiential media platforms enable persons across a diverse array of disabilities to increasingly engage in customizable, interactive, immersive and multisensory globally connected and mobile learning environments."

Ryan (2018, p. 66) claims that her approach to multisensory rooms has "created an advanced blend of treatment activities with the power to rewire the brain." Ryan goes on to make a great many more claims, all echoing those made by McCormack and other proponents of multisensory room usage. But with this initial claim we have the opportunity to take a little tangent into the tangle that is sensory integration theory, a theory that proposes that certain therapies can retrain the brain such that it is better able to integrate sensory information.

Botts et al. (2008, p. 139), in discussing sensory integration theory, explained that "the efficacy of the programs designed to repair or retrain the brain was largely laid to rest by the research of Hammill and Larsen in 1974." Going on to point out that "because of the research-to-practice gap," that same dangerous gap multisensory rooms currently teeter upon, "many programs remained in use long afterward."

Bott et al. (2008) explore recent criticism of sensory integration theory, which is often used itself to justify the use of multisensory rooms. They cites the lack of empirically sound research studies to justify adoption of the theory before coming back to a conclusion drawn by Hoehn and Baumeister (1994), which declares that "the current fund of research findings may well be sufficient to declare Sensory Integration Therapy not merely unproven, but a demonstrably ineffective, primary or adjunctive remedial treatment of learning disabilities and other disorders" (cited by Botts et al. 2008 in Jacobson, Foxx and Mulick 2005, p. 348).

As I write, a team at Cardiff University (Randell 2019) are looking to evaluate sensory integration further. They too note the lack of research into this particular therapy. I wait keenly to see if the people in their study will be offered sensory integration therapy or nothing, in which case I would expect the group that received stimulation to show improvement, regardless of what that stimulation was, or whether the participants in the study will be offered sensory integration therapy, nothing, or another sensory stimulation programme with matching levels of 1:1 attention and time, as is involved with sensory integration therapy.

No one is immune from bias

Enser (2017) advises that "teachers have needed to become more research informed to respond to the masses of misinformation presented to us. Even when a teaching approach is exposed as incorrect, it can continue to influence how we work." This is not just the case in teaching but applies across the board. We are all influenced by the past, and being aware of its influence can help us to make informed choices.

There is a big difference between simply not knowing you have been influenced and not having been influenced. Anyone believing themselves to be uninfluenced by the practices and attitudes of the past is deluded. It is not just ideas that have been shown to be wrong that pose a threat. Non-reflective adoption of any idea is dangerous.

The highly controversial claims of sensory integration theory are not the only ones we might want to hold up to the light when examining our practice in multisensory rooms. In many rooms (and outside of them), the legacy of behaviourist B.F. Skinner's theory of operant conditioning is still largely at play. This is a theory with a solid evidential basis, but the existence of solid research alone should not be enough for you to adopt something into your practice. Skinner showed that by positively or negatively reinforcing behaviour, you could effect behaviour change in both humans and animals. The token economy systems run in settings whereby tokens of some kind or another can be swapped for rewards spring directly from Skinner's work. The practice of encouraging people to press buttons in order to be rewarded by a sensory experience also comes directly from behaviourist theory.

The process of rewarding behaviour with external motivators has the secondary effect of increasing extrinsic motivation and decreasing intrinsic motivation; in other words people no longer do something because they want to do something, they do it to get something else. The something else becomes the focus of the behaviour, rather than the original object of it. Many educators will tell you that teaching a child to press a switch gives them access to technologies to enable them to communicate further down the line, but is this true in all situations?

Some children may be able to learn to press a switch but may never be able to learn to operate a computer in a meaningful way. Switch work can be confusing; we ask a child to engage with an object, but then require their engagement with a different object in order for them to do this. "Here is your switch, now look at the bubble tube." Some switches are an end in themselves, for example a Big Mac switch that plays a recorded message when pressed; others are a means to an ends and so demand greater cognitive understanding in order to make the link between object and the effect triggered through interaction with that object.

Do children necessarily have their life experiences enhanced by being conditioned to hit a switch? Imray and Colley (2017, p. 19) contend that "incessant switch work" may be motivated by an "overriding need to show 'success' within a linear, academic, developmental model" and an "over reliance on mainstream target-driven curriculum model." If we were looking to support their ability to communicate, might not intensive interaction, with its lack of any external motivators aside from communication, itself be a better approach?

In his presentation for the Nordic Network on Disability Research, Dr Ben Simmons, author of *The PMLD Ambiguity* (2014, p. 166), describes the following vignette about "Sam" as he takes part in a switch-based activity:

> Sam is sat on the carpet. His head is tilted back as if he is looking up at the ceiling, but his eyes are rolled back. He gargles and shakes his head left and right repeatedly whilst vocalising (". . . aaaaah aaaaah uuuuuh aaaaah . . ."). An LSA [Learning Support Assistant] walks over to him, puts her hands under his armpits, picks him up, and carries him a short distance to his wooden chair on wheels. She places him in the chair, straps him (seatbelt around his waist, feet in the stirrups), and clips a tray to the chair. Sam is then wheeled to the computer desk. The LSA connects a switch to the computer, places the switch on Sam's tray, and loads the software. All this time Sam is passive and slouched, almost like a floppy rag-doll. The LSA tests the software to make sure the switch is working. The switch press activates a sample of loud acid house music. The beats are fast and repetitive; the synthesiser rifts [sic] are high-pitch and frantic; the vocals are shrill. Animation accompanies the music. Lights flash creating a strobe effect; silhouette figures dance; and "trippy" patterns unfold in the corners of the screen. The LSA has left me to work with Sam. He makes no attempt to press the switch and looks increasingly frustrated, moaning to himself and shakes in his chair (is he trying to get out?), looking everywhere but the screen. I encourage him to press the switch, vocally at first, and then by holding his hand and placing it on the switch. I repeat this several times. The music plays and the graphics flash. Sam becomes aggressive towards himself. He snatches his hand away from me and slaps himself in the face, pulls his hair, pinches the side of his

neck and flaps his arms. He repeats in various combinations, over and over. I pat Sam on his back and speak jovially to him, trying to calm him down. He becomes less "self-active." I ask him to press the switch again and avoid touching him. He is not looking at the screen. He shakes his head left and right, wiggles in his chair, and slaps his face occasionally. Several minutes pass. I press the switch hoping that he will look at the screen. He only briefly glances at it. He keeps raising his flapping arms and hitting the table with them. He presses the switch with his forearms (but was it accidental?). He repeats the action, but does not hit the switch. Sam is now hitting himself over and over again. His skin is becoming red. Despite holding apart his arms, I can feel him fighting me. Eventually an LSA walks over, removes Sam from the chair and places him on his favourite vibrating rug. He keeps hitting himself and it takes a lot of effort to sooth [sic] him.

Why is Sam being expected to work on learning to press a switch, and why are children like Sam asked to do the same? By "like Sam" I do not mean of a similar level of disability; I mean anyone who so clearly does not want to do a thing.

I cannot possibly hope to unpick all of the foundations, good and bad, that multisensory room practice is balanced upon. All I can reasonably aim to do is point out that it is worth questioning what you do and why you do it. It is very possible that you have made an assumption along the way somewhere that, were you to catch it in the light, you would think twice about.

OVERVIEW

Without easy access to clear evidence from research, advertising becomes a source of information. Without clear guidance from research, advertisers are relatively free to make bolder and bolder claims. We have seen the claims made by the manufactures of multisensory rooms increase to almost ridiculous levels and we are beginning to see claims of a similar scale being made about the new immersive multisensory rooms.

Much of the information we have is from advertising and although we may be aware of this we underestimate our own bias and how swayed we are by what we hear. No one is immune from the hard sell of a well-written advert. We need to question where we get our information from and look into the history of that information. Is it fact or faith that is being proclaimed? Taking any piece of information at face value leaves us open to being misled.

F.I.S.H.

How do you find out about equipment and practices within multisensory rooms? Do you look to people with a vested interest in the rooms to guide you?

Do you ask peers who have experience of the rooms?

Do you look to the research archives to validate the claims you are hearing?

Do you have a method of testing the veracity of the claims you are hearing for yourself?

How do you evaluate the information you receive about multisensory rooms?

Do you consider the motivations of the person sharing that information with you?

Do you look back into the history of that information?

Do you inspect it for evidence rather than opinion?

ORIENTATION

Multisensory rooms promise to answer a great many problems, but have we considered other solutions to these problems? The evidence to show that being in nature offers valuable sensory stimulation is stronger than the evidence supporting multisensory room practice. Various behaviour management strategies have been shown to be far more effective in managing troublesome behaviour than exposure to a multisensory room. Even if multisensory rooms provide the positive outcomes they claim, are these enough to justify their large price tags? Are we being lured by a resource that promises to solve all our problems when actually different provision for different needs could be more effective?

Is there another way?

A good question to ask yourself is whether something else might be a better use of your time, money, staffing and resources for this particular person than a multisensory room. Mount and Cavet (1995) noted we tend to focus on the positive aspects of multisensory rooms without necessarily taking into account the range of other sensory approaches out there. Along with Ayer (1998), Mount and Cavet (1995, p. 53) postulate that everyday or community experiences could have greater benefit, and say "the paucity of published research into the educational applications of multisensory rooms should be a cause for concern especially in view of the amount of resources they absorb."

When we choose to expend a large amount of funds/time/space/staffing or other resources on one thing, we are putting our eggs very much in one basket, risking a lot. Would the risk be as great if we placed eggs in different baskets? I asked people on social media what they would spend the money on if I could reimburse them for just one-tenth of the cost of their current multisensory room. Answers ranged from music materials, good speakers and music therapists to intensive interaction practitioners, forest schooling, massage stories, intervenor training and sensory integration assess-ments, and even a small paddling pool with coloured cellophane panels to place over windows.

Deciding on what another way might be is tricky. Multisensory rooms are sold with promises that they will do everything for everyone; if we want to find evidence-based practice we may have to do different things for different people, to each according to his need rather than a one-size-fits-all-approach. In *Inclusion is Dead: Long Live Inclusion*, Imray and Colley (2017) argue vehemently that provision for people with profound and multiple learning disabilities should be fundamentally different from provision for other populations. A one-size-fits-all approach in the classroom, care setting or multisensory room benefits no one.

Here are two examples of researched-based practice that could plausibly be an alternative to multisensory room provision: nature and behaviour interventions.

Nature

A multisensory room looks impressive; it gives the impression of *something* being provided, of things being done. But impression and actuality are different things. The outdoor environment is freely available – it does not look particularly impressive, and yet researchers comparing its impact with multisensory room usage have found it to be superior at reducing stereotypic behaviour (repetitive seemingly unproductive behaviour) and increasing engagement (Cuvo et al. 2001; Fowler 2008; Hill et al. 2012). Hussein (2010) reports anecdotal evidence that sensory gardens are effective as a tool to enhance the educational development and social interaction of children with special needs. An outdoor education centre local to me installed a multisensory room but found visitors chose not to use it, preferring the natural experiences already on offer. An attempt to extend their provision revealed to them the worth of their pre-existing provision.

Lynsey Robinson (2018), who works for the Sensory Trust, an organisation that seeks to enhance the accessibility of nature for people, explains: The outdoor environment is always full of multisensory opportunities. No matter what the surrounding environment is like if you are outdoors you will be experiencing a range of sensory stimulus. For a start, there is always weather, there is always temperature, there is always sound.

We have been hearing for a number of years that children access the outdoors much less than they ever have done, and that the shift from being active outdoors to being sedentary indoors is having a damaging and lasting impact on our young people (Palmer 2006). We have also gotten used to terms like "nature deficit" (Louv 2005) and we are beginning to understand how a disconnect with nature impacts our physical health and emotional well-being.

There is a wealth of research sharing the benefits of spending time outdoors, from forest bathing (time spent in a forest to help reduce stress and increase well-being, a Japanese practice known as *shinrin-yoku*) to blue gyms (using water-based environments to increase health and well-being and connection to place). We are aware that spending time in nature not only makes us feel better but can also help to reduce blood pressure, alleviate symptoms of depression, and reduce heart rate and muscle tension (Stamatakis 2011; Mitchell 2008).

Nature can alter our physiology, but it can also support cognitive ability, helping us to clear our minds and complete different tasks. For example, it has been demonstrated that children with ADHD are more able to concentrate on focused tasks following time spent in nature (Taylor & Kuo, 2008). This research supports the ideas Hussein (2010) alludes to, namely, that you can indeed support educational development by using the outdoors.

The ideas around supporting social interaction of children are also valid when you look at the field studies conducted by Coley et al. (1997) at the Human-Environment Research Lab at the University of Illinois. Their work highlights that spending time in nature connects us to each other and to our place in the world. This type of understanding is key for many people who struggle to relate to each other or understand how they as an individual fit into the wider world. We need to be smarter about how we use school environments and give educators the tools to engage with nature.

It is clear that if we are considering alternatives to a multisensory room, the natural world is a very strong contender.

Behaviour

With regards to the use of multisensory rooms as a tool for managing behaviour, Hogg et al. (2001) point out that there are behaviour management techniques that have very solid research foundations and question why any setting would ever choose a strategy with no foundation in research over one already proven.

"Evidence on the effectiveness of behavioural approaches to challenging behaviour far outstrips that from multi-sensory room studies." Therefore, "the use of multi-sensory room as a first choice for dealing with challenging behaviour must be viewed as highly questionable" (Hogg et al. 2001, p. 370).

McKee et al. (2007, p. 306) agree that multisensory rooms are a poor choice when it comes to the management of behaviour as "there is no evidence of generalizable, specific therapeutic benefits for disruptive and aggressive behaviour." They advise that funding behaviour training for staff would "be far more effective than an elaborate multi-sensory room."

A cynical person might consider the motives behind the choice of a room over a well-evidenced and proven strategy. It would be easy for a purchaser of a multisensory room, sold to them as an ideal environment within which to help people in crisis, to think that the purchasing of a one-off big-ticket item was a savvier economic choice than the endless training and retraining of staff who may leave their roles and take all their carefully spent money with them. They own the room and keep it.

The idea that a one-off big-ticket item can adequately provide for behaviour needs and is a cost-effective way of doing also neglects the necessity of ongoing training and support for staff using multisensory rooms. But as so few settings actually provide training for their staff in how to use a multisensory room, it is rarely seen as a necessity. Training on behaviour management techniques is also terribly specific: it is about behaviour, whereas a multisensory room for people to use – when they express through their behaviour that they need it – can also be used for other people and other purposes. Again, it could seem like the more cost-effective answer to the unreflective purchaser.

Even if they work, are they worth it?

Lancioni et al. (2002) go a step further than questioning whether it is worth spending considerable resources on multisensory rooms without a solid evidence basis being in place and ask, regardless of whether or not they have a positive impact, if can they be considered cost effective. Speculating that they may only be so in large settings where many people get to use the equipment, they recommend that sensory stimulation sessions could be a viable, cheaper, less space-expensive option for small settings or for individuals. Haegele and Porretta (2014, p. 31) say that "research into the use of multisensory rooms must become more rigorous if their value is to be justified." Are multisensory rooms worth the financial and space costs?

OVERVIEW

Using multisensory rooms as an answer for a multitude of challenges from engaging the senses to dealing with behaviour might seem cost effective, but placing all our eggs in one basket is unlikely to yield the best results.

Decisions made without consideration of alternative options are unlikely to be finically sound in the long term, however economically savvy they may appear on the surface. Multisensory room practice has no solid evidence base, yet alternative targeted strategies have a wealth of research underpinning them; for example, the use of nature as a sensory stimulant, or the use of behaviour management programmes for reducing the occurrence of problem behaviour.

Making a large, expensive purchase simply because it promises to solve all your problems is not a wise choice. We need to look for evidence. However, even if we could show that multisensory rooms have the effects they claim, would their large price tags (with cost being measured in terms of space, staffing and time as well as money) be justified?

F.I.S.H.

What do you want to use your multisensory room for?
How many alternative provisions have you considered?
Which of your options has the strongest evidence underpinning its effectiveness?

ORIENTATION

Characteristics indicated by research as being significant to the effects witnessed in multisensory rooms are shared by smaller, improvised environments. In this section, you will be introduced to a range of alternative sensory spaces, big and small.

Alternative spaces

The research that yields positive outcomes indicates that it is the being in a different space, and the opportunity to relate to another person, that are the most powerful drivers of change when using multisensory rooms. My own research highlights the importance of this space being free of interruptions and the benefits of being able to control the lighting in the space.

If we are looking for a space with the following criteria, then there are many ways we could go about providing such a space:

- A space notably different from our day to day environment – answering the researchers that speculated that it could have been the novelty of the experience rather than the experience itself which was the catalyst for the responses witnessed.

- A space in which it is possible to control the light levels – in answer to the findings in my research that indicated that being able to reduce lighting was a key factor in creating engagement.

- A space where we are not interrupted – again in answer to findings from my own research about what practitioners currently using multisensory rooms found to be significant.

A multisensory room certainly answers these criteria and is likely to be more robust and to last longer if availed of by multiple users (Hirstwood 2017), but the alternative spaces listed in the following paragraphs could also be used whilst satisfying the criteria listed here. Challis (2014, p. 216) remarks that "acknowledging the effectiveness of ad-hoc, small-scale spaces built around the needs of the individual and gently moving away from the generic commercial resource may well be the way forward."

Alternative sensory spaces are not a new idea; if we were describing the very first multisensory rooms, the descriptions of these spaces would fit far better alongside descriptions of alternative sensory spaces than they would alongside descriptions of current multisensory rooms. Lilli Neilsen's "Little Rooms" and resonance boards were initially homemade, improvised environments. Flo Longhorn's rumpus room was wonderful, and wonderfully homemade; she describes its creation thus:

> It cost about two thousand pounds, funded by local pubs. Two men from Wales came and slept in the school hall and feasted on school dinners as they built it. I designed it around the children. It had a copy of the book "Where the Wild Things Are" hung on the door to remind staff that there were no rules in the room. The children were liberated of the tyranny of adults hovering and supervising them through the use of a stable door.

Examples of some of the items on the list, and some items not on the list (including a multisensory room made out of empty milk bottles and another out of papier-mâché), can be viewed in a public Facebook photo album shared by @TheSensoryProjects entitled Alternative Sensory Spaces (www.thesensoryprojects.co.uk/books).

Big spaces

A tremendous tent

A simple pop-up tent can provide an instant small immersive world. Cutting the bottom out of a tent can enable it to be positioned around a person who uses a wheelchair – so long as the tent is big enough. A browse around your local outdoor adventure store will tell you all you need to know about the different types of tents, include ones in which full blackout is achieved. Being in a small space promotes feelings of security and can lead to greater engagement with people or objects.

In his fabulously titled article "Loitering Within Tent" (1997, p. 24), Keith Park talks about his experiences supporting a child with complex needs to engage in communicative responses within a tent: "With a blanket over the tent to give a dark interior, and a pen torch to illuminate the material, the effect was similar to Greenwich Planetarium – as well as being cheaper and quieter!" Park notes that the tent afforded them the opportunity to personalise the multisensory environment according to the needs of the particular person who would be using the tent, and that they would be able to have more regular access to the tent than they would the multisensory room. It was felt that there was more potential for development in the tent that there was in the multisensory room.

In his equally fabulously titled sequel article "Loitering Within Tent T(w)o" (1998, p. 5), Park reports on the continuing success of the tent in his setting. Park explains that "in the energetic bustle of home, nursery or school, the physical environment can distract a child with a visual impairment and additional disabilities" and highlights how a tent can play a role in supporting such a child: "A tent, like a quiet corner of a room, offers a calmer and less distracting environment for the child who may experience difficulty in blocking out the inessential sights and sounds of everyday commotion."

A yomping yurt

Yurts offer you the opportunity to create a bigger space that more people can share in together. A well-set-up yurt will provide the opportunity for people to orientate themselves to the space and prepare for known activities that take place there; that is, people coming into the space will be able to recognise that it is the yurt and associate this with the activities they usually take part in there, and so enable them to ready themselves for the activities better.

The hugely successful campaigning organisation PAMIS (Promoting A More Inclusive Society) began using a yurt as a sensory story sharing space in 2016 and have continued to use it to share sensory stories with people with profound and multiple learning disabilities and their families.

An improvised tent

If you do not have a tent, what about tying a washing line across the room and hanging a blanket from it? Get fancy and tie two washing lines and you can have a flat-roofed tent with more space inside.

Pop over to your local haberdashery store and peruse the amazing fabrics they have there and consider what camping beneath each would be like. My advice would be to buy at least two large swaths of fabric for your washing-line tent; one plain in a colour that will create a great background against which to experience people or objects, and another fabulous one, where the colours themselves are the object of wonder and engagement.

A hygge home

"Hygge" is a Danish word meaning to gather with friends and to feel warm and snuggly together. Typing it into Pinterest will get you plenty of inspiration for items you might include in a hygge space: soft textured fabrics, warm glowing lights, everything gentle and muted. A great place for relaxing and chatting and sharing sensory conversations.

A gorgeous garden

The outdoors is already a wonderful sensory experience, but with a little insight and some green fingers you can create an augmented outdoor space. Consider, as you create your space, how plants will be positioned to ensure access; planting up a wall can help provide access to people unable to bend to the floor. Consider plants both as experiences in themselves and as background for experience. For example, you might grow vines up a wall to create a green canvas against which to present the bold red of a particular flower. Textures, sounds and scents are all easy to provide horticulturally alongside the glorious visuals nature has to offer.

A withy wonder

Withies are tough, flexible branches often cut from willow trees; they are commonly used for sculptures. Withies are a wonderfully versatile material to work with; you can bend them into any shape you like and secure with tape or cable ties. Once you've made your structure, cover it with papier mâché effect. In the Facebook photo album shared by @TheSensoryProjects you can see an example from a woman who made an entire multisensory room in this manner!

Beautiful blackout

One of the most powerful features of a multisensory room is the ability to control the lighting. If you can achieve blackout on any space then you can do the same. There are many ways of doing this, from the relatively elaborate, such as installing shutters across windows or blackout blinds, to the more improvised, such as draping heavy blankets over windows or using self-adhesive blackout plastic (Magic Blackout™ uses static electricity to adhere to windows).

Once you have blacked out a space, the small amount of UV light cast from a single bulb or torch or small self-illuminating toys become very powerful indeed. Hunt for items that the person experiencing them can have an effect on, such as items that fluoresce under UV light that the person can manipulate or move, or self-illuminating items that are responsive to sound or movement so that the person experiencing them can set them off.

Simply space

Another often overlooked power of multisensory rooms is simply the association of a space with an activity or atmosphere. The person recognises the multisensory room as the place where they do a particular task or the place where they get to relax. The association of the space with the activity contributes to making that activity more accessible, as it enables the person to mentally prepare for what will happen. Simply creating a designated space can achieve this.

I discovered the strong association of space with an activity or atmosphere most powerfully early on in my teaching career when I created what was ostentatiously called a "Numinous tent" (you can see pictures of this tent in the Facebook photo album shared by @TheSensoryProjects). My numinous tent was in fact four pieces of plumber's pipe joined together with cord so that they formed a 2mx2m square. The pipe was plastic and lightweight so it was easy for me to hang this square from the ceiling of my classroom. I purchased an 8m length of fabric from my local haberdashery and hung this from the pipe to create a fabric box.

I experimented with this fabric box: I tried telling stories within it and projecting lights on the outside of it. I played music and sang. But ultimately I found the most powerful way of using the numinous tent was to simply allow the children I was the supporting (all of whom were classed at the time as having "severe special educational needs and disabilities") to just go in the tent.

As the children were free to use the tent as they chose, my staff and I witnessed some wonderful things. I remember one little 8-year-old girl electing to sit quietly on her own in the tent for upwards of forty-five minutes; she appeared so contented and calm to finally get some time on her own. She led, necessarily, a very observed life. I saw a young man, ordinarily oblivious to the presence of his peers, sit down in the tent next to one of his classmates with his shoulder touching theirs and after a while he reached out to put his arm around his friend in a half embrace. The two boys stayed like that in the tent for some while.

Notable people from my local county council came to visit the tent and to witness its magic in action. It won a local award in recognition of its impact, and yet it was only four pieces of plumber's pipe and sixteen pounds worth of fabric. That was all I needed to create: a space. And sometimes all you need is space.

Superb shadows

An improvised shadow theatre is easy to create and can provide a wonderfully responsive sensory environment. You need a large white sheet and a light source. Any light source will do, but an old-fashioned overhead projector offers extra ways to augment this space.

Suspend the sheet so that it hangs flat. If you have one with a wide hem, sliding bamboo canes into the hem can weigh the bottom of the sheet down as well as keeping it flat.

Position the overhead projector (or alternate light source) so that it illuminates as much of the sheet as possible.

Now play!

There are so many options; if you position the person you are inviting to explore the shadows between the light source and the sheet, facing the sheet, they will see a bold, high-contrast image of their own shape, their shadow, and this will move when they move.

Placing items on the projection plate of the overhead projector can add interest to the shadowscape they perceive and can encourage them to move so that their shadow is cast in different positions on the sheet.

Laying coloured cellophane over the light source can create different atmospheres. It's also possible to create a variety of puppets, moving scenery and shadow costumes to further augment your play.

Glorious gazebos

Pop-up gardens or beach gazebos can be purchased for under 100 pounds and be used to create a room outside or a room-within-a-room. Dressing the gazebo with coloured fabrics can create different atmospheres. Using fairy lights strung from the struts of the gazebo can create visual interest. Similarly, items to be explored can be hung from the struts of the gazebo to create interactive components. Remember that Hulsegge and Verheul's first multisensory room was a large tent outside.

My most memorable moment inside a glorious gazebo was on National Multi-Sensory Storytelling Day in 2018 when, together with The Sensory Trust, I led the co-authoring of a sensory story with close to sixty students with profound and multiple learning disabilities at National Star College. Over the course of a day the students "wrote" their sensory story through their interactions with various sensory experiences on offer in a large theatre setting. One of these experiences was a gazebo, draped in black fabric and strung with tiny star fairy lights beneath which we had a 3D print-out of the moon to explore. Students lay beneath the stars and passed the moon from hand to hand, marvelling at its beauty. Many students, upon entering the shelter of the gazebo starscape, spontaneously began to dance or move. Our final story saw lovers dance by the light of the moon beneath a starry sky.

A gazebo might seem an everyday experience to you, but dressed for the senses it can be just as awe inspiring and beautiful as the most expensive multisensory room and nearly as magnificent as the night sky deep with stars.

Water worlds

Many of the respondents to my research, when asked if there was another space where they saw increased engagement and responsiveness from people with complex disabilities, highlighted the hydro-therapy pool as equalling or exceeding the responses they saw in the multisensory room.

The experience of being in water, and of the sensation of wetness, is a very unique one in the sensory world. Being submerged in water not only gives the body extra support, enabling movement, but also provides the body with extra proprioceptive awareness, which also enables movement.

Whether you have access to a hydro-therapy pool or simply a paddling pool (or a bath tub or a hot tub), you can think about how to use the aquatic space as a sensory space. Finding a way to dim the lighting in the area of the pool or adding lights under water can create gorgeous visual effects. Looking for toys that are suitable for exploring in the water can provide the person you are supporting with objects they can manipulate in a place where they are best positioned to use their physical skills.

Think a little outside the box and try your hand at creating some new sensory experiences. For example, a rubber bath mat with suckers on the bottom can be attached to the bottom of your pool. If you then tie to this coloured plastic fronds, you create a reed bed that can tickle the limbs of a person moving through it. I made one of these using the plastic weaving threads known as Scoobies, which formed the basis of a teenage craze in the early 2000s. I discovered that the threads became illuminated beautifully in UV light so that when submerged in a darkened pool lit with UV light, we had the tentacles of some amazing, glowing underwater creature.

One final fabulous trick you can do with water is to get the water itself to glow in UV light. This is simply achieved by dissolving vitamin tablets in the water. Vitamin B50 fluoresces naturally in UV light. I have had lots of fun creating glow-in-the-dark water-play scenarios for people in my life.

Small spaces

Creating sensory environments does not have to be about creating big spaces. Small opportunities for sensory exploration are also extremely valuable. Here are a few to get you started.

Brilliant brollies

Using decorated umbrellas to create pop-up sensory spaces that can easily be positioned on a floor for a person to lie beneath or held aloft to hide a person or two people beneath are an invention made famous by the likes of Flo Longhorn and Richard Hirstwood. The possibilities for these simple sensory spaces are seemingly endless: use a black brolly and suspend UV florescent materials from it, project onto a white brolly to create moving scenery, use themed brollies to hold sensory conversations about different topics beneath, decorate a clear brolly with coloured marker pens to create a highly personalised stained glass effect, find brollies with amazing patterns to spin and create hypnotic visual effects, and so on and so forth. Add to this list by sharing your pictures in the Facebook photo album shared by @TheSensoryProjects.

Lovely "Little Rooms"

Lilli Neilsen's "Little Rooms" have made a massive impact on provision for people with complex disabilities. Simply described, they are small spaces/boxes big enough for a person to lie or sit inside. Hanging from the ceiling of the Little Room are various items that if interacted with offer sensory feedback. The walls and the floors of the rooms can also be constructed to offer feedback. Moving within such an environment is an education in locating yourself in space, as you discover that moving *that* limb creates *that* sound, whereas moving that *other* limb creates a particular sensation.

You can now buy purpose built Little Rooms from a variety of websites, but construction can be simple; you just need to make a space that is sufficient for the person you intend to share it with to be able to move freely within it but also to be able to reach all of it. People have made them out of large cardboard boxes. Of course they will not last as long as a purpose built item, but a lot of fun can be had in them before moving on to a new one. It helps to be able to see a person inside a Little Room, so be sure to cut holes into your box if you plan on using one.

A search of Pinterest or Google Images with the terms "Lilli Neilsen" and "Little Room" will return thousands of images to inspire your creation.

Activity arches

An activity arch can be built around a space already occupied by the person for whom you are making the arch, such as an armchair or wheelchair. Essentially you are creating a seated version of the baby gyms that babies explore before they can crawl. Use anything you like to create an arch that will allow objects to be hung within the person's field of vision and in a position easy for them to reach. You do not have to position the arch over the hands; it could go over their feet if they are more able to use these to explore items.

The beauty of a small and simple sensory space such as an activity arch is that it will be very easy for you to customise to the interests and abilities of the person exploring the arch. For example, for someone who is great at hearing but not so great at seeing, you might choose to find lots of items that each create a different sound when interacted with, and look to see whether the sounds created encourage exploration. For someone who struggles to piece together memories, you could create an activity arch relating to an outing. For example, a trip to a fairground could be recorded on the arch through souvenirs collected during the day, a ticket for a ride, a striped bag of sweets (preferably with a few sweets still inside), a bright yellow plastic duck from the hook-a-duck stand, and so forth.

Sequence strings

Sequence strings are similar to activity arches but can be explored by people across a wider space. All you need to create one is a long piece of cord and around a dozen bulldog clips. Attach the bulldog clips to the cord at regular intervals and tie the cord up at a height that will allow for easy interaction.

Your aim with a sequence string is to tell a story as you move along the string. This might be a very simple sensory story, for example, one about colour as the colours of the items clipped to the string shift slowly from one tone to another, or it could be one about sound, with bells clipped to the string that will chime with increasing or decreasing pitch as you progress along the string. It could be a more elaborate story, perhaps the items from a sensory story, or items gathered from a recent walk displayed in the order in which they were discovered on the walk.

I had my breath taken away once when I first witnessed the creation of a sequence string. I was walking along the city wall that encircles the tiny medieval town of Göttingen, Germany, in the spring. I was not so much walking as waddling; I was heavily pregnant and moving very slowly. Coming towards me in the opposite direction was a woman pushing an old-fashioned perambulator, the type in which the baby lies flat on their back with a large hood over them.

As she walked towards me pushing her child, this woman kept stopping. At first I thought she was looking for something she must have dropped. But as she came haltingly closer to me, and I waddled slowly closer to her, I realised what was happening. She pushed the baby along a little way and the branches of a tree, green with spring growth, brushed against the pram. Prompted by this brushing she stopped, came around to the front of the pram, and played with the bow of the tree for a while, brushing it on the pram's hood and reaching it down into the pram so that the child inside could grasp it in their hands. After a while she snapped a small piece of the branch off, and clipped it to a simple string of bulldog clips that were suspended across the large hood of the pram. As I passed them, smiling to myself, the small child inside was reaching for the fresh leaf hanging before them.

Happy Hula-Hoops and stupendous shower curtains

Hula-Hoops and shower curtains can be used to make instant small spaces in which to cocoon people. Find a large, light-weight Hula-Hoop and tie string across it so that you can hang it from the ceiling, and then clip a shower curtain to it. Hoop worlds are a more flexible way of creating a tent-like environment. It does not have to be a Hula-Hoop – by using coat hangers hung from different points on the ceiling you can create a wider space. Do not worry if your ceiling hasn't got any points for you to hook onto; just tie a cord across the room. In the past I have used window handles, the tops of doors and well secured shelving for this purpose.

It is possible to purchase a wide range of printed shower curtains, enabling you to instantly create a forest scene or an underwater scene which can be interesting for people who understand the significance of the imagery to play within. Consider offering someone a sound-responsive bird toy to "fly" within a forest space. Oftentimes plain curtains offer greater potential (and are cheaper to purchase). A plain curtain partnered with a small, sound responsive light can create a cave of light that is controlled by the vocalisations of the person within it. You can hang things into the hoop to be explored or use small torches to project onto the outside of the shower curtain to encourage skills such as visual tracking.

Examples of happy Hula-Hoop spaces, and many of the other smaller sensory environments listed here, as well as some not listed, can be viewed in the Facebook photo album shared by @TheSensoryProjects and there are still more examples I have yet to list or find photos of, especially ones not represented visually – remember, the visual denotation of space is very important to people who access visual stimulation. To those who have less access to it than ourselves, other representations of space are just as important; consider a different sound space, or a different smellscape. Resonance boards offer a vibratory space, hammocks offer a cocooning space supportive of proprioceptive input, and things as mundane as small airers and pop-up laundry baskets can be used to create sensational small sensory spaces.

Affordable

Considering the spaces mentioned in the list of alternative spaces, both the big and the small, you would struggle to spend even 100 pounds creating most of them. If I were to give you 1,000 pounds to create one, you could create the gold-standard version with knobs and bells on. And for the price of your multisensory room you could probably create a new gold-standard version alternative sensory space once a year for life, personalising each to the needs of the particular people in your care at that time. With a mention or two in your local newspaper, it's likely you could attract volunteers and fundraisers to help you with your projects; art students and other creative individuals could take you as their muse and step in to help you create awe inspiring spaces that everyone would want their photos taken in. With a little bit of effort to maintain communication with your community, the creation of the spaces could become self-sustaining. What a wonderful sensory adventure that would be!

Considerations

A sense assessment

Prior to accompanying anyone into any multisensory space or expecting them to access and engage with any form of sensory stimulation, it is worth knowing as much as you can about their sensory abilities. Has the person you are supporting had a sight test and a hearing test? Have their sensory capabilities been assessed by the professionals best placed to pass judgement on their abilities?

SeeAbility (2016), an organisation dedicated to providing specialist support, accommodation and eye care help for people with learning disabilities, autism and sight loss, reports that children with learning disabilities are twenty-eight times more likely to have serious sight problems than typically developing children. Yet when they reviewed the eye care received by students in special schools, four out of ten students had never even had an eye test, and ninety percent of the children with disabilities who had been under the care of hospital eye clinics had been discharged and had no history of sight tests within the community.

There is a tragic misunderstanding at large with people thinking that sensory tests, such as sight tests, are reliant on a person's cognitive or communicative skills; that is, people think "there is no point taking them for an eye test as they cannot say whether the letters they are shown are clearer with or without the lenses." But there are many ways to test sensory skills, and organisations such as SeeAbility are well placed to advise us.

Why would they want to go into the space?

I am not advocating improvised multisensory spaces over multisensory rooms. The risks of mistaking the space around you for the thing that is important is just as great with an improvised space as it is for a purchased space. Ensure that your decision to enter the multisensory space, whether it is an improvised one or a purchased one, is founded on your relationship with the person you are accompanying in that space. Ask yourself why *they* would want to go there.

If your answer to the question "Why would they want to go there?" is "Because it is great," or "Because we have made it," then think again. We have plenty of multisensory rooms around that have been designed by brilliant individuals and companies, who have equipped them with a wealth of resources, announced them to be wonderful and handed them over fait accompli. Equally I've seen gorgeous, creative, inspired improvised rooms made by talented artistic people, equally presented as "done." The sentiment is "I have made this for you. It is good. You will like it." The sentiment did not begin with the question "What do you like?" or "What would you like?" The rooms are *done to*, rather than *made with*.

The idea of co-designing a multisensory room with the user or users of that room allows me a little tangent into one of my projects: the Sensory-being Project, which at the time of writing is in its third year of running (and hopefully there will be a good few years to come). It has just won a National Award for Visual Arts and Design from the Creative Learning Guild in recognition of its co-design methodology.

The Sensory-being Project sees consultant teams of Sensory Beings advise design teams of sustainable design students on the creation of new sensory resources. The consultations occur through a process of spending time together and sharing sensory experience. The advice given is meaningful, not tokenistic, and not only helps with but is necessary for the creation of the products which are the end goal of the project. You can read more about the project on www.TheSensoryProjects.co.uk/the-sensory-being-project, where you can also access online photo albums which give insight into the consultation process.

A room that is finished before its user has been enabled to express an opinion about it is always going to lack something when compared with a room that grew from a relationship with its user. It is worth noting that when I refer to enabling a person to express an opinion I do not mean we must act to enhance their communication skills. It is our communication skills that need enhancing; we are, after all, the ones not listening.

What do I want to explore in this space?

My detour into the Sensory-being Project gives me an opportunity to share a little of the consultant's advice with you. The consultant team is made up of people between the ages of 4 and 19 years old (we have on occasion been assisted by an 18-month-old and a 64-year-old, but the core team falls within these age ranges). Many members of the team have advised on the project for three years, although a few are new to the project and have only given their advice this year. Three team members have died during the running of the project. We miss them enormously but we work to ensure their advice is still heard. At its biggest, the team numbered over thirty, and at its smallest, fewer than fifteen. The team all hold exceptional insight into the sensory properties of resources, and into their physical accessibility for those with atypical mobility.

Each year the design team considers which of the materials they could use to construct their designs might interest the consultants. They bring these materials to the consultants who all consider them carefully and feedback their insights to the design team. After our first round of consultations the design team takes what it has learned from the consultant team and comes up with a prototype resource. The prototype resource then gets taken back to the consultants to get their advice and is updated in accordance with their guidance.

Through witnessing this consultation process for three years now I can report consistent feedback given by the consultant team as to what makes for an interesting sensory resource. This advice is particularly interesting as the consultant team has a wide range of interests and abilities. As with any sampling of so many people, they are not naturally people who would agree on what is interesting and what is not – each person has their own tastes – but the following feedback has been seen year after year:

1 I want something that is of interest to my senses. The resource must appeal to the sensory systems of the consultants; this is their start point to being interested in it. It needs to appeal to the senses alone; representational appeal is no use. I will not be interested in looking at something because it looks as if it contains information or it looks as if it means something. I will be interested in looking at it if the experience of looking at it offers stimulation to my sense of vision, and the same applies for my other senses.

2 I want to be able to effect the sensation I get from the resource. I want something about the sensation I get from this resource to change because of my interactions with the resource.

3 I am more interested in the resource if the change I can effect is dimensional. For example, if you offer me a bright red switch that appeals to my sense of vision, that when pressed illuminates and further stimulates my vision, that is great, but it will only hold my interest for so long. Whereas if you offer me a red tube that lights up when I touch it and I can manipulate that light into many different shapes, perhaps of different levels of brightness, I will be interested in exploring this for far longer.

4   I they respond particularly well to designs that can be taken apart; several of the consultants who work on the project are particularly interested in finding out how things work. They want to open up the resource and see how it functions.

This advice has been consistently given by the consultant team as a whole through three years of the Sensory-being Project. Some members of the team are all about the first piece of advice, whilst others are all about the fourth piece (but only if the first three have been met). Sometimes the design team brings resources to share with the consultants such that I can easily predict the latter's response. I know that a design team member offering a piece of space blanket is going to have a great conversation with a member of the consultant team, just as I know that a design team member bringing something small with subtle colour changes is likely to struggle to engage the visual sense of the consultant by whom they are being advised. However, a few of the stranger offerings work as examples of this advice. A crystal goblet was a huge success, because of the unusualness of the tactile experience to the consultant team. A sparkly belt was equally wonderful, this time because of the multitude of ways the visual effect of the sparkles could be adjusted by our interactions – sometimes it was pulled taut, straight, other times it was a small heap of sparkles. A boring resource partially hidden inside another could suddenly become interesting as we worked out how to get it out.

Consider the consultant team's advice as you consider what resources to offer within your multisensory space. Better yet, ask the people you will be sharing that space with what they find most interesting or would most like to explore.

OVERVIEW

Many beneficial aspects of multisensory rooms are also exhibited by small improvised spaces. Indeed, the original multisensory rooms were themselves improvised spaces. Creative use of improvised multisensory environments may well be as beneficial as, if not more beneficial than, use of large commercially produced multisensory rooms, and will certainly be more cost effective.

F.I.S.H.

Have you tried creating an improvised sensory space? Why not have a go at one of the ideas listed here?

Section

ORIENTATION

The following sections provide an overview of a research project that looked into the current use of multisensory rooms in the UK and its findings.

Report from research: how are multisensory rooms currently being used?

Of greater relevance perhaps than how particular people, or particular schools of thought, *intend* multisensory rooms to be used is how they are *actually* used. I sought to find this out by conducting a series of semi-structured interviews of people presently using multisensory rooms in the UK. Each interview was a maximum of one hour long. I asked questions, not to get answers to those particular questions, but to get people talking about the room they used. I wanted my interviewees to say what was most relevant to them, rather than to give me answers to specific questions. Everyone talked until they had nothing further to say on the topic, or until the allotted hour had run out, although many interviews ran over the hour marker.

I sent out invitations to be a part of this research through several channels: I handed out flyers at the TES SEN show (the UK's largest special educational needs conference); I emailed the SLD forum (an email network that connects special schools across the UK); I posted across social media, using Twitter (reach of 8,443), Facebook (reach of 2,765) and LinkedIn (reach of 8,546). Through people sharing my invitation across social media platforms, more people had the chance to respond than I am able to track.

I conducted the interviews over a period of three months, allowing interviewees to sign up for time slots either during work hours or in the evening. More time slots were available for the daytime than for the evening, which may have limited the ability of people to take part who could only do so outside of work hours.

Many potential interviewees expressed a fear of not knowing enough to be able to usefully take part. Everyone was told that the purpose of the interviews was to find out how the rooms were being used currently and that there was no requirement for a certain level of knowledge in order for their participation to be useful. However, it is likely that many potential interviewees self-excluded from the process, believing their knowledge not to be significant enough. The flip side of this is that it is likely that my sample comprises people who feel relatively confident in their knowledge of using their particular multisensory room.

In the first phase of the research twenty-five people were interviewed formally. One person asked to conduct the interview by written correspondence but provided only very concise answers to the initial questions and did not respond when asked follow up questions. A further eight people signed up for interviews but had to cancel due to work or personal commitments.

A multitude of additional people provided information informally. For example, when I was handing out the leaflets at the conference, often the handing over of a leaflet would prompt a small discussion of multisensory rooms, and the insights people shared with me helped to shape the research. Similarly, as people at events I attend and those who knew me online became aware that I was conducting this research, they raised issues they had encountered around multisensory rooms or told me about examples of great practice they knew about.

My interviewees included parents, teachers, sensory specialists, tech specialists, foster carers, teaching assistants and adult care workers, with several people falling into more than one of these categories.

Once the three-month interview process was over I began to digest the information and examine it for themes. During this time I continued to have conversations with people on the topic of multisensory rooms. These conversations have informed the writing of this book but were not used to supplement the data drawn from those initial twenty-five interviews. In conducting the interviews a new question emerged, as you will read in Section 5. I posed this new question to some of my original interviewees and to many more people after the three months of interviews were over, asking over fifty people in total. You can read more about this question and the findings drawn from it in Section 5.

At the start of each interview I informed my interviewee that it would be anonymous and encouraged them to speak freely. During the interview I aimed to restrict my speech to just the questions or prompts to clarify what had been said, and to not add my own insights or opinions. Of course I am only human, so it is likely that I have affected the interviews in some way; for example, it was noticeable to me that a great many of my interviewees, when asked what activities they liked to do in multisensory rooms, said "sensory stories" before they said anything else. Now, it could be that sensory stories are extremely popular in multisensory rooms currently. Hirstwood (2017) notes them as one of the key uses of multisensory rooms. Or it could be that they knew I have written a book about how wonderful I think sensory stories are (Grace 2014).

I typed notes on what my interviewees said as they spoke, recording the main thrust of what they said in as much detail as possible. I type at a rate of more than 100 words per minute, but of course speech can be quicker. I left out from my records anything that might identify particular people or places. Speech is rarely without fluff around the edges, so for example someone, in describing taking somebody to a multisensory room, might have said "Well we have to get them ready and there is always stuff everywhere, dishes, and we have to remember to take their meds with them and when you go over to that cupboard you see any number of other things that need tidying or remembering, so you are always making notes and it takes a while," and so on. And I would have recorded "classroom logistics slow departure to multisensory room – medication/mess." In instances where I felt something particularly pertinent was being said (and of course what I consider to be of particular pertinence may not be what the next person considers to be pertinent and so in doing this I introduce a bias), I asked the interviewee to pause so I could record it in full. Similarly, if I was not keeping up with my typing, I would ask the interviewee to pause so that none of what they said was missed.

I used the following prompts to get people talking:

Tell me about your multisensory room.
How did it come about?
Does any particular piece of equipment stand out to you?
How is the room used?
What is a typical session?
Do you have a particular aim or purpose in mind when you go into the room?
Do you have any other strategies you use for that end?
What effect does the room have?
What do you think causes the effect?
Does the effect last?
Have you seen similar effects elsewhere?
Have you had training in using a multisensory room? (Using – as in what to do in there – rather than Operating – as in how to operate the equipment).

Results

Overview table of interviewee responses

Interviewee number	Directive (D) or Non-directive (N) approach	Noted aspects of the room*		Intent to relax (R) or stimulate engagement and response (S)	Lasting effect noted Y/N	Training received Y/N
1	D	A	F G H I	R	Y	N
2	N		G J	R	Y	N
3	N	A F		R	Y	N
4	N	B C D	I	R	N	N
5	D	D	k	S	N	N

Interviewee number	Directive (D) or Non-directive (N) approach	Noted aspects of the room*	Intent to relax (R) or stimulate engagement and response (S)	Lasting effect noted Y/N	Training received Y/N
6	N	B D I k	S	/	N
7	D	B E I	S	N	N
8	N	B F I k	S	Y	N
9	D	B C E k	S	N	Y
10	D	B C E k	S	Y	N
11	D	B E G	S	N	N
12	D	B E H J	R	/	N
13	N	A F	R	Y	N
14	D	B D E J	R	/	N
15	D	B D	S	N	N
16	D	A B D	S	Y	N
17	D	C D E	S	N	N
18	D	B C D E	S	N	N
19	D	B C D	S	N	N
20	D	B H J	S	N	N
21	N	B D G	R	Y	N
22	D	B C D E	S	N	N
23	N	B	R	N	N
24	N	B I	S	Y (But bad)	N
25	N	B C E I	R	Y	N
26	N	C	S	Y	N

*Key: noted aspects of the room
  Any aspect of a multisensory room mentioned by more than two interviewees has been listed in the grid below, together with the number of people who mentioned it.

Letter ref.	Description	Total
A	Active space – somewhere people could move about vigorously.	4
B	Dark – somewhere that lighting could be highly controlled.	19
C	Uninterrupted – somewhere that people did not interrupt activities.	9
D	Control – somewhere people could exert control over effects.	11
E	Focused – somewhere free of distractions.	10
F	Safe – somewhere people were safe from injury.	3
G	Vibration – somewhere people could access vibratory sensory stimulation.	4
H	Personalised – somewhere that it was possible to adjust sensory experiences to suit an individual.	3
I	Sensory – somewhere that sensory experiences were available.	7
J	People – somewhere that people could be better connected.	4
K	Impressive – somewhere that impressed people, causing the expression of "wow."	5

Overview of themes identified from the interviews

Next to no one receives training on how to use a multisensory room, but pretty much everyone gets taught how to turn the equipment in a multisensory room on and off

Four percent of the people I interviewed had received training on how to use a multisensory room. Spending on the rooms people were interviewed about ranged from a few hundred pounds to over 125,000 pounds. Considering that there had been such an outlay of funds to provide the equipment, it is shocking to see that this financial commitment to resources was not matched by a financial commitment to ensure people knew how to use the resources.

Consider other situations in which an organisation might spend large amounts of money on resources. Would you expect an office to buy a new set of computers without also providing the training to enable staff to use them? Would you expect a building site to buy new machines but then not train staff to drive them? In such scenarios the staff is trained to use the new resource because the people who have bought the resources want them to be used to their maximal capacity and to be used safely. What would it mean if they bought the resources but did not provide the matching training? Presumably those resources would just be for show. Or would it mean they did not really care about the outcome of using the equipment and just wanted to be seen going through the motions?

You would also expect in both of my hypothetical scenarios, new office computers or new building site machinery, for there to be a program of training that was ongoing, with refresher courses available and all new staff having a full introduction into the use of the equipment. Why do we not expect the same from multisensory rooms? It could be, as other researchers and commentators have said, that we wrongly think that the rooms will do the work for us (Hirstwood and Gray 1995). If the room is doing the work, then we do not need to know how to use it; we only need to know how to switch it on.

Non-directive users of multisensory rooms were more likely to see long-lasting effects from using the rooms

Forty-two percent of the people I interviewed were using their multisensory room in a non-directive, child led way. Sixty-two percent of the people I interviewed reported no lasting effect from using the multisensory room. More interesting than these statistics was the correlation between directive and non-directive use of the rooms and the longevity of the effect of the rooms. Of course correlation does not imply causation, but it does give us reason to speculate about whether there could be a link.

Twenty-seven percent of the people I interviewed reported both using the multisensory room in a non-directive way and finding a lasting positive effect from using the room. This compares with only four percent of the people I interviewed who reported finding a lasting positive effect from using the room in a directive way.

This correlation is very interesting to note when you consider that the rationale often given for using a multisensory room in a directive way is that the person wants learning to occur, and for there to be some lasting outcome from using the room rather than just a pleasant time had within the room. Interviewees who advocated a directive approach often did so with great forcefulness. For example one interviewee stated that "we rail against multisensory rooms being used in any different way to the classrooms," and another explained that they were not allowed to use the room "unless we have a clear objective for each child going in there."

Of course, as is traditional, it would seem, with multisensory room research, my study is too small to generate conclusions. But it is interesting to consider the question that these results beg: is using a multisensory room in a non-directive way a better conduit for learning than a directive approach?

Multisensory rooms are used with the intention of furthering engagement or promoting relaxation

When considering what people hoped to be the outcome of time spent in a multisensory room, two answers dominated: relaxation or greater responsiveness and engagement, with thirty-eight percent of the people I interviewed considering the multisensory room to be the ideal place to promote relaxation and sixty-two percent viewing it as a place conducive to inspiring increased responsiveness and engagement. Again it is interesting to note the numbers when compared with directive/non-directive approach. Twelve percent of the people I interviewed were using the room in a directive way to promote relaxation, whereas twenty-seven percent were using the room in a non-directive way to promote relaxation.

Questions prompted by these findings

The results cited in the previous section lead to some interesting questions and points for us to consider, for example:

Is the multisensory room more likely to contribute to a lasting positive change if used in a directive way or a non-directive way?

Eighty percent of the people I interviewed who reported a lasting effect from using a multisensory room were using it in a non-directive way.

Research has shown that neural pathways are formed quicker through play than through repetition perhaps this could account for the lasting change seen by people using the rooms in a non-directive manner?

Is lasting positive change from using a multisensory room more likely to come about if the focus of the room has been relaxation compared to if the focus has been on responsiveness and engagement?

Of those reporting lasting positive outcomes from using the room, 86% were using it with a focus of relaxation.

In *Another World* (1986), Hulsegge and Verheul advocated a non-directive approach to multisensory rooms, hoping that people relaxed within them would become curious and enjoy their surroundings. This could be taken as confirmation that their approach is right and that other more directive, structured approaches do not achieve as much as they think they do.

However, as is always the case, if we ask a different question we might get a different answer. For example, 100 percent of the people who reported using the rooms in a directive way reported getting the responses they hoped to see from the people they engaged with in the rooms. Several teachers commented that the rooms were the ideal learning environment for their students or "the only place" they were able to engage.

Imagine a person with a level of vision that means they are only able to see the very brightest of things in the very darkest of places. Within a multisensory room they may learn to track an object across their field of vision from left to right and up and down. Over time they may begin to show anticipation of where the object will be. They may even start to look for it when they come in the room, scanning their surroundings to find it. This person has clearly learned whilst being in the room but their new found skills will not "last" outside the room, as once outside they are in an environment where it is not possible for them to demonstrate their skills.

When we consider people for whom a multisensory room is not only an optimal learning environment but possibly the only truly accessible space for them, we face two more questions: what is the point of skilling someone up if they can only display their skills within a darkened room lit by fibre optics? Gray (1994) identifies the biggest problem with multisensory rooms as being the "lack of transition of skills to other areas." The frustration in his tone is underpinned by the assumption that it is possible for the person in the room to apply their skills in other places. For example, a person with autism who successfully learns to use a picture symbol communication strategy within a multisensory room in order to request their favourite piece of equipment should rightly be expected to be able to use that skill in another environment and its use should not be restricted to the multisensory room. But what of the person I asked you to think of earlier, the person who can only see the brightest of things in the darkest of places? Are we frustrated by their lack of transitional skills, or excited by the development of those skills? The goal of transitional skills is very much dependent on who the person is who is using the room and what their skills and capabilities are. Which leads me to another question: if someone is able to show certain skills in a certain environment, should we not either be seeking to allow them to spend more time in that environment, or looking for ways to adjust the other environments that they spend time in such that they can be skilled throughout their life? Bleming (2019a) says, "The access points in multi-sensory rooms should spill out of the rooms and into every aspect of life."

To draw a comparison: if a person who uses a wheelchair discovers that their friend's house has ramp access to the front door and a lift instead of a staircase within it, does that mean they should live at their friend's house, or should we be seeking to provide them with ramps and lifts wherever they go? One ends up as a restricted life; the other as a liberated life.

Access is well understood when it comes to lifts and ramps and wheelchairs, but when access to life is contingent upon sensory measures, people understand it less, often returning to their own experience to judge (e.g. "it is not too noisy in here" or "we need to switch the lights on, it has gone dull"). Recognising that a person is able in one environment but not able in another should be a springboard compelling us to make accessibility adjustments to those other environments.

Further findings relating to room accessibility

Multisensory rooms can be surprisingly inaccessible – design

Considering that the accessibility of all environments leads us to considering the accessibility of the multisensory room itself. Many of my interviewees reported problems that hindered access to multisensory rooms for the people they support. Researchers also highlight the need for better design. For example Challis (2014, p. 197), after reviewing how multisensory rooms are used within the UK through the course of 2012, said, "there is a need for a more coherent approach to the design of these spaces" and later noted the lack of literature advising on design. Indeed, some of the access arrangements were so bad they could form the sequel to my stand-up act in Section 2. The content that follows is all directly lifted from insight from my interviewees who work within the rooms mentioned:

> Have I told you the one about the multisensory room where the bubble tube had been plumbed in across the door such that wheelchair users cannot get into the room whilst in their chairs?
>
> What about the many rooms with padded floors that impede the mobility of those unsteady on their feet?
>
> You must have heard the one about the multisensory room built at the end of a narrow corridor; the wheelchair users were able to wheel into the room but

the mobile hoist required for them to exit their chairs and explore the room does not fit down the corridor, so all they can really do is view the equipment that they might have had the benefit of using had the design of the room been better thought out.

Oh, and there is the classic of the gorgeously equipped room with all manner of interesting thing to look at and explore on the walls, but the point of access is the waterbed where people lie facing the ceiling; the ceiling that has nothing on it and is so high that staff cannot reach it to even attach a mobile. The users of that particular multisensory room lie staring into oblivion, whilst nearby, stimulation that would have been accessible to them flashes away to itself.

Or the opposite one, where the room is controlled by the site manager, who comes in bright and early in the morning and switches every piece of equipment on and then locks the switch box so that none can be switched off until everyone has gone home! People needing to adjust to the sensory stimulation in the room, or people desiring focused stimulation, are sent into instant shutdown or meltdown by the bombardment of effects that hits them the minute they step foot inside the door of the very room meant to cater to their sensory needs.

None of these examples are made up; all are directly lifted from the interviews I conducted for this research, with issues such as the padded flooring being noted by more than one interviewee. Each of the design issues is shocking in itself, but what is more shocking is just how many of my interviewees reported such design issues. Design flaws such as in these examples were not rare; they were a regular occurrence.

Many of the most catastrophic design flaws could have been avoided by simply involving the people who would be using the room in the design of the room. Presuming that people with profound and multiple learning disabilities cannot advise on design is a false presumption, as has been demonstrated by the Sensory-being Project.

Co-design can be simple and inexpensive to do; the main requirement is for human contact. If done routinely as a part of multisensory room design, it would lead to more accessible multisensory rooms with more engaging resources within them.

To avoid a great many of these design faux pas, read Richard Hirstwood's (2017) "The Multi-sensory room/studio . . . How to design" before planning your multisensory room, and work in collaboration with the people who will use the room as you put it together.

Multisensory rooms can be surprisingly inaccessible – usage

Aside from commenting on the design of the room, many of my interviewees and others I talked to as a part of this process reported that access to their multisensory room was hindered by how it was being, or had been, used. Problems commonly reported included the following:

Trigger-happy facilitators switching everything on and interpreting the subsequent overload experienced by the people in the room as relaxation occurring.

Items within the room being broken and out of use, either as a result of the room being used by people in a state of meltdown or through lack of maintenance – some people had bought rooms without factoring in maintenance costs, others had found the maintenance contract unaffordable and had not realised that the nature of the equipment meant that they could not shop around for other maintenance options.

Difficulties with the journey to the multisensory room; these included rooms so far away that people visiting them had to be readied with coats for the journey and the time taken to make the journey ate into time in the room. Difficult journeys also meant that the requisite journey back to base was enough to obliterate any residual increase in engagement spurred on by the room. I also heard stories of rooms positioned in inaccessible locations, for example, upstairs with no access due to broken lifts, or at the end of corridors too narrow to allow mobility equipment along them.

Timetabling issues including time in the room being allocated unilaterally regardless of need; not being able to be in the room for enough time for it to be meaningful or regularly enough for it to be meaningful; not being able to take people into the room when they were ready and able to access it; the ridiculousness of the room being a relaxation space used not when one needed to relax but only at 11am on a Wednesday.

People being parked in the rooms – this is a reflection of the "holding bay" or "dumping ground" previously referred to by researchers and commentators.

Rooms being used as cinemas, blocking use for those who would want to use them in a more interactive and responsive manner.

People not having the technical skills or the confidence to use the room; many people worked in situations where one person was able to operate the room confidently and everyone else either used it as it appeared when first switched on or was unable to use it at all.

Not having set up time; people reported having multisensory rooms that could be personalised to suit particular people's needs but not having the time prior to that person arriving in the room to set up that personalisation, rendering the capacity for personalisation meaningless.

Rooms being used as containment zones for people in a state of meltdown. As multisensory rooms are viewed as secure padded spaces, people exhibiting violent, explosive behaviour have been shut into them. Using the rooms in this way not only endangers the equipment in the room, it endangers the person in a state of crisis. If a room is needed for this kind of use, it should be devoid of electrical equipment and so forth, and settings should be honest with themselves about their need for such a room and not avoid the issue by pretending that the multisensory room is solely a place for fun.

OVERVIEW

Interviews with users of multisensory rooms revealed that factors other than the equipment within the room were more influential with regards to the impact of the room. It is notable that with regard to both the accessibility of the space and the effectiveness of the space, the human influences on the design and use of the room were of equal, if not greater, significance than equipment choice and the capabilities of the equipment within the room.

F.I.S.H.

How is your multisensory room timetabled?

Are there access factors that affect your multisensory room aside from the physical nature of the space?

Is your multisensory room regularly used as a containment space?

A detailed look at limiting factors influencing multisensory rooms

ORIENTATION

In this section we are going to take a closer look at the commonly identified access problems to multisensory rooms caused by the usage of the rooms. Having a better understanding of the problems created by misuse of a multisensory room can help us to dodge these problems for ourselves.

Trigger-happy facilitators

Many interviewees and indeed many of the people I spoke to more informally commented upon staff operating multisensory rooms as being trigger happy and there being a tendency to switch everything on. Jacques (2016, p. 31) observes that it seems to be instinctive to turn the equipment on; one of his interviewees reflects this when they say, "*It's almost natural instinct because that's what's happened so it's almost now embedded . . . you turn everything on* **because** *everything needs to be on*" (italics in original; bold emphasis added).

The reporting of people switching everything on is often said with a note of disdain, implying that the people doing it are foolish or careless. But when the only training you have had is in how to switch equipment on and off, it stands to reason that you would expect to enter the room and switch on equipment; you are not being unthinking, but are doing as you have been shown.

Actions speak louder than words for everyone, even people who understand language. Staff may have been told "do not switch everything on," but what have they been shown? Was it, by any chance, how to switch everything on?

The message "do not switch everything on" will come through more powerfully if it is accompanied by being shown how to use the room with a single thing switched on. Yet, often training in using a multisensory room is fitted in around other essential training and so staff will move from an hour's first-aid training to an hour's multisensory-room training and it is only possible to fit in the functional essentials, that is, a quick flick through of all the switches and settings for the room, into that hour.

Understanding comes into play here, too. One of my interviewees who works in the adult care world reported teams of carers hiring out a multisensory room to use with the people who lived in their care home. Having paid for an hour's use, they were determined to stay for the whole of that hour and to use everything in order to have gotten their money's worth from the time.

You can see why people would feel that using everything and staying as long as possible was the most frugal approach to the situation. Unless informed otherwise, how would they know? Using a multisensory room is not an instinctive act.

Similarly, people who supported parents reported that they too often switch everything on, wanting to discover it for themselves and wanting to use it all. Parents hiring a multisensory room for their child are not people who lack care; they are people wanting the most for their child and it is easy to see why they would think "the most" is everything.

Finally, people tend automatically to judge sensory stimulation by their own standards. Sensory differences are generally invisible and so less taken into account than visible physical disabilities. Someone who is ambulant who supports a wheelchair user in getting to a place will recognise the need to take the lift over taking the stairs. However, someone who processes visual stimulation quickly and efficiently will not recognise the need for a low-stimulation visual environment for someone quickly overwhelmed by visual experience in the same way. Although these differences mean the same in terms of access, the sensory differences are much harder for people to understand and remember. Detailed and empathetic training is needed in order for people to appreciate the significance of these differences, and ongoing support and monitoring can ensure that the differences are being respected.

Turning everything on in a multisensory room is far more likely to spoil the benefits of being in the room than to add to them. With one piece of equipment on, a person using the room may be able to focus. If it is a responsive piece of equipment they will be in a position to recognise that their actions cause the change. If two pieces of equipment are on it will take them longer to know what their actions are effecting. Likewise, if there is more than one person interacting with the equipment at a time, how are they to know which action it was of theirs that produced which response? If the lights change when I move my foot and the sounds change when I move my hand, how am I to know that the lights are actually being controlled by someone else's hand? Bleming (2019b) remarks that "A quiet, dark, comfortable, odourless ambience is optimum to help differentiate (in-focus) sensory experiences from background noise. This is useful if you are zooming in on specific sensations with people who have trouble filtering things out."

Park (1997, p. 5), reflecting on the limitations of multisensory rooms when compared to smaller improvised environments, says: "The noise produced by even a small group of children and staff in the multisensory room may neutralise any potential benefit."

Some people, when faced with sensory overload, will let you know about it in a very clear and expressive way through their behaviour. Others will simply zone out and become passive. This passivity can be viewed by people as relaxation when it is in fact a stress response.

Broken items

> People have been sold a dream but find themselves living a nightmare on a daily basis. Broken stuff. Devices not pairing. Lost remote. Etc. No money to fix anything.
>
> *(Bleming 2018a)*

Many interviewees reported issues with items being broken. Several interviewees had expensive projectors smashed by people who had been forced into the room when their behaviour had become too much to cope with elsewhere. One interviewee had a bubble tube out of action for months because modelling clay had clogged up its parts and no one could fix it aside from the manufacturer and they were not able to come until the new year. Others reported switches broken through a lack of respect; in one situation a picnic had happened in the multisensory room and pieces of food had gotten into electrical equipment and broken it, including a switch priced at 800 pounds.

It is easy to see why broken items would affect the running of a multisensory room; in any situation if your equipment is broken it is going to cause problems. But there are further nuances to this that may not at first be apparent.

Many multisensory rooms can only be maintained by the companies that installed them, meaning that once you have purchased a room, the company you have purchased it from holds a monopoly over the maintenance of that room. A few of my interviewees reported needing to have new multisensory rooms installed because they could not afford the maintenance contract for the old room. One of my sensory techie interviewees reported being called in to fix a rival company's room and not being able to do so as they had used bespoke switch mechanisms, not only on the equipment that they installed, which was their own, but also on equipment brought in from other companies. The replacement of the original equipment switches with their own switches invalidated the warranty on the original equipment, such that it could not be replaced when broken, as the setting had initially thought.

There are no industry standards that companies are obliged to adhere to when installing multisensory rooms, not even those you might expect, such as fire safety standards. Two of my interviewees reported well-known companies installing expensive multisensory rooms upwards of 20,000 to 30,000 pounds each, and them not working and in one case catching fire! Another interviewee commented that with just one or two companies out there creating multisensory rooms, they had not really had a choice about what type of room to buy. There are actually a great many companies that will create and install a multisensory room, small and large, specialising in different equipment and different set ups; so the choice is there, but it is not there in reality if settings are not aware of it.

Hirstwood and Crabtree (2018) identify forty-two responsibilities of a multisensory room co-ordinator that they feel are essential to the effective running of a multisensory room. Many of these are maintenance practices or checks that need doing daily or weekly in order to persevere the safe operational running of the multisensory room, from simple things like wiping fibre optics clean to procedures that require a little more knowledge, such as adding conditioner to a waterbed. I would be surprised to find more than a handful of settings in the country where all forty-two of these responsibilities were being reliably fulfilled. How many settings even have a designated multisensory room co-ordinator?

Difficult journeys to the multisensory rooms

Many interviewees reported trouble with getting to their multisensory rooms. For some this was so significant that they were unable to go at all. For example, there was the room with the bubble tube, which was plumbed in across the door in such a way that made it impossible to get wheelchair users in whilst in their wheelchairs. There was also the room that prohibited the use of a mobile hoist, meaning that people could get in the room to view it but not get out of their chairs to use it effectively. There was also the room on the first floor accessed via a lift that was broken.

For others, a lack of access to their multisensory room was more of a logistical problem than a physical one. One room was a long way away, requiring a trek that took a while and required multiple members of staff because pushing a person in a wheelchair safely requires one member of staff for each person in a wheelchair. This setting did not have 1:1 staffing ratios, which meant they could not safely get to the room. Another room required you to go outside to reach it and for some of that setting's more medically fragile people, this was a big barrier.

People often reported the time taken to get to the room and get ready to use it as making it an almost pointless effort; one interviewee remarked that "by the time we've got everyone there and got out of our wheelchairs there is only about ten minutes before we have to make our way back."

More significant than the difficulties getting to the rooms was the impact that leaving them had on the benefits reaped within the rooms. One interviewee remarked, "You can have a brilliant session and no matter how sensitively you bring the lights back up you still have to hoist them and do the transfer, and it is all lost in the transition." Another interviewee forlornly reported:

> Last year we did see some benefit from being in the room as we had the morning slot and we would go back to class and some of that engagement would last, but this year we have the slot before home time and they go straight from the room to the bus and it is all lost. There are not many good slots, the one before lunch is just as bad it is such a bump to go from that space to the dinner hall!

In planning for a visit to a multisensory room, practitioners need to consider the time it takes to journey to and from the room and if there is any way to smooth this transition to allow users of the room to bring away with them some of its magic.

Speech and language therapist Sharon Cross did a beautiful piece of work creating a meaningful journey to a multisensory room for one little girl with profound and multiple learning disabilities in a special school. Sharon identified points of sensory interest along the girl's route from her classroom to the multisensory room, and then composed a simple song to go with these points that began "This is the way to the multisensory room, let us stop" and continued with, for instance, "feel the wall" or "hear the door handles" and so on.

Just pushing that girl in her wheelchair to the multisensory room would have taken less than a minute; she would not have known where she was going and would simply have arrived in the space. On the journey she would have been little more than a parcel, an item being shifted from place to place. Sharon's journey took over five minutes; it was repeated every time the girl went to the multisensory room and after a few weeks the difference showed. As the song started, the girl showed visible signs of excitement, knowing she was going to one of her favourite places. As she progressed through the various sensory engagement points along her journey to the room, you could witness her becoming more active, lifting a hand in readiness for the door handle she knew was coming.

Each step of the girl's journey contained her as a person, not a parcel; it was meaningful and it was communicative as she and Sharon shared responses. Making the journey meaningful takes a lot more time, but it is worth so much more than its alternative.

Timetabling

The majority of my interviewees were accessing a multisensory room that was shared with other people in a school or adult care setting. Typically, timetables had allocated an hour a week to each class or group, regardless of individual needs and abilities. In a few school settings students with profound and multiple learning disabilities or students with autism had been given priority over other students and had a daily slot. Other places operated a sign-up process for their timetable, allocating spaces on a first come, first served basis. If you were the group that got to the timetable last, you got the slot no one else wanted, usually the one that overlapped with lunchtime or with home time.

Letting everyone have a turn is a very obvious first thought when considering fair allocation of a shared space, but it is a very short thought. What was clear from my interviewees was that no one was working somewhere where a lot of thought had been given to timetabling.

It is nonsense to say that your room will be used to help someone calm down, but then specify that they can only do that at 2pm on a Wednesday. If it is going to be needed to assist people in calming down, and it has to be timetabled, then the obvious thing to do would be to examine that person's week and see if there are particular times when they are likely to need that time. For example, some people may need to recover from their journey to school or care setting and time spent in the multisensory room on arrival could help them to do that.

You should also be asking whether it is the right thing to do to let everyone have the same amount of time in the space. One of my interviewees spoke about her class of students, explaining that for half of them *the only place* they could access learning was in the multisensory room. The classroom environment was too bright and busy for them and they tended to sleep or shut down, but in the multisensory room they "came to life."

Those children – who only learn in the multisensory room, who "come to life" in the multisensory room – only get one hour a week in the multisensory room. And part of that hour is taken with the logistics of setting it up and hoisting them from their wheelchairs. In their school are other children who are able to learn within their regular classrooms. Is it fair that they spend one hour a week in a learning environment that suits their needs when their peers spend thirty hours a week in a learning environment that suits their needs? Of course all of those students benefit from being in the room, but for some those benefits are far more significant, considerable enough to warrant being called a need.

Park (1997, p. 6) advocates the use of smaller improvised multisensory spaces for children who require a sensory environment in order to be able to engage. In talking about his use of a tent as a personalised multisensory space for one young man, he reflects that it "seemed to offer far more potential for development than could be exploited by a once weekly visit to the multi-sensory room." If timetabling does not allow you to make the most of your multisensory room, then there is an argument for considering whether improvised spaces could be more effective. You will find suggestions for such spaces in Section 3 on page 127.

Timetabling for a multisensory room should not be quick and easy. If you are doing it right and considering the people who will be using the room as people with different needs and abilities, then it will be a long and tricky process requiring a lot of thought and difficult decisions – one you will need to repeat and evaluate and redo on a regular basis. Used effectively, multisensory rooms can be so powerful as to appear miraculous. If you have the privilege of having such an incredible resource, do not nullify its benefits with such a simple mistake as careless timetabling.

Parked

People reported members of staff taking people to a multisensory room, switching on a few things and then leaving them to it. I do not mean that they leave the room; they simply disengage from the person they are there to support because they understand that the person is doing something in interacting with the room and they do not see that they are a part of that process. They remain in the room and just relax. One interviewee said: "We have had a couple of incidences of staff falling asleep in there, they view it as a place to relax." Another teacher commented "I ban chat in the multisensory room, multisensory rooms can be very chatty places."

Once again this disengagement of support staff is not as simple as it looks on the surface. These are not careless people; they are people who are overworked and under-supported. They have been told to take the person to the room but have not been told what to do when they get there. When not in the room they have fifty other things they have to be doing at any one time, so they are naturally exhausted. A space where they do not have anything to do and can catch up with their friends, a space where they finally get a moment to themselves, is precisely what they need, so it is no surprise that when they are presented with it, they take it.

Staff members need careful, gentle support to understand what is expected of them in a multisensory room and to realise that their role, whether the session is directive or non-directive, is an active one. One of the people who fed into my research fondly remembered a head teacher they had worked under who would not allow staff members to facilitate in the multisensory room until they had proven their observation skills.

This particular head teacher would take sensory-based lessons in class and talk staff through the responses he was looking for and the time he would wait to get them. Over time he would back off from explaining and begin asking staff to explain to him the responses they had seen and to describe how long they were going to wait and how they were going to manage waiting. Once he was convinced that they could sensitively support someone to engage with a sensory experience, they were given the privilege of being allowed to support students in the multisensory room. Consequently, attentive, sensitive facilitation within that multisensory room was a badge of honour amongst their staff team and the impact of that showed clearly in the practice within the room.

It is very sad that nearly four decades on from when commentators and researchers first remarked on people using multisensory rooms as "dumping zones" or "holding bays," we are still tackling the same issue. What this tells us is that our current approach to trying to prevent this kind of practice is not working. Simply telling people not to park people is not enough; we need to tell them what to do as well as what not to do, recognising as we do so that what comes naturally and easily to some people does not to others.

One of my interviewees said they found it easier to interact with their students in the multisensory room because they were not being watched there; they felt less inhibited. Relating to a Sensory Being requires the kind of communication strategies a parent might use with a very young child; a lot of these are very intimate and require one person to be close to the other person and to make shapes with their faces and noises that they would not ordinarily make. To feel comfortable doing this requires a person to feel quite self-assured in the first place; not everyone does, and our confidence levels peak and dip over time.

If we want to see a more caring response to people with profound disabilities from the staff who are paid to look after them, we need to demonstrate that care for those people first. They cannot give out what has not been put in, and simply telling them they are doing it wrong only perpetuates the problem.

Cinemas

All of the interviewees I spoke to who had access to a modern, immersive multisensory room with multi-wall projections reported it being used at times as a cinema. Here's a representative example of what was said:

> Staff will bring a group in, set everyone up so they can see the screen, pop a film on and then just sit there and chat. They say they are watching, but how do they know? That child is just there in the room. And if they are focusing that focus is going to be disrupted by people chatting around them. They bring food too and I end up with bits of picnic stuck in expensive equipment.

I am sure an immersive room makes for a wonderful cinema experience and if that is meaningful and engaging to everyone, then there is nothing wrong with using it as such. The problems come when we consider the timetabling issues earlier. If you are watching a film whilst somewhere else a person who can only access stimulation within that space is blocked from being in there by your film, which you could also access on a TV screen elsewhere, then something is going wrong.

Immersive multisensory rooms can cost a lot of money. One of my interviewees had access to a room that cost over 45,000 pounds for just six square metres of floor space. Settings pay out that kind of money expecting to be able to do particular things with the rooms; it is unlikely that they have paid that with the intention of creating a cinema. A large, flat-screen television would have been enough if that were the case.

If your multisensory room is being used as a cinema, go back to what your original intentions and hopes were for the room and educate the people who work in that setting as to what these are. Help them to understand why they are important and show them how to use the space to be more than a cinema.

Tech fear

"It takes a degree in astrophysics just to operate it so we all just use the pre-set functions," said one interviewee, which is the equivalent to buying a keyboard in the 1980s and then only ever using it to play the demo track.

Another interviewee commented that the tech becomes a barrier to the sort of interactions you are hoping the room will inspire as the potential communication partner gets stressed by their inability to get the room to do precisely what they wanted it to do. Whilst it is true that the technology at our disposal today can create incredible immersive sensory experiences, it is also true that it can only do that if people feel confident using it. No one feels confident after a single training session, no matter how brilliant that training session. Several interviewees reported feeling less confident about their use of their multisensory room as a direct result of inspiring training that had shown them what the room was capable of, which only served to highlight to them their own incapability with regards to achieving such effects.

Many settings reported having, or wanting, rooms that would link to iPads, primarily because their staff members were not frightened of iPads. One of my sensory tech company interviewees pointed out that this is not because iPads are simple and the tech his company supplied was tricky; it was just that people had more practice at operating iPads at home, so they were better versed in the functioning and consequently not so worried about using them.

In spite of being someone who sells multisensory rooms, he went on to say that he believed that sensory equipment was more useful than multisensory rooms. He said he was seeing "more and more money sunk into the rooms when they cannot even tell me what they are or what they are for, they just know they want one because they have seen one somewhere else."

We need to recognise the clash between those who love tech and those who will always be frightened of it. One interviewee who had been responsible for the redesign of the multisensory room at their setting confessed, "I got caught up in all the new tech, and bought more than I should. No one could use it and I was always getting pulled out of class to show them how to do it."

The sense of being "caught up in" tech came through in some of my interviews too, such as when I asked people "tell me about your multisensory room." Several went off on long, lavish descriptions of all the equipment they owned. What was noticeable about their descriptions compared to other interviewees who also listed the kit available to them in their multisensory room was that they only spoke about the kit and what it could do, whereas other interviewees linked the capabilities of the kit to responses they saw in particular individuals.

My interviewees expressed very conflicting messages. One person said that "people just do not see the value of the equipment we have, they think it is lovely and that's nice but they do not appreciate its true value and what it can do for people." Whereas another said:

> Multisensory rooms are not worth the money. A human can be so much more interesting. There is such a message in that, if people see you using specialist equipment they think they need specialist equipment and to be a specialist. You do not need fancy kit, it just disables and disenfranchises the people, and it is them: they are your best piece of kit always.

On both sides of this argument we find a plea for people to be more informed and have more understanding so that they are empowered to do their best by the people they support. The importance of the person in a multisensory room is something we address in Section 5.

Set up time

Not allowing time for a multisensory room to be set up ahead of a person arriving is a surefire way to make null and void any of the fabulous personalisation abilities of the room. Arriving in a space that is set up in a welcoming fashion with appealing sensations on offer is very different from arriving in a space where the lights are initially too bright, the sounds too loud and equipment is responding unexpectedly, but which then becomes a pleasant space. For some people this difference is just one of inconvenience and lost time; for others the stress of the non-preferred space will be enough to block them from being able to appreciate the preferred space once it is created. If multisensory rooms are as valuable as their price tags command, then practice within the rooms should respect that value.

Containment zones

Many of my interviewees reported that their multisensory rooms were used as containment zones for people who had become violent and were in a state of extreme distress. Multisensory rooms are used this way because they have more padding than a typical room. Some multisensory rooms have soft walls and floors, and rooms often contain beanbags or waterbeds. For this reason they are seen as safe spaces. But, as we know from the section on broken equipment, it is not safe to be in a space with electrical appliances that you could potentially break and injure yourself upon.

My interviewees reported agitated people becoming more agitated in response to an overly stimulating sensory environment. "Staff drag them in there, switch everything on hoping it will calm them down and all you have is a stressed child who gets more wound up by everything going off." A setting using a multisensory room to contain people who have become violent is not being honest with itself. Either acknowledge that you need a safe space (in which case build one that is completely safe, free of breakable equipment and designed such that it offers low levels of stimulation), or acknowledge that your current behaviour strategies are not working effectively and take a closer look at them.

Researchers have found mixed results with regards to whether multisensory rooms have a positive or negative effect on behaviour in the long term. Certainly you need a clear plan if a multisensory room is going to be used to manage behaviour. You should not be taking people there in an emergency situation more than once. Once that emergency has happened, you plan for what you would do if a similar situation were ever to arise again.

You need to be recording how emergency situations unfold to make sure you are alert to patterns forming. For example, it is easy to see how someone who gets taken to a multisensory room that they enjoy being in as a result of a violent act might be tempted to produce more violent acts in order to have more time in the room. Access to a multisensory room can have a powerful calming effect, but only when it is handled sensibly. It is not simply putting someone in a room that has that effect.

If you are looking to a multisensory room as a way of dealing with the behaviour of a person that you find challenging, then there is a question to answer as to why you are looking to a multisensory room to provide for those needs. Hogg et al. (2001) show that the evidence for the effectiveness of behavioural approaches to challenging behaviour far outstrips the scant evidence there is to suggest that multisensory rooms might help.

OVERVIEW

Taking time to consider some of the simple decisions that impact the access and effectiveness of your multisensory room can help to maximise it as an asset within your setting. Failure to take account of these things can nullify the potential positive benefits of even the best equipped multisensory room.

F.I.S.H.

Consider each of the identified points in turn and question whether it has an impact on your multisensory room:

How are the people who use your multisensory room shown how to use the equipment? Is the demonstration one of everything switched on at once, or is it a more sensitively modelled affair?

What is the maintenance provision for your room? What steps are taken to ensure equipment within your room is not broken?

What journey do people have to take to reach your multisensory room? How could this be improved?

How is your multisensory room timetabled? How could this be improved?

How does the underpinning philosophy of the people using your multisensory room effect the likelihood of someone experiencing being "parked" in the room?

Does your multisensory room get used as a cinema? Is a cinema space what you hoped your multisensory room would be?

How confident are the people who use your multisensory room in operating the equipment and getting the most out of the space? What can you do to enable them to feel more confident? If what you are already doing is not working, how can you do it differently?

Do people using your multisensory room have adequate time to set it up according to the needs and preferences of the people whom the space might benefit?

Is your multisensory room ever used as a containment zone? Do you need an alternative space for this purpose, or do you need to readdress how behaviour within your setting is being managed?

The limitations of my research and the positive findings

ORIENTATION

This section discusses the limitations of the research I conducted into the use of multisensory rooms in the UK and looks at some of the positive findings it turned up, namely, aspects of the rooms that people felt were particularly beneficial.

The limitations of my research

In the reporting of my research I have created binary responses out of conversational data. In doing this I am exacting my own judgement and creating a layer of bias. I have tried to evaluate what was said on face value but regardless of my possible personal bias, some answers are very hard to judge indeed. For example, in the case of someone who tells you confidently that they use a directive approach but goes on to say they is always responsive to the child and explains that if the child does not want to do the activity proposed they move to a different one, is that person using a directive or a non-directive approach? Similarly, for a person who describes their intent for the room to be inspiring of playfulness, are they seeking for a person to relax or to be stimulated? The risk of presenting data in a numeric or binary way is that it suggests firm answers, and as we know by now in the land of multisensory room research, rarely do we encounter anything methodologically rigorous enough from which to draw firm conclusions. I am afraid my research is no different; it is "indicative of," not "evidence of."

My research, as I have highlighted throughout, is not exempt from bias. I have done my best to draw your attention to where bias may be taking hold, for example my interviewees' mention of sensory stories. Clearly the questions I chose to ask reflect my own interests, and although I tried to make them as free from bias as possible, in the asking of certain questions and not others there is always bias of a kind.

Another problem we have when evaluating the validity of my findings is that the answers given may not reflect the true situation, as I am reliant on the reporting of people involved in the situation, who themselves are likely to be biased. For example, when an interviewee reports that the person they support in the room becomes relaxed in the room, how do I know whether that is a genuine relaxed state or whether it is a shutdown state caused by sensory overload? Quite simply, I do not.

My research is weakened by the small sample size, with just twenty-five people completing the full interview process. However this number is in line with similar studies, as discussed in Section 2, and although only twenty-five people completed the full interview, over fifty answered the "get it" question reported on in Section 5 and a great many more fed into the writing of this book as a whole.

The small number of respondents to my broadly advertised appeal for interviewees is a finding of sorts in itself. But indicating what? A lack of time? A lack of confidence? A lack of priority? A lack of interest? The relatively high dropout rate is another finding of sorts, but again we cannot be sure what it indicates, although the same possibilities would apply.

Positive findings

I have reported many of the limiting factors people experienced when trying to get the most out of their multisensory rooms. In this coming section I look at features of the room that people commonly reported in the positive. One of the noted features was one we might expect, namely, the ability to control stimulation. Three of the noted features were perhaps more surprising, as they were not related to the unique nature of the equipment within the multisensory rooms or to the effects that could be created by said equipment. These were the ability to black out the rooms, the uninterrupted nature of the rooms and the way the rooms inspired focused attention. One final feature was, to me, even more surprising: the impressiveness of the space.

Control

Being able to control the stimulation offered in a multisensory room was an aspect of the rooms that was noted by a good number of my interviewees. In general, people used their ability to control the sensory stimulation on offer within a multisensory room as they set up the room prior to an activity starting. People rarely mentioned using their control of the room during a session. Using the controllable elements of the room to personalise experience was only mentioned by three people.

Becky Lyddon from Sensory Spectacle (2019) notes that for people with sensory processing difficulties, we might recognise a characteristic of needing to feel in control in order to help them regulate themselves throughout the day. Having a sensory environment where someone is able to feel in control is so important. Yet no one I spoke with, either during the semi-structured interviews or during any of my conversations surrounding this work, mentioned handing over control of the room to the person using it. It was always controlled on their behalf.

Furthermore, it is interesting to consider whether control in itself is a support for self-regulation. Suppose I am someone who craves a particular type of visual stimulation, for example, the flickering of light between my waving fingers. If I enjoy this stimulation to such an extent that it blocks out my access to the world around me and the people in it, is it good for me? Am I going to be supported by an environment that offers me further opportunities to explore this flickering of light? To suggest that my support would come from the environment is akin to suggesting that an alcoholic would be supported by ready access to a wine cellar. The support on offer to me comes from the possibility of a relationship within that environment, by offering me access to the flickering of light with, or via, another person; what you are offering me is not the magic of control over my own self-stimulation, you are offering me a relationship with that person. It is that relationship which will be key to me learning to self-regulate, not the opportunity to access stimulation for myself.

Darkness

It may come as a surprise to some people that the most noted feature of a multisensory room by my interviewees was the darkness of the space, not the sensory nature of it or the ability to exact control over equipment and experience cause and effect. The ability to make the room dark was most commonly cited as being *the thing* that made the difference in causing the response or promoting the relaxation.

Uninterrupted

Next to the darkness of the rooms, the fact that they were uninterrupted and focused was very important to my interviewees. They often commented that in their usual spaces – their classrooms, dayrooms, living rooms and so forth – it was common for other people to pass through. In a school or care setting this could be other professionals, and in a home setting it could be other family members. The relatively uninterruptedness of the multisensory room was seen as being key to the increases in engagement witnessed within the rooms.

Focused

My interviewees also commonly highlighted that because there was only a certain set of things that could be done in a multisensory room, this made the room a more focused place. In a classroom, for example, staff supporting a student in engaging with a sensory activity could be distracted by the needs of another student, by a toy dropped on the floor in need of picking up, by dishes unwashed, by a cupboard in need of tidying, by a note that needs writing, by any number of things, whereas in the multisensory room there is just the task in hand of being in the room. Likewise, the association of the room with a particular activity helped people going into the room to ready themselves for and engage with the activity.

I often clarified this answer with my interviewees by asking "If I could give you a dark, sound-insulated tent where no one interrupted you, do you think it would be as effective as your room?" Everyone I asked this of said yes. As you consider the significance of this, it is worth taking a look back through the alternative sensory spaces suggested in Section 3 to see if they hold this magic.

Multisensory rooms are dazzling. They promise to perform like magic wands and we believe the promises because we want the magic. Do not be disappointed that closer inspection reveals no wands. You are the magic.

To create the magic of a multisensory room, set up a space where the sensations within are at a pitch ideal for the person you intend to take into that space. Choose a space where it is possible to make it dark if you want to, one free from interruptions and solely dedicated to the creation of wonder. That is all you need. If you have more than that, and you have wonderful awe-inspiring bits of technology at your disposal, then that is grand; you can do magic with them just the same. But you do not need them. Your heart, your connection, your responsiveness . . . these things are the essential elements of magic. Be empowered by the simplicity, not disappointed by it. You are more amazing than any room.

Wowness

Before we move on, there is one other noted aspect of the rooms that I want to address: the wowness of the space. I confess I did not actually expect people who had installed rooms to tell me that they had chosen the equipment within the rooms or the design of the rooms based on wanting to have the same as or, more often than not, better than another setting. Clearly I am naive, as several of my interviewees said things like "We wanted to make sure ours was better than such and such a nearby setting's." Once stripped of this particular piece of naivety, I confess to inwardly rolling my eyes when any of my interviewees began to tell me how their room was better than someone else's room.

A particular trigger for my inward eye roll was the phrase, "It's great for showing visitors around." This was a phrase that came up so often, both within my interviews and within my wider conversations, that I began to wonder whether people were installing these elaborate spaces purely to entertain people on tours of their school or care facility – until one of my interviewees, just as I was beginning the upward motion of that eye roll, qualified what he had said with "and we need that."

I brought my eyes back to their correct alignment and asked him to explain.

It's great, it's such a resource. It's one of the things I talk about most when showing visitors around because it's really nice to be able to show them what special education can be like. In contrast to other things they may see around school it is a very non medicalised environment. They are just getting used to the idea that their son or daughter might have to come to our school, and how different it is here to the school their other child goes to, and in the other rooms they see pumps and medicines and chairs and stuff, here. In here it is all fun. It is an easy positive thing to show them. It is the place in the building people have the least preconceptions about. We battle everyday against people's misconceptions of what special school is like.

And in saying this he reminded me that the multisensory rooms of today are very much deployed against the backdrop of the provision of the past. If this is what we are using our multisensory rooms for, should not we also be focused on additional ways to battle those misconceptions?

Consider your local community. Where do they get their information? It is likely that it is a mixture of local news outlets, like papers and the local news on the television and social media. How much information would your local community find about your setting through those outlets? Do just as you would do with the people you support and use the channels of communication they prefer. Get into your local paper, be interviewed on the local news or share a post on social media. Do this often. Battle those misconceptions that still linger.

Of course it is not just large, professionally installed multisensory rooms that can trigger the "wow" response in outside observers; improvised spaces can do the same. One of my interviewees told me:

I have a curtained off area where the walls have been painted black, and there is an overhead wooden frame from which I can hang objects. It is used a lot every single day and has attracted pupils from other classes, e.g. at lunchtime, and it is often shown to visitors.

The interviewee goes on to say later: "I think that being creative with a few cheap items has absolutely been more stimulating than the very expensive multisensory room which I do not think can justify its expense, even with excellent training." A glance through the Facebook photo album shared by @TheSensoryProjects (www.thesensory-projects.co.uk/books)will give you plenty of opportunity to be wowed by inexpensive improvised multisensory environments.

OVERVIEW

The ability to control stimulation within a multisensory room was commonly reported as being a positive feature of the rooms by my interviewees. However, this reporting was done without passion, expressed more as something a person has learned to say than something they feel. Three further features were identified which were spoken about with greater passion: the darkness that was possible within the rooms, the uninterrupted nature of activities within the rooms and the ability to create a place of focused activity. The novel and impressive nature of the rooms was highlighted as being an important tool in tackling preconceptions surrounding provision for people with learning disabilities. Alternative sensory spaces may be able to provide many of the noted aspects of multisensory rooms and can also wow people with their novelty value and their inherent creativity and dedication.

F.I.S.H.

What would you identify as being the key features that contribute to the impact of your multisensory room? What could you do without? What do you long to have the capacity to do?

How do people respond to being shown your multisensory room? Is it used in a way that changes perceptions? What else could you be doing to change these perceptions and how would a change in perceptions benefit the people you support?

Section

5

ORIENTATION

The most important piece of the kit in a multisensory room is the person facilitating in the space. As with any piece of a kit, this one can operate well or it can operate poorly. This section reports findings from a thematic analysis of over fifty conversations as to what stops this piece of the kit from working at its best. Despite being widely recognised as being of critical importance to the success of experiences within multisensory rooms, the people facilitating the spaces have been very little discussed in the literature surrounding them. In addressing this topic I endeavour to remove a little of its taboo nature.

The most important piece of the kit

It is a well-known right answer when asked what the most important piece of the kit is in a multisensory room to say "the person facilitating the space." And it is clearly true that the way someone is supported in accessing the sensory experiences available within a multisensory room has an enormous influence over whether the experience of being in the room is positive or negative. The most important piece of the kit in the multisensory room is the person facilitating and their relationship with the person they are supporting.

The strange thing is that in spite of this being such a well-known right answer, almost as soon as the answer is given it becomes a taboo topic. In conducting my research I began, at first spontaneously and then later on more purposefully, to ask my interviewees a very simple and very vague question: "Do you find, when supporting people with profound disabilities, that some people get it and some people do not?" I asked over fifty people this question; some were my existing interviewees who took part in the semi-structured interviews described in Section 4, others were people I met at events I travelled to, even people I met on the train whilst travelling, and many were people I hold in particularly high regard, whom I sought out as I was especially keen to hear their answers and learn from them.

What all of the people to whom I asked the "get it" question have in common is that they all work directly with or are family members of a person or people with profound and multiple learning disabilities and appeared to me to be passionate about their role in that person's or those persons' lives.

Everyone instantly understood the distinction between those who "got it" and those who did not. I purposefully did not define what these statements meant because part of what I was interested in was people's individual interpretations of the vagueness of my question. But nearly universally people reported having their practice thwarted by a person who did not "get it."

If the most important piece of the kit in a multisensory room is the person facilitating another person's access to that space, then surely we should be talking about those people. What is the difference between those who get it and those who do not, and how can we turn those who do not get it into those who do, and is this even possible?

I took notes on all of my "get it" conversations and typed them up on the same day as having the conversation to ensure my memories were as fresh as they could be. I conducted a thematic analysis of these conversations in a very rustic way: I printed them all out, cut them up into small sections and then laid them out on a giant sheet of paper, placing similar expressions together. The process of doing this revealed ten to twelve common topics within the answers.

What I will present to you in the coming section is an overview of what was expressed to me during the conversations I have had around doing this research. I have no answers; this is the start of the conversation. In beginning this conversation I hope to dispel a little of the taboo surrounding the topic of talking about the people facilitating in multisensory rooms.

Good practice within a multisensory room is relational, as it is with other forms of support offered to people with disabilities, and as it is in any situation where people cooperate. Researchers have sought to look at the impact of attitudes and relationships on the success, or otherwise, of support offered to people with learning disabilities (e.g. Lewer and Harding 2013a, 2013b). Other researchers have noted that the social engagement of people supporting individuals with profound disabilities is contingent upon their view of them (e.g. Simmons 2019a, 2019b). Crombie et al. (2014) note that aspects of provision found in an outstanding special school were implicit in the staff facilitating that outstanding care, that is, the staff "got it."

As my research into the use of multisensory rooms unfolded, I became increasingly aware of a taboo surrounding this topic. If we look honestly at the people in multisensory rooms and how they are relating to one another, then we will be better able to set up and use multisensory environments as spaces whose benefits are wholly realised, rather than have them remain as they are: spaces whose incredible potential remains unrealised.

First, hear the voices of parents and professionals describing coming up against the person who does not get it:

After supporting a student in their music therapy sessions for a year I asked a member of my team to give me feedback on that student's communication whilst in the session. Their response was "You can tell by looking at her that she cannot do anything." It made my blood boil, I had to walk away.

A higher level teaching assistant has been leading our sensory story sessions and getting some great responses from our students. It has been really lovely to see their confidence blossom. Then last week another teaching assistant questioned her, midway through a session, saying "What is the point in doing this, they cannot learn anything?" Not only did she hold such an opinion in the face of their clear progress she felt it okay to voice it in front of other staff and in front of the students themselves.

They see their role as just "changing bums" and do not see anything else. They do not recognise that person's inherent value so they cannot CARE as they provide care.

Some people just cannot get it. I have seen great people work alongside useless people for years and it just does not rub off. It is in them. They do not get it.

There are always people who do not get it, often it is people in management which makes my job all the harder.

For me I can see it in their handling of the children, those who do not get it. I have lost count of the number of times I have seen staff arrive at reception and begin pushing a child's wheelchair without so much as a hello, moving them as if they are a parcel to be got from point A to point B as quickly and efficiently as possible.

If you support a person with profound disabilities it is likely that these comments, although shocking, are not surprising to you. I expect you could add a litany of your own examples. It is clear that with regards to our support of people with profound disabilities, there clearly are people who "get it" and those who do not.

I am well aware that I am continuing to avoid defining these criteria. I think reflecting on precisely what it is we personally mean by "get it" can help us to tune into ways of sharing our understanding with others. What would you mean by someone who "got it" or someone who did not?

It is innate

Having asked people the "get it" question, I tried to encourage people to unpick what they meant by "get it" and what caused one person to get it and another to not. Nearly everyone began by saying that the distinction was innate. They believed that the ability to understand and respond appropriately to someone with a profound disability was either something that someone had, or that they did not have, and that no amount of life experience or education would change this fundamental aspect of a person's character.

People felt that the ability to "get it" was somehow already in a person before they acquired any experience or received any training. When pushed about the nature of this innate ability or inability, people began to explain in ways that opened up possibilities for change. For example, one interviewee said that, "Introverted people live a more viscerally experienced life so they are more attuned to small responses." From their start point that you needed to be an introvert in order to be able to fully relate to someone with complex disabilities, we now have two clues: maybe if we could connect people with their own visceral experience it would accentuate their abilities, or maybe if we could clue them into the tiny responses that were presented by others, it would awaken their abilities to react to them.

Another explained, ""Anyone who uses the phrase 'in my day' automatically assigns themselves to a different time, they opt out of the current age and sign themselves up to the perceived core values and principles of a particular time." This interviewee's answer points towards generational shifts in understanding, and if this entrenched person has shifted their understanding once, perhaps they can do it again.

Wheat from chaff

Many people advocated a sorting the wheat from the chaff approach of identifying those who "got it" and those who did not and then using them according to their skills. Examples were given of using particular people for administrative tasks or ensuring they were always in the company of someone who did "get it." Some people even advocated firing those who did not "get it," or wished aloud that it were possible to do so.

A couple of providers of care notable for their high standard of provision explained to me processes whereby they did just that: over a set period of time, usually a year, the person who appeared not to "get it" would be supported with training and feedback, but ultimately if they did not demonstrate a shift in their attitude, they were fired. These settings argued that indulging these people with further support was simply throwing good money after bad and to do so would be to waste the time of those in their care who would suffer for a lack of better support.

I was unwilling to simply chalk up the distinction between those who "get it" and those who do not to something people are born with. Surely it could not be. Could we honestly go around a baby unit and audit those newborn infants according to which could be empathetic, responsive, reflective and compassionate? Is there a particular gland or protein or part of the genetic code missing from those people who seem to see no personhood in people with profound disabilities, such that it makes it impossible for them to ever do so? It seems very unlikely. As fundamental as the distinction between getting it and not getting it may seem, it must at some stage have happened to a person. But how?

A dozen clues

I asked my interviewees to think about a person they had known who clearly did not "get it" and speculate on what it was about that person that made it difficult for them.

After conducting a thematic analysis on the myriad responses I received, twelve themes emerged. It is important that I again state that I am in no way suggesting that this list is definitive; this is the start of the conversation.

The issue of people not "getting it" is not one restricted to multisensory rooms but is one we face across the whole of provision for people with complex disabilities, and keeping it as a taboo does not help. So let us explore. The twelve topics my interviewees identified fall broadly into three categories:

* Characteristics of the person who does not get it.

* Characteristics of a person who does get it that are lacking from a person who does not get it.

* Ways of enabling someone who does not get it to get it.

Four characteristics of people who do not get it

My interviewees identified four characteristics of people who do not get it. These were identified as separate entities, but there was no suggestion that someone who did not get it would have all four. These four things represent the conclusions different interviewees drew when speculating upon why a particular person they knew did not get it.

Toughened

Lots of people described the person who did not get it as tough, in some way hardened by life. They felt that when this person had met adversity in their own life they had made a choice to harden themselves against it so that, were they ever to experience the same thing again, it would not hurt them next time.

Toughened people were known for saying things like "I have had enough" or "I do not take shit from anyone." These phrases were quoted frequently by people trying to explain the conflict they felt within their provision.

We speculated that if someone has managed to make their outer self, the part of their personhood that is in touch with the world, so tough as to not feel the day-to-day blows of life, it is likely that their toughness also equates to a lack of sensitivity such that it makes it difficult for them to respond to the subtleties of someone whose communication is different from their own.

The way to connect with a toughened person could possibly be to find a way to enable them to identify aspects of their own vulnerability with the inherent vulnerabilities of the person in their care. Their toughness then could potentially be put to good use protecting the person they support.

Power

Commentators have highlighted issues with workplace bullying within education (Kettle 2012; Akbar 2018 and many more) and social care (Clements 2014; Cook 2017 and once again many more). In his article, Clements (2014) cites Murray's (2009) description of the bully: "The bully has an extreme need to have complete control over an individual or environment." Imagine such an individual: one with this extreme need to have control over other individuals. Where might such an individual be drawn to work? Would a setting that offered vulnerable individuals who are potentially easier to have control over than other people be an attractive offer?

The idea that a bully might be drawn to work supporting people with complex disabilities was one reflected by people as they wrestled with my "get it" question. Answers included the following:

> It is about the power balance, where else is someone like that going to feel in control? Where else are they not going to be the stupid one?

> It was the only job they could get, it is the only place where there are people who they are cleverer than.

Could a problem such as this one be made worse by a job role in which one feels themselves to have very little power, such as when there is no ability to decide upon aspects of their work, for instance, how a task will be done or when it will be done? Could a problem such as this one be mitigated by giving a person clearly defined places in which to exhibit power, for example, responsibility for a certain area or task within a setting?

Could there be a way of using their need to dominate and control as a positive force? I am thinking of one of the best responses I have ever seen to playground bullying: I was on my very first teaching placement, working in a rural school whose population doubled in the summer term when a traveller encampment set up on a field near the school. There were many tensions between the traveller population and the local population and some of these were shown in bullying in the playground. I was waiting outside the head teacher's office for a meeting. The head teacher came to her door and called me in and as she did so two little girls left her office chatting pleasantly to one another and doing that very fast, I'm-not-running, skippety walk back to their classroom.

The head teacher apologised for the late running of our meeting and informed me that she had had to deal with an incident of bullying. She nodded towards the two girls. I was confused. The girls were clearly friends. The head teacher explained:

> Last week Ellie's Mum came in to say that some of the traveller children had been giving her trouble on the playground. I spoke to Ellie and she said it had all been led by Lucy. So I called Lucy in to see me and we had a chat. I told her that I knew that Ellie had been having difficulty on the playground and that she wanted to be friends with everyone and be able to play with everyone nicely. I said to Lucy that I thought she would be just the girl for the job. So I put her in charge of making sure that Ellie had nice playtimes. That was them coming back a week on to report a week of happy playtimes. I have given them both a sticker and I'll write a note home to their parents tonight, to tell Ellie's Mum she's had a good week and to tell Lucy's Mum what a star she has been.

My example features children, but a similar message of showing respect and trust might enable others to use their power for good.

Ended up here

Interviewees discussing the power imbalance between people in a caring or facilitator role and the people with profound disabilities for whom they were caring often went on to discuss the lack of freedom in deciding to take on the role. The interviewee who said it was the only job people could get went on to explain:

> How many of them set out to work here? They have non inquiring minds, no genuine empathy, they are educationally below average. That's a limited choice: hair dresser, workman, but all of those you still have to go to college for, what if you could not be bothered? What role could you walk into? It is this one, and it is wiping arses, that is all they will see it as because they think that is all they are qualified for. There is no respect in society for this work. Why are these people, who are the most vulnerable among us, the bottom rung of the job ladder? The people doing the work loathe their role because they are looked down on, and the individuals themselves are traded as commodities by companies who make money out of them. Those people could not change because to do so they would have to recognise what they have been and they could never forgive themselves for that.

This interviewee was particularly candid with their responses and saw themselves as being on both sides of the fence as they had worked in the care industry themselves and also had a family member in care. Although their position reads as extreme, when I shared it with other interviewees most nodded in recognition and no one spoke against it. Lots of interviewees echoed the sentiment that the job had been "ended up" in, not chosen.

Another interviewee reflected: "Some people get it but the trouble we have here is when someone like that comes along, someone proactive, they do not tend to stay long, they move on to better things." If people are "ending up" doing a job they do not value, perhaps showing them the value in the job would help them both to recognise the worth of what they do and value themselves more highly. Valuing the job more highly could also mean people do not feel such a need to move on to "better things." If they value themselves more highly they may have less need to dominate others in order to feel valuable.

Chailey Heritage Foundation School, a national, if not global, leader on the provision of education and care for people with profound disabilities, has spent considerable time and effort creating a list of competencies for their teaching assistants. The extensiveness of this list is not intended to daunt potential candidates considering the role, but to provide a means by which Chailey celebrates the extraordinary talents of their team and lets them know that their role is valued. As I write, Chailey is looking to gain continuing professional development (CPD) accreditation for the competences to further endorse the capabilities of their staff.

Short thinking

Many interviewees described people whose chains of thought when interpreting the behaviours of people in their care seemed remarkably short, ending almost as soon as they had begun. Here are some examples that I was given:

> It's like he thinks, oh he has made that noise, if I made that noise it would not mean anything, so it does not mean anything.

Or even non-existent:

> The way they see them is that they cannot do anything, do not mean anything, do not have any views, they do not even ask the question of what does this mean because in their minds they have already answered it: these people cannot do anything.

Finding ways of extending these thought chains through worked examples could begin to open out the possibility of self-reflection. Judicious use of video footage and discussion could get people into the habit of questioning responses and looking for meaning beyond what they would typically ascribe to the action in their own life.

Characteristics of people who do get it that are lacking from people who do not get it

Many of my interviewees when asked to reflect upon a person they knew who did not get it spoke of characteristics they lacked. My interviewees found it easier to note what was lacking than to speculate as to how these deficits of character had occurred.

Reflective

When we explored the way that people learn in an attempt to understand what those who do not get it lack, my interviewees and I often fell on the topic of being reflective. The description of short thinking is itself a description of people not reflecting on their actions or the actions of others.

People commented that some people are best able to reflect when they are sitting still and given time to think, whereas others may need entirely different circumstances to prompt reflection. Nearly all of my interviewees identified being able to reflect and evaluate how a particular interaction had gone as being critical to being able to learn how to better support someone with complex needs. The ability to be reflective was valued more highly than, for example, knowledge about particular conditions or memory for certain procedures.

One interviewee was clear about this from the very start of our "get it" conversation:

> If I had a penny for every example I had of someone not getting it! What makes someone get it is a combination of. . . . Fundamentally . . . it is about a person's ability to reflect on a situation or look at a situation and be aware of their role in their having an effect on that situation. You can take someone who works with a child with PMLD and even in the way they naturally speak about how an interaction has gone its very much there: some will reflect on it and list what they did and there is no indication of a "maybe I could have done this" or a "in responding to this I triggered that." Part of it is self-reflection, thinking about what you do and do not do, and part is reflecting on the other person and what their responses were. It is the same with training, it's not just being able to go on a course, but being able to reflect on it and think about it when you are there.

What stood out to me from this person's response was how they saw the reflective nature of the people who "get it" as being there at every level of that interaction, extending it to how they spoke about an interaction and how they engaged with training as well as the interaction itself and their reflection on their own role and the responses of the person they were supporting.

The ability to be reflective is one that can certainly be enhanced by training that models the reflective process and invites participants to take on aspects of it bit by bit. Ware (1996/2003) describes how through the Contingency Sensitive Environment Project she was able to enhance the reflectiveness of staff by exploring with them the types of responses they were looking for from their students. Simply modelling reflective thought processes can be a good way to start. For example, you could video record an interaction and ask everyone watching the video to reflect on their own role within the interaction. Lead by example, by ensuring you are in the video and passing a reflective comment about your part. Encourage people who give brief answers, like "I did that wrong" or "that was good," to extend them, supporting them to give reflective answers.

They see personhood as separate from functionality

Personhood was a topic many interviewees danced around but struggled to put their finger on directly.

> They do not see the inherent value in people, they want something in exchange for their efforts.

> They think they are being really good, but they are not. They are just doing things to them.

Others were exceptionally blunt:

> They just see them as bits of meat.

The clarity of that particular interviewee's assessment of a particular member of one care team gave me a lens through which to look as I re-inspected conversations I had taken part in recently in a care setting. At the time of having those conversations, something about them had felt uneasy to me, but they were cheerily and openly under-taken. I could not place what it was that I found unsettling, and then that interviewee said that and it became clear. Looking back through those conversations in my mind and evaluating what had been said, if I imagined that the person being talked about was simply a piece of meat, a well-liked piece of meat and one that it was recognised should look nice and be well presented and moved about at different times to different places, there was nothing in what was said that would give me any cause to suppose that the subject of the conversation was anything more than a piece of meat. Nowhere in any of what these people had said to me was a reflection of the personhood of the people in their care, and nowhere was any mention of their innate humanity. I had not been able to place it before and noticing it was very chilling.

Simmons (2019a) challenges us to reflect on our understanding of personhood, pointing out that we are biased towards certain concepts of the mind and define people in terms of how well their minds function when concepts of mind themselves are contested as are mainstream definitions of personhood that focus only on the mind.

Believing the embodied and relational understanding of profound and multiple learning disabilities to be undertheorised, his work looks at how relationships between people are affected by the way the people involved in those relationships framed the lived experience of the other. In his study he observed that "differences in social engagement were contingent upon the framing of the body as living or lived" (Simmons 2019a).

Clearly our attitude and our underpinning philosophies (even if we are not aware of having them) have a massive impact on how we relate to others in our lives. I began to wonder how people who cared so closely for people with profound disabilities could possibly miss their personhood or humanity. How, when spending so much time in such close proximity, could you fail to see it? Once again the conclusion was less about the presentation of the people being cared for and more about how the person providing the care viewed themselves.

What they all had in common were lives in which their own identity was tied up in their function. They were busy people who carried out many roles, often very practical rather than creative: they made the dinner, they picked the children up from school and took them to their clubs, they remembered what was to be put in which bag, they attended to the care needs of someone, they hoovered up and kept everything nice, and they helped out with such and such on the weekends and so on. When they talked about the quantity of stuff they had to do, they, in a sense, came alive, and it was when their expression was most animated. Their own identity was in their function and where they saw no function, they saw no identity. The people they cared for did not "do" in the way that they did, and so they were objects of function, not people.

As with the fear of difference, this type of "not getting it" has negative consequences for the person themselves, as well as for those in their care. Imagine their life when their family has flown the nest, or perhaps when in later life they find they need support. Who are they when they no longer "do"? Will their identity be lost when the busyness of their life fades? Encouraging their attention to non-functional aspects of life may well enhance their ability to appreciate the personhood of someone with fewer functional abilities than they possess. It is likely that these aspects of their personal capabilities are under-developed and need a lot of nurturing and support. They may be worried about doing something they are not confident in doing well. Perhaps a gently taught art class would have more impact on their provision than a targeted training session!

It is worth noting that the responsibility for deficits such as those described here does not rest solely within the individual. At times within our discussions about functionality and personhood, as well as in our discussions about other topics, interviewees pointed to situations where established policy and procedures were in conflict with the personhood of the individual being cared for. One interviewee commented:

> Clinical ethos and policy and procedure take away from individuality. We have
> lots of positive care but it has a big paperwork burden and if you have not done

something then you get questioned and the individual gets lost. For example if you tuned into what that person needed and they did not want a flannel in their face at 8am but procedure demands it then you either get in trouble or you squash that person out.

Another commented on how a shift in institutional focus has effected how people perceive those they care for:

Generations ago special education was less about the learning profile and more about care. And giving care, however compassionately, can easily be misunderstood as being about the mechanics of the body, not about a person. There has been a massive shift towards more reflective practice, plan, do, review, but I am not sure it has captured everyone.

Another interviewee suggested that the apparent lack of perception of personhood could indicate a fear of acknowledging personhood more than a lack of recognition. They said:

We know from psychology that anyone who uses that phrase "I could not cope if it happened to me" is removing themselves from the possibility of having to imagine themselves in that scenario.

As with the "they just see them as bits of meat" comment, this remark really stood out in my mind. I have an active presence on social media, and on Facebook in particular I am connected with many families who support children and adults with complex disabilities. I have seen so many of them post comments in frustration in response to someone having said to them "I could not cope if it were me." It is something I commented on in my TEDx talk – "Inclusion: for pity's sake?" (Grace 2018) – when speaking about families coping with the death of a loved one.

My interviewee went on to explain that of course we could all, through accident or illness or simply through aging, find ourselves in a highly vulnerable and dependent state, which is alarming to consider. By saying "I could not cope if it happened to me," the observer of a situation instantly opts out of imagining themselves in that situation by identifying the person within the situation as one type of person, namely, someone who copes, and themselves as another type, namely, someone who cannot cope – they are claiming difference. And in that difference is an idea of protection. I am not like you. These things happen to people like you. They do not happen to people like me.

Perhaps facing people with stories of just how possible it is to have our life circumstances change would, in a sense, force them to remove that false barrier of difference and occupy a more compassionate stand point.

The same interviewee who made the "could not cope" observation at the end of our chat gave a wry smile and offered a technique that they had used for circumnavigating this issue, saying, "You can of course try planting facts." I requested more information about this cunning and they went on to explain:

> If you know something about the person, say they are a football supporter, you can tell them that the individual they are working with is a fan of the same team, and that plants a "like me-ness" in them from the start. I find it works better.

Another interviewee, this time someone who regularly ran workshops inviting people of different abilities to take part in an activity together, also reflected this point.

> People need relatable moments, we manufacture them sometimes, for example blindfolding someone and inviting someone else to guide them. Every now and then we see a penny drop and someone will make a link to a person in their own life, like "It's like my mum her sight went at the end of her life." And once they have made that link how they respond to the person changes.

It was another great insight and shows the importance of shared stories, narratives in which we both take part, like the success of a football team, or a change in fashions. It does not have to be manufactured, just noticed. For people who are not able to communicate their interests verbally or through traditional means, finding ways to present their interests can enable others to form more genuine connections to them. Even simple things like t-shirts with logos or stickers on a wheelchair frame can be very powerful tools for enabling people to connect with one another.

One of my interviewees spoke of a time when things changed for them:

> You get to a point in life where you recognise your vulnerability and it is at that point that you stop seeing them as others. Luck and time are the only things that separate us from being them. You think of it as being someone else's problem, it's not until you are there and you realise the finality of it. I always had a way out before. Even just knowing you did not understand would be useful.

Here is something a little different for you to try: a thought experiment. Sometimes when dealing with concepts that are hard to pin down, it can help to examine them from a different point of view. By embedding these concepts into a story you can reflect on how you feel about them independent of your own circumstances. Of course this is not a perfect science. There may be places where you feel the story is not an accurate reflection of the concepts we are dealing with, but this is good too, as it provokes you to think of why that is, and in doing so you hone your own opinions and ideas. The following thought experiment relates to what we were considering with regards to personhood and functionality.

> Long ago in a faraway place, a King and Queen were blessed with a child. Sadly the child died at birth and the King and Queen were grief stricken. Looking for a way to ease the grief of the royal family, the court soothsayer ordered that an ornate statue be created.
>
> A sculptor was called to court to carve the form of the dead infant from oak. The sculpture was oiled and dressed and wrapped in the blankets meant for the royal baby and handed to the Queen. Her grief seemed to ease as she gazed down onto the familiar face, and adjusted the bonnet upon the small head.
>
> The King at her side softened to and leant across to put his finger to the cheek of the wooden baby. Soothed by the carved child, the King and Queen regained their strength. The Queen beckoned for the court nannies to come and take the child to the nursery, and the court swung into the rhythm of life they had been expecting prior to the death of the baby. The nannies cared for the wooden child by day in the nursery from time to time the Queen, and sometimes the King, would pop in to look upon the child, and every evening the child would be brought to court to be given the blessing of a kiss from his parents.
>
> The nannies in the court knew the King and Queen thought well of them if they treated the child as if it were alive and so they were seen to coo over the baby and sing it lullabies, but only when they knew the King and Queen were likely to be present.
>
> Over time the Queen became unsettled. The soothsayer came to her side and whispered "What ails your majesty?" "The child does not grow," complained the Queen. The soothsayer understood immediately and called for the sculptor once again. This time he was commissioned not to create a single carving but to prepare for a lifetime of study as he would be expected to deliver a new wooden child annually upon the day of the birth of the dead baby.
>
> The court instantly understood the ritual and on his birthday courtiers would gather to remark upon how his majesty had grown and how proud his parents must be of such a strapping young man.
>
> The nannies continued to care for the succession of wooden children, keeping their bodies oiled and dressed for the duration of the year that they were the royal child and then storing them out of sight thereafter.

Spend some time in the landscape of this story by discussing how it might continue.

If you are facilitating these discussions in a group, aim to have the group chat for as long as they need to start talking about the situation as if it were real.

What happens to the sculptor? What happens to the retired babies? What befalls the wooden boy?

Once you have considered the story as a whole, focus in on the nannies. Have people discuss their work and how they might carry it out. What is thought of them for doing it? Is it an honourable role or a mocked one? How would they feel about their work?

How does caring for this royal baby differ from caring for other royal babies?

Move on to asking groups to imagine a scenario in which a nanny gets into trouble for not caring appropriately for the royal baby. How might such a situation come about? Justify the situation from the nanny's point of view and from the point of view of the offended party. Would it only be the King or Queen who would be offended or might another nanny be offended? Why?

Now share the story again, but this time with a difference:

Long ago in a faraway place, a King and Queen were blessed with a child. Sadly the child died at birth and the King and Queen were grief stricken. Looking for a way to ease the grief of the royal family the court soothsayer ordered that an ornate statue be created.

A sculptor was called to court to carve the form of the dead infant from oak. The sculpture was oiled and dressed and wrapped in the blankets meant for the royal baby and handed to the Queen. Her grief seemed to ease as she gazed down onto the familiar face, and adjusted the bonnet upon the small head. The flame of love that she had felt for her child at birth leapt up from the ashes of his death and burned in her heart.

The King at her side softened too and leant across to put his finger to the cheek of the wooden baby. Soothed by the carved child, the King and Queen regained their strength. The Queen beckoned for the court nannies to come and take the child to the nursery, and the court swung into the rhythm of life they had been expecting prior to the death of the baby. The nannies cared for the wooden child by day in the nursery, and every evening the child would be brought to court to be given the blessing of a kiss from his parents.

By day, governing the land kept the King and Queen fully occupied, although both found time occasionally to sneak away from proceedings to the nursery to check upon their child. But at night lying awake in bed, the Queen felt that blaze of love for her child burning such that it kept her awake, and long after the rest of the household were slumbering, she would rise and take the stairs down to the nursery, tiptoeing softly past the dozing nanny to where her wooden baby lay. She would lift the child and clutch it to her heart. And although he was hard and did not move, still that loved blazed within her. One particularly dark night, it blazed so bright that a spark flew out from her own heart and embedded itself in the wood. The ember burned its way down into the sleeping heart of the wooden child.

In the morning the nanny on duty noticed the small burn on the chest of the wooden child and was afraid that she would be reprimanded for sleeping when she should have been protecting the child from harm. She lifted the baby, by habit holding him the way she would a living child, whilst she searched for an outfit sure to cover the blemish. Holding him close for a moment, she felt her own heart beat with increased heat as the flame in the baby's heart called to the fire dormant in her.

The following night when the Queen crept into the nursery to lift her ever sleeping child, she felt something different within her. As she lifted the wooden baby, her own heart lifted. Their flames danced together, each making the other brighter, and she returned to her bed feeling nourished, not desolate.

Night by night the Queen met and held her child. She took to adding a little something to the nanny's nightcap to ensure they would not wake her, and her time with her child grew in its richness as she told him stories and took him to the window to gaze together upon the stars.

After a year she felt sure that the fire inside him would burn all the way through his little body and he would be consumed, so she had the soothsayer commission a larger child from the sculptor.

She was afraid the first night that she stepped into the nursery to see the new sculpture, but she needn't have been; as soon as she lifted him she felt the flame alight inside of him.

Each year when delivery of the new wooden child was taken from the sculptor, the Queen would conduct the courtly ritual of his birthday. Dead-eyed courtiers would mutter platitudes as she held her beautiful boy. The King at her side was still so blinded by the grief of his loss that the fire in his own heart had gone out and he felt cold when he touched her arm. But at these occasions the Queen's interest lay not with the King, nor even with her child, but with the nannies. She did her best to eavesdrop on their gossiping, for although they all knew not to talk in court there was always the thread of a tale being woven somewhere.

Through the years the Queen came to be aware of a number of nannies who saw her son as she did, nannies who spoke to him, who cradled him, who blessed him with stories and tickled his wooden form. She even heard rumours of nannies who believed they had seen his wooden eyes blink or his tiny toes wriggle.

At night she wondered at the magic her love had brought about; she wondered about the speculating nannies and the love they seemed to feel for her child. She began to suspect that if she could cultivate an environment in which her son was surrounded by people who believed in him and loved him, that she would see him truly live. This was her dream for her child by night, and by day she worked to make it real, even though the passion with which she strove to make dreams reality led tongues to wag and call her mad.

How does the Queen know which nannies know the truth about her son and which don't? What is the difference in the way that they speak about him? What is the difference in the way they handle him?

Empathetic

The word "empathy" was much used by interviewees describing people who did or did not "get it." Although only a couple of interviewees picked empathy out as a theme in itself, so many used the word that it became clear when I went back through the notes of the interviews that it was seen as fundamental to getting it.

One interview that stands out in my mind with relation to this topic was with a prominent member of an organisation that is noted for its excellent practice in supporting people with profound and multiple learning disabilities. This interviewee identified empathy immediately as the distinction between those who got it and those who did not, defining it simply as the ability to understand that one should look at things from the other's point of view, not from one's own. They explained how, after a few bad experiences with staff members who lacked empathy, they had developed an interview process to identify empathy in candidates and no longer employed people who were not empathetic.

It was interesting to find out that this interview process included asking people how they would tackle someone who did not get it. Some candidates, they explained, responded to this question with an impassioned speech about how wrong it was of the other person not to perceive the things that they could perceive, whilst others noted the fault of the other person but in doing so expressed empathy for their situation saying, for example, that perhaps they had not had the same opportunities in life that they had, or perhaps if they had been shown they would be better able to understand. My interviewee explained, "A person who is truly empathetic will display it in all aspects of their life, not just in those places they think you are looking for it." Whilst aiming to convert people from the "do not get it" camp to the "get it" camp is noble, in the real world we may need to behave more pragmatically, and certainly it would seem that if there is a process whereby we employ only staff who get it from the outset that would be immediately appealing.

It is worth noting that if asked, most people would describe themselves to be empathetic and would believe themselves to be so. Many a self-absorbed person claims that their own fatigue is the result of carrying the burdens of others. However, those known for carrying the burdens of others often exude energy, leading us to perhaps question whether their fatigue might be more indicative of selfishness than of empathy.

Confident

In line with the description of those who get it being people who are empathetic in all aspects of their life, not simply in relation to people appointed as deserving of empathy, most of my interviewees at some point in our conversation would halt in their explanation of the deficits of the person we were discussing to mitigate on their behalf in some way. Oftentimes they cited a lack of confidence as underpinning, or relating to, whichever failing they were describing. The lack of reflective nature was ascribed to a lack of confidence in their own thought processes, the tough attitude was linked to lacking confidence and needing to self-protect, and the lack of academic success was seen to cause a lack of confidence and so on.

Some interviewees followed that line of thought and reflected upon how a lack of confidence impinged on people's abilities to relate to the person they were supporting.

> They are worried about looking silly.

> I can see she knows what to do but she just lacks the confidence to initiate it, sometimes she will join in if I get things going.

> They have been so burnt in the past now they are fixed. Change is scary, to change is to accept that the way you are is not enough and that you need to grow and learn, some people are frightened by that, it's a confidence thing.

Some interviewees went on to explore how this lack of confidence was not simply something inherent in that particular individual but was affected by the set up in which they worked.

> Staff morale is low, a lot of people are just here because it is their job and they have not got the confidence to leave, and the way we work at the moment is not good for anyone's confidence.

Positive feedback could do a lot to support a person who lacks confidence in their practice. Feedback was highlighted by my interviewees as being particularly needed by some people in order to maintain good practice, as you will read in the next section.

Where my interviewees cited a lack of confidence as underpinning other previously identified deficits in their colleagues, it is interesting to consider where else it might be having an effect. My research indicates that non-directive playful approaches are often highly effective in eliciting engagement and response. Katie White, founder of The Best Medicine, an organisation that teaches people therapeutic laughter skills, is a playful person who often invests time and money in becoming more playful. I asked her to reflect on the significance of play in relationships and she said:

> I think to play you have to show some kind of vulnerability, especially as a grown up. When you are vulnerable you are more likely to connect with people on a deeper level. When two people play they are both in that play together, until one person decides to drop out. The invitation to play can mean the risk of being rejected. But if you are brave enough to play and get past the inherent vulnerability in the act of play, then you get to a magic place where you are not only creating together in play but also connecting and interacting on a deeper level.

Katie is someone who takes play very seriously, and in this one insight you can see how confidence might thread through so many things, and equally how a willingness to be vulnerable might also be a key component to understanding the distinction between those who get it and those who do not. Someone who has toughened themselves up to meet the challenges of life is someone who is refusing to be vulnerable anymore.

Strategies to enable someone who does not get it to get it

There are lots of ideas for how to support someone who does not get it in learning to get it, contained in the descriptions of the characteristics of getting it/not getting it. For example, within the descriptions of short thinking and reflectiveness is the idea that reflective thought patterns could be taught and modelled. Another example mentioned is the use of video recording as a tool to aid reflection and feedback. The strategies listed in the following sections are those that were specifically highlighted by my interviewees as ways to change mindsets, not an exhaustive list of possible strategies. They are not necessarily the best strategies and they are certainly not the only strategies. The F.I.S.H. at the end of this section contain a good overview of reflective points covering all the strategies discussed within this section.

Feedback

Several interviewees, in talking about a lack of confidence in the individual who did not "get it," attributed this directly to a need for feedback, whilst others very honestly appraised their own feelings of exhaustion within their current role in relation to a lack of feedback:

> They lack confidence and when they do not get an instant response they lose heart.

> It is such a hard job, it's not paid well, it's not valued in society, and when you do not get any feedback from staff or students it is hard to maintain your confidence.

> Some staff need a response from the students they are okay with the ones with whom they can strike up some form of banter, but with the students with PMLD they really flounder.

> You are doing something great, but no one would notice, so why would you do it again?

The benefit of learning to recognise the idiosyncratic feedback supplied by someone with a profound disability and also being able to receive feedback from colleagues or even simply from yourself via video observation is something highlighted within Jean Ware's (1996/2003) seminal work, *Creating Responsive Environments*.

Increasing the modes and frequency of the feedback received by people supporting individuals with complex disabilities would serve to benefit not only those who need such feedback in order to function sufficiently but also those who manage to survive without it but whom would be given wings by receiving it.

One person I interviewed, who had previously been identified by several other people as being someone who "got it," described how they built feedback into their daily routine in order to encourage the team they worked alongside to engage with intensive interaction:

> I struggled for years to get support staff to engage with intensive interaction. I had a break through last year, I built five minute sessions into the day at four or five key points. Everyone had a partner and together we fed back. I made a point of being very positive about what staff did. It got people on board.

> I also made sure we swapped partners, and that gave me the chance to model how I would interact with each of the people we were supporting. I found a form that gave a breakdown of the different types of interaction really useful in getting staff to be aware of the responses they were getting.

Another interviewee reported success with his "catch them at it" approach to feedback:

> Even the most rubbish person does something right sometime. You just have to catch them at it. With some mind you will be waiting a long time. But if you can catch them doing something good, even if it is just the tiniest thing and then big them up for that, I find that works. It can take a while. But you do get more "with-it-ness" from them after a while.

Teach in the way they learn

How people responded to training was one of the most discussed topics within the "get it" conversations. Initially people would say that the person who did not get it needed more training, but then quickly reflect that the training they had received thus far had seemingly little impact.

My interviewees reflected upon the experience of education had by the person whom they had identified as not getting it. They recognised the not-getting-it person as someone for whom education was not easy or was not pitched according to their personal way of learning. Upon entering a training environment, the person with previous negative experience of education instantly relates the set up to previous negative experiences and puts up a mental block even before the training begins.

Other interviewees commented on the need for training to be given in accordance to the different ways people learn. Several people insightfully reflected that rather than being productive, training for these people could be counterproductive, serving only to reiterate to them their own failures in education. Reminding people of past failure is rarely the way to inspire them to future success.

Becky Lyddon from Sensory Spectacle (2019) creates immersive learning environments alongside children and adults with sensory processing disorder (SPD). She says that gaining an experience to feel how someone with SPD may be feeling is something which she could never teach people unless it's through their own experience and reflection. Many teachers and parents have said that it has helped them to understand why their student may do the things they do. Learning through experience promotes a form of empathy which we can then relate to the other person better.

Other people may learn better through reading, or through chatting to people. Professionals who support people with profound disabilities often go to a lot of effort to personalise learning experiences for them, but find they receiving training, which is very much one-size-fits-all.

Generate awareness: experience, micro-steps and acceptance of difference

Interviewees discussed what they felt might penetrate the lack of awareness in the minds of people perceived to be not getting it. Three themes sprang from these conversations.

The first was the necessity of experience for those who do not learn through traditional teaching methods. The general opinion amongst my interviewees was that without feeling something for themselves these people were unlikely to budge in their opinions. Some felt they could learn from clear evidence that they merely witnessed, and others felt more strongly that they would only shift if they had personal experience. Training organisations that offer this kind of first-person experience, such as Sensory Spectacle, which provides training on sensory processing difficulties, were held up as examples. Crombie et al. (2014) cited experiential learning as critical for developing the implicit skills that led the staff team they studied to provide outstanding care to the young people with complex disabilities they supported. One interviewee recalled their experience on a "Dementia bus," an immersive environment where she experienced treatment that a person with dementia in a care setting might experience from day to day. A few minutes on the bus had been enough to bring her to tears.

The second was people felt that those who did not get it were not seeing the subtleties of the engagement of those they were supporting. Several interviewees used the phrase "micro-steps," commenting that the person who did not get it did not seem to be able to perceive the micro-steps towards a particular goal or that made up a particular communication. The importance of recognising micro-steps was highlighted by Crombie et al. (2014), who refer to staff's granular understanding of students with complex disabilities.

This particular difficulty could potentially be answered by training procedures that highlighted these micro-steps in a multitude of ways – describing them orally or in writing, demonstrating them through witnessing in person or via video, or becoming involved in them by, for instance, asking someone to act out the different stages to put themselves in the other person's shoes.

Finally, interviewees commented on how at ease the person who did not get it was with difference as a whole, noting that they were quite conformist in their outlook and seemed alarmed by difference, and often citing examples of other prejudice, for example, against particular races or sexual orientations. We speculated upon what could make someone so afraid of difference and what effect that fear might have on their own lives. Someone afraid of difference in others is likely to be afraid of it in themselves. We are all different. When we embrace the differences in others we free ourselves to express our own differences. Perhaps tackling the person who fears difference is less about explaining the differences they object to and more about showing your acceptance and celebration of their own differences.

Develop their view of their role: moving people on from being stunned or stagnant in their practice

Several interviewees described people they had worked alongside who did not "get it" but whose lack of getting it seemed to come about not through a lack of reflective skills but more through a kind of stunned response to the situation. They people they described had, in their descriptions, a "rabbit in the headlights" quality to them.

> They felt our classroom was not somewhere they could be playful. You can be playful, they just did not know how.

> You can get by on just knowing how to do one thing, this teacher just kept playing songs, she did not know how to do anything else with them.

Others were described as less stunned, more stagnant – unchanging in their ignorance as they did not recognise it as a lack of knowledge in themselves.

> They are patronising, they do everything for them. They see that as their role. They think they are good and nice because they are helping them and they cannot do anything. They do not know how to support them to do anything.

> There has been little evolution from that mindset of spastic pity, they devalue them and pity them, they do not know how to do otherwise, that's the way they have always thought about them.

The feeling within these discussions was that the skills could be learned but the initial demonstration of them would need to be exceptionally bold in order to counter the resistance formed through years of inaccurate belief or the inertia born out of being so overwhelmed by a seemingly impossible task. Providing narrative from the point of view of the individual who is the recipient of this care can be very powerful. This is something Hirstwood and Gray (1995) do in their book, as they highlight how a person's experience of being handled can be very different from what the person doing the handling thinks it is:

> In the morning I'm touched by hands. They are big. Sometimes there are hands both sides of me, on my shoulders and feet, lifting me into the moving chair. Most of my time is in the moving chair. I do not always like it when it moves as anything can happen when it stops. Today the chair stopped in the wet place. I know the smell of this place it smells of the stuff they put on me with wet stuff and it stings my eyes. Sometimes it's above me and goes down my head and places, other times I'm moved into it. I'm always scared before it comes as its hot or cold, sometimes it's both when it's the wet stuff on my head. When it stops they rub me in clothing stuff but I do not wear it. I think it's the same hands but I'm not always sure. Afterwards the moving chair moves and material is put into my hands, other times I wear it. The moving chair goes to the food room. I like the smells, I wish I could eat the smell that's my favourite. Sometimes I do, other times it's there but the spoon in my mouth has something different on it.

Hearing even an imaginary voice can be a very powerful tool for enabling people to understand that someone else's view of events could be different to their own. Staff reading this might be prompted to say "Yes, but we know he likes X because we see him Y," and these types of observations can be built upon. Staff can be praised for giving clear observations and can be asked for comments as a way of habituating this type of reflective observation. In doing this you encourage people to check their understanding of the emotional response of the person they are supporting. Bleming (2019b) points out that our opinions of the value of a multisensory room directly underpin our decision to take someone to a multisensory room:

> When person X takes person Y into a multi-sensory room it is because person X has made a judgement that it is worth person Y's time to be in there. We need to think about it from person Y's point of view: Why would person Y they want to go in there? What does it mean to them? What is it worth to them?

If we are spending other people's time with our decisions, we should be attempting to think from their point of view.

The wow space

This strategy for inspiring behaviour change was not addressed directly by any of my interviewees but was the subject of all of our chats, because, after all, we were talking about multisensory rooms. All of the promises made about the rooms are to do with change: a person will change in this room, will do more, will see/feel more, will be more relaxed. A change of space promises a change in behaviour. And this is true of all of us. We change how we act according to the space we are in. Part of this is learned through social expectations, and part of it is pure reaction. How we feel changes in different spaces.

Changing a space changes the people within that space. And when a change in space happens, part of the change within the people will happen instinctively through their senses, and part of it will be learned. A new space demands a new set of social responses and people look around to see what they will be. Installation artist and disabilities researcher Jill Goodwin's work at Tingly Productions (http://tinglyproductions.org) is based around the power of changing a space. She explained to me that when staff members enter a new space, you have an opportunity to set the tone of behaviour and relationships within that space. She explained that getting people to dress a little differently, through the use of token items of fancy dress, and encouraging them to join in with songs helped her to create immersive sensory environments in which those supporting access for others did so with full attentiveness, almost becoming part of the environment themselves.

Reflecting on the question

The binary nature of my original question, dividing people up into those who "get it" and those who do not, creates an inaccurate picture. It was a useful question to ask, as it instantly drew to mind for my interviewees people with whom they had experienced particular problems, and although everyone felt the problems were innate, it seems unlikely that they are.

Rather than an innate capacity to "get it" or not, it seems more reasonable to presume that the problems experienced are partly about the particular capabilities or incapabilities of the person identified as not getting it, and partly about a mismatch between that person and the environment they work in. For example, an interviewee who naturally gives their staff oodles of feedback about their responsiveness to the people they are supporting is unlikely to report a problem with a member of staff "not getting it," because they are feedback dependent. Similarly, an interviewee who has taken the time to explain a particular manner of working in a way that their member of staff understands is unlikely to complain about people not being able to take information on through training.

One of my interviewees remarked that they did not work with people who did not "get it," but did regard some of their colleagues as being on the way to "getting it," citing age and understanding as a part of flourishing into "getting it." This particular interviewee was well known for being able to change mindsets. Were they just, as they put it, "lucky never to work with anyone like that," or was the reason they never worked with anyone like that found within the way that they worked? My bet would be the latter, not the former.

Although the question was useful, dividing people up into those who "get it" and those who do not is not useful. What is useful is recognising what is needed in order to get it, and some of the clues shared by my interviewees start us off on the path of finding out what is needed.

Why employing only those who get it does not exempt you from needing to provide ongoing support

In that original division of those who get it and those who do not, a simple approach to selecting staff might be to say that you only want to employ those who already get it as you have not got the time to carry out the delicate and complicated negotiations that would be needed to shift the views of people who have misunderstood their role. However, I do not think that people who "get it" are automatically the right people for the job. It is likely that they need just as much attention and maintenance as those who do not get it – they just need a different kind of support.

Reflecting back on the people I have met and worked alongside through what is now nearly two decades of working within inclusion, I can think of many examples of people who cared enormously for those they supported but very little for themselves. These people often suffered health problems that inhibited their ability to provide support. What use to you is the person who "gets it" wonderfully if they are off sick all the time?

I have known people who latch onto the problems experienced by a particular person or particular family and clearly want to rescue those people from that situation and will doggedly put everything into an attempt to do that, even when the possibility of rescue is so tiny as to be reasonably considered impossible, for example, in the case of people with aggressive degenerative conditions. How useful is your "getting it" person if their whole life gets absorbed into a mission to find a cure for an incurable disease? Clearly we want cures for awful diseases, but we need to be rational about where these will come from. Will it be from the world of science or from someone who cares enormously but has none of the underpinning knowledge that is likely to be required to come up with such a cure?

Similarly I have known people who, when working in a team, see the failings of others and try to take on their responsibilities. They "get it" and so they want to do it all, and they exhaust themselves with their efforts and suffer burnout. What use is your "get it" person if they are signed off with a long-term mental health complaint?

Finally, I have known people who "get it" and in getting it feel they have a right of access to every point of that person's life. They begin as someone in a supporting role, and become a friend, then a counsellor to the family, the one person turned to in a crisis, the person looked to for advice on all aspects of care. They end up trying to be more than they are, and they want to be everything to all people. But again, realistically we can each only do our bit. We should do it to the best of our ability, but

139

we should also recognise when something is outside of our role and look to others to provide that (as illustrated in Figure 5.1).

Ultimately, what is best for a person is to have a network of support. Doing everything for a person can seem kind, but in doing that you place all of their eggs in one basket, and how sure can you be that the basket will not break? Over-involvement may feel super supportive, but in the long term it can turn out to be a very risky strategy.

The support we provide to enhance people's practice bolsters those whose practice is already good and develops the practice of others. We must be vigilant to signs of people taking on too much and look to have friendly, supportive conversations with them about the balancing of their role.

Ultimately the difference between those who get it and those who do not might not be so great. Being able to connect with people (including people who have profound disabilities) is less about having a particular strength or skill and more about having a connection to your own humanity. Understanding your own humanity is more often than not done by coming to accept your own vulnerabilities and weaknesses. "Getting it" is not a strength, but a glorious manifestation of our appreciation of our own imperfect humanity.

For some people, the "not getting it" will be deeply entrenched and although the suggestions within this section and the extra ones you come up with will go some way towards changing their responses to people with profound disabilities, you would expect this change to be slow. At some point we must make pragmatic decisions, recognising that it is not okay for someone with a profound disability to be subjected to care that equates to them being treated like a piece of meat devoid of personhood.

Although the person who doesn't get it may complete care routines accurately and be able to administer medication in accordance with guidelines, if they do not recognise the personhood of the person in their care, then their "care" is an abuse of that individual and we should act to remove them from that position. It is not okay to accept provision for the body alone. It is concerning that many of the assessment or inspection criteria that such a person may be evaluated by only address the bodily aspects of care. We need to ensure that we have robust procedures in place for removing people from their roles if they do not "get it" in order to protect people.

OVERVIEW/F.I.S.H.

The following thinking points provide a quick overview of some of the strategies highlighted by my interviewees or implied through their insights. It is the start of a list, one to which I hope you will, in time, be able to add a great many more items:

- Be aware that training works for some, but for others it can increase their feelings of inadequacy and so have a counterproductive effect. Address this by offering different styles of training according to how people learn.

Figure 5.1

- Disciplinary procedures are necessary when we face extremes such as abuse. But as a strategy to develop a workforce, disciplinary procedures that let people know they did wrong generally lower self-esteem and in doing so increase the risk of that person becoming less caring in the future. Identifying bad practice needs to be done in an incredibly supportive manner, with full training given on how to rectify that bad practice to ensure the person fully understands what was wrong about what they were doing and how to get it right next time.

- Showing people what to do, rather than telling them, can be very effective. Finding ways to provide experiential learning can be very powerful.

- Put into people what you want to get out of them. For instance, if you want to see an increase in empathy, demonstrate your own empathy for their situation.

- Catch them at it. Be sure to notice people doing good, identify it, explain why it was good and celebrate it. Even if you can only notice a few small acts, the noticing, explaining and celebrating of these acts will enable them to spread and grow.

- Value and celebrate – acknowledge the role that is being carried out. Value it and celebrate it both within your organisation and without. Internal recognition of good practice will bolster the self-esteem of staff; external recognition will contribute to a shifting of public understanding of their roles and in the long term lead to more general social regard for their work, which will also be good for their self-esteem.

- Develop the non-functional aspects of people's lives. Offering staff the opportunity to take part in seemingly frivolous things such as art, dance, music, theatre, craft activities and so on may seem unrelated to their role, but if you develop their appreciation of non-functional activities and their recognition of themselves within these, then you increase their capacity to recognise the identity of people who do not have access to the same level of function as themselves.

Focus on the positive

ORIENTATION

Which is a greater driver for change: the example set by someone who does the wrong thing, or the one set by someone who does the right thing? Throughout history, are our leaps in progress caused by our collective response to someone we do not want to be like, or to someone we want to emulate?

In the following paragraphs, I offer some examples of wonderful practice from within multisensory rooms.

The sensory story

Sensory stories were commonly mentioned as a great activity for multisensory rooms. I am fortunate enough to have witnessed many a wonderful sensory story being told. The following account is of a wonderful session for which I once had the privilege of being a fly on the wall.

Five children and three members of staff are preparing to go to the multisensory room to share a sensory story about an ocean crossing that they have been sharing together for several weeks. In the classroom a simple projector is casting a blue watery light over the ceiling and doorway and a sea shanty CD is playing. The staff members supporting the students are moving subconsciously to the rhythm of the music as they quietly gather the resources they will need for supporting the students in the multisensory room.

In the multisensory room the teacher is setting up the resources for the sensory story within easy reach of the storytelling position; they have checked that all the switches that will be used are working and had a quick run through of the effects that they will use to create the story. The room is lit with a blue colour wash that mimics the blue light in the classroom and the same sea shanty CD is playing.

One by one the students are brought to the multisensory room. Two students stay in their chairs whilst in the room. Their chairs both have trays attached. One younger student is lifted from their chair to sit on a member of staff's lap and the other two students are hoisted from their chairs to lie together on a large waterbed in the corner of the room. Arriving in the room takes the best part of fifteen minutes with staff working for the most part in silence, maintaining the calm of the space. Occasionally someone will speak to give orientating prompts to a child being hoisted or to ask another member of the team to support them in lifting or moving a piece of equipment out of the way.

The teacher greets each student as they enter by approaching them at their level and saying their name together with the greeting "Welcome aboard." This greeting is given prior to any physical handling, lifting or hoisting taking place. It is a moment's pause upon entry into the room. Once the student is in position in the room, the staff who facilitated their arrival leave to collect another student from the classroom and the teacher steps forward to offer them a sensory item to explore. All of these items have an aquatic theme but are linked to that student's own sensory interests and abilities. One student is given some silver strands that reflect light in a way that is reminiscent of light shining through water. The students on the waterbed are helped to lift and drop their arms to set the bed wobbling. This provokes evident delight and they are able to continue this activity without adult support, with the less physically able child clearly enjoying the movements of the waterbed triggered by the wriggling of the more physically able child. Another student grasps a wet flannel whilst the student seated on the adult's lap is supported to put their fingers into a bowl of water.

143

Once all the students are settled into the room, the teacher fades the music on the CD out and she and her staff begin to softly sing a sea shanty about hauling ropes and casting anchors away. The rhythm of the song translates into the interactions between the staff and students. The two students seated in their chairs are supported by one member of the team, the two on the waterbed by another, and the smaller child seated on the adult's lap looks to the teacher for interaction whilst being supported physically by the adult they are seated upon. The teacher moves between all the students, joining in with their exploration of the resources they have been given.

The sea shanty grows louder and the movements of hauling, of rocking back and forth, become more pronounced. One of the seated students vocalises in time to the singing. Staff members' eyes twinkle with mischief in anticipation of what is to come, and one of the students lying on the waterbed appears to be anticipating with them. As attention shifts from the objects being explored to the shared movement of hauling and rocking, the staff clears away the resources previously being explored and encourages students to link up. The students on the waterbed lie with their arms overlaying one another, and the teacher rocks the bed steadily on one side whilst reaching across to hold hands with the students seated on the lap of another member of staff. The staff member seated between the two students in their chairs links hands with them both and together the class hauls upon the imaginary rope to raise the anchor and set sail.

When the anchor is finally flung on deck – signified by the teacher raising a shiny tin foil anchor into the light cast from a small spotlight torch directed onto the anchor by another member of the team – it splashes all aboard, facilitated by the support staff all dipping their fingers into the bowl of water and flicking droplets onto the students. For some students the droplets are copiously distributed and clearly enjoyed, and for the student who clasped the flannel droplets are delicately scattered across the back of their hand. This causes them to grow still and drop their head to their hand, mouthing the back of their hand where the water fell. The staff member next to them allows this to happen but gently moves their hand away from their mouth before the exploration with lips becomes biting.

With the anchor hauled the teacher begins the tale of adventures on the high sea. Some of the sensory experiences supporting the story are provided by the room, with lights going out and fibre optics waved to signify a thunderstorm, with the sound of the storm coming from the speakers in response to a switch pressed by one of the students seated in their chairs. Others are provided by resources brought into the room for the story – for example, a crate of gold coins, pirate treasure through which the more physically able students push their hands.

At the end of the story the pirates gather on deck to sing of their adventures and the collective swaying from the start of the story is mirrored as staff members sing a sea shanty about passing the barrel around, whilst supporting students to clink the tin mugs that have been passed out. As the shanty continues the teacher gradually brings the lights back up in the room, and staff move around to be in front of the students they have been supporting so that they have time to reconnect with them, moving out of the story and into the real world, ready to go back to class.

Leaving the multisensory room takes as long as arrival. The teacher sits engaging in brief intensive interaction conversations with students about particular resources or parts of the story whilst everyone waits for their turn to get off the ship.

A clipboard with a recording sheet is passed amongst staff who each take it in turns to note down observations pertinent to the students they have supported through the session.

Developing sensory awareness and ability

In *A Sensory Curriculum For Very Special People* (1988, p. 62), Flo Longhorn describes a partial visual stimulation programme for a child with profound learning difficulties and little sight. The child is recorded at the start of the programme as being interested in objects presented at eye level, and as bringing her hands to her mouth and attempting to feel objects she comes in contact with and also attempting to bring them to her mouth.

The level of detail in the programme described is superb. What is particularly noticeable is that this is not a programme solely for use in the multisensory room (which in this situation is a dark room). It has sections for the classroom environment and home environment as well. The essence of the programme is to help the little girl, Alice, to become more aware of her hands, through showing her her own hands, by lifting them to her face or making them more visually interesting, for instance by shining torches on them or putting sparkly gloves on them and by playing hand games, such as clapping games with her. The long-term aim of the programme is for Alice to be able to use her hands to play.

Observations are recorded from November 1983 through to February 1984. These observations are a tiny snippet of all the opportunities Alice must have been given through this time to learn about her hands.

Initially, observations record responses such as "Looked at light rather than hands at first. When I touched her nose with her hands, her eyes turned inwards" (p. 64) and "Did not appear to be actually regarding hands and fingers" (p. 65). Alice had daily opportunities to practice her hand awareness skills and the records show she visited the dark room weekly, sometimes having more than one recorded visit in the week, and as the dark room in this situation was actually just a small painted cupboard adjoining the classroom, it is more likely that Alice's opportunities to spend time there were daily in their frequency than weekly.

Adults support Alice in a 1:1 ratio, playing games with her that draw visual attention to her hands. Their rationale is that if she can notice her own hands and see the movements she is able to make, she will be better able to direct those movements for her own ends.

After over a year of stimulation, the observation records show the progress that has been made: "Eyes looked towards her hands, vocalized, and brought her left hand to her mouth" (p. 70). "When had knocked bells, fingers opened, she looked in direction of her hand and bells, and smiled and vocalized" (p. 70).

Longer records indicate just how much more Alice is doing a year on from the start of the programme:

> Calling out "oooh" with big smiles. Right leg lifting on and off block. Brought hands midline across her chest, head back. Right hand lifted silver paper and knocked suspended red paper, looked and laughed at the resulting movement. Head back to midline, stilled, turned left eye to suspended silver paper, turned head to right in order to use left eye, probably for preference for red. Opened mouth, thrust out tongue, lifted head and cooed, appeared to listen to the crackle of paper.
>
> *(p. 71)*

Over the course of a few pages, Longhorn (1988) details the year's worth of effort. Interesting visual stimuli are hunted for. Large boxes are turned into Little Rooms, small sensory spaces offering interesting visual stimulus. The improvised dark room is strung with new items, and new resources are taken in there. Torches are played with. Gloves are worn. All sorts of hand games are played, by the girl's parents, teachers and support assistants. The activity continues for more than a week, more than a half term, more than an entire school year. Everyone working together with the hope of enabling one little girl to partner her visual understanding of her hands and their movements, with her visual picture of the interesting world around her and reach out and interact with it, results in one little girl, Alice, being able to use her hands purposefully to play. The multisensory environments, the dark room and the large cardboard boxes play a supporting role, but it is the persistence and dedication of those around her which ultimately gives Alice access to playful movement.

Hugh learning to see

Emma Murphy blogs in the LittleMamaMurphy blog about her experiences of raising her son Hugh, whom she refers to as Happy Little Hugh. Emma gave me permission to share one of her blog posts with you. In it she describes the incredible benefits Hugh has reaped from time in a dark den in their living room:

> I remember the day they told me Hugh was blind. I went home and I sat on the stairs and wept. I called my mum. And she cried too.
>   Of all the challenges he faced, the developmental delay, the seizures, the hypotonia, his feeding difficulties . . . it just seemed so unfair that he was hit with another blow.

And blind? Well, blind seemed so final somehow.

When Hugh was a new-born I was concerned that he never made eye contact and that he was so disinterested in the world around him. In a dark room, he would not turn towards the light, even light up toys, right next to his head in the cot, held no interest for him.

But slowly, painfully slowly, almost so slowly you would not notice, Hugh started to "see" things. There'd be brief glimpses of recognition or attempts to reach towards things; shiny things and red things usually. We borrowed a dark den – a huge tent that blocks out all the light – and I would sit in there endlessly with light up bouncing balls and fibre optics trying to *teach* him to see.

The thing with Hugh's kind of blindness is that it's all to do with the brain and less to do with his eyes. There's very little wrong with his eyes really, but his brain just cannot make sense of what they see. This is called a "brain based visual impairment," or "cerebral visual impairment."

In a funny kind of way, this is good news. Or less-bad news. It gave us something to work with, something we could try and improve – hence the hours sweating in the dark den. Hugh's brain could try and learn how to see. Hypothetically anyway.

The dark den, lived permanently in the corner of our living room; a large tent-like cube constructed of plastic poles and covered in fabric designed to block out all light. Inside we had a vast array of items that lit up, some picked up cheaply in the pound shop, others borrowed from the Visual Impairment teacher or on loan from charities. Unable to sit independently, Hugh would either lie on his back or sit propped against me in my lap, whilst one by one I would activate the light up spiky balls or the fibre optic fountain lamp and encourage Hugh to track and follow them, reach for them or hold them. Often Hugh's older brother, Sean, clambered into the tent too and, tightly squeezed in together, we'd all play with the light up balls, rolling them forwards and backwards to each other. Sometimes we'd all just sit or lie in there together surrounded by the lights; fairy lights dangling from the ceiling and a multitude of flashing bouncy balls around our feet. We used the tent as often as we could, fitting it around Hugh's frequent ill-health and the other therapies he was doing at that time. We aimed for at least daily although that was not always possible and the heat meant we rarely managed more than 15–20 minutes at a time. Hugh found it quite tiring too so we let him guide us. At times it felt like he was not making any progress at all, which was soul destroying, but we persevered, hoping that one day he'd be able to see.

Although Hugh, now 9, is still registered blind (severely sight impaired), we've seen tremendous improvements in his ability to see. He certainly recognises his favourite toys and he will reach and grab for them. When I lean towards him, he always pulls my glasses off and I have watched him whip a stethoscope from a Doctor's neck once. He loves playing with helium balloons and has mastered the art of spotting and catching the shiny string to pull them towards himself. He can track and follow objects with his eyes and now looks towards faces and makes fleeting eye contact. He's progressed so much that he now wears glasses to help ensure the image reaching his brain is as clear as it can be. From the baby who could not see a light shining in a pitch-black room, these are fantastic achievements.

Finding rest

This section was written by Esme Turner, a physiotherapist at Hope House Children's Hospices.

James has a diagnosis of dystonia and is often in pain. He visits the hospice for both respite stays and symptom management.

James experiences powerful dystonic movements that are clearly painful and distressing for him. Pain triggers his dystonia and his dystonia causes pain, becoming a vicious cycle. He can become frightened and it is very difficult to find ways to help him calm and reduce his discomfort.

On one particular stay James was in the dining room, a busy, noisy environment full of the sounds and smells of people talking and eating. James loves his food; it is very important to him. He has a huge appetite due to the number of calories his dystonia burns. On this occasion James was not interested in food, turning his head away, arching his back and groaning. He had not had a good night with frequent episodes of dystonia. This had continued through the morning and he was not happy to be sat in his chair.

It became apparent that food was not James's priority at that moment, and that he needed help to get more comfortable.

James was taken to our multi-sensory room and hoisted onto the swing. The ceiling's fine fibre optic lights were switched on as well as one warm, gentle light. The swing was set in motion (our swing continues to move gently for half an hour after a single push).

I lay next to James, my hand resting on his chest. James began a low vocalisation when breathing out, I mirrored this and slowly extended the duration of the sound. James's breathing slowed and gradually his vocalisation stopped.

The linear vestibular stimulation, low lighting and closeness to a trusted adult calmed James and he drifted off to sleep.

Using the multi-sensory room in this minimal and calm way has consistently had a positive effect for James. Information has been added to his care plan and symptom management plan to allow all staff caring for James to facilitate appropriate use of the multi-sensory room as a form of symptom management.

Multisensory room with preschool-aged children

My work at The Sensory Projects brings me into contact with many marvellous, twinkly eyed people and Christine Waterman, a teacher at the Early Years Specialist Development Centre in Hertfordshire, is one of them. What struck me about Christine when we met was how she was able to balance the needs of the young children she supports with the needs of their parents. Many researchers point to the increased risk of mental ill health that parents of children with additional needs experience (e.g. Ghaziuddin et al. 1998; Count Us In 2002; Davies and Hogg 2004; Goward et al. 2005; Making Us Count 2005; Smith and Grzywacz 2014; Colley 2015; O'Brien 2016). Christine works with families when their children are very young and her ability to make connections with the children and with their parents, and between the children and their parents, means that she provides a wonderful foundation for their relationship and for sharing sensory experiences together. I asked her to write and tell me about some of the children she has supported recently. Notice how her account is about the relationships more than it is about the resources and the space:

> Our sensory room is a different space in which to interact with a child, to enable them to interact with us, and with their environment. It is attractive, calming, less busy, more predicable than our busy classroom. The sensory equipment allows for a more noticeable and often more exciting and rewarding response, especially to small movements. It allows us to increase the contrast between one object and its background and make that one thing stand out. However, what we do in there is the same as we do in the rest of our room. We start with the child, where they are now, what interests and excites them and what we hope to offer that child. The switches, the lights, the ball pool are tools to inspire and support that interaction either between the child and the adult or the child and their environment.

Making connections and gaining independence

The following is from Christine Waterman:

> For Laura the attraction in the sensory room is the fibre optic lights. She loves to hold them up to her face and watch the strands moving, the lights changing colour. She waves her hand, and the little lights dance. She is happy doing that and it absorbs her attention. Crawling, Laura can make her own way into the sensory room. It takes her a little while to go up the small step created by the padding on the floor, but she is motivated by the lights, and has kept working at it until that skill is mastered. She crawls into the padded "den" with its lit-up ceiling, and mirrored walls, smiling at the reflections of the lights in her hand as she sits in this tiny space. As she became more confident walking, she did not want to drop

down to crawl into her favourite room, but the step is difficult for her. We stood by, offering a hand, until, with much practice and concentration, she could do it unaided. Now, as she arrives in the classroom, she looks towards the sensory room, and goes straight to it. She has a mental map of our room and knows where she wants to be.

Sitting on the floor, Laura grasps strands of the lights. I pick some up and wave them in the way that she is doing. We have some undisturbed quiet in this room, and Laura notices the lights moving in my hands too. We do this together. Sometimes she stops and watches my hands. Sometimes she takes the strands from me. She has started to look at my face when I do this. At times we will do the same thing without anything in our hands. She will pat her hands against mine, make eye contact, smile with recognition at my voice. She babbles more and more, and watches me. Often, when she has had enough of this game, she brings her head right up to mine, with a smile. Her mum tells me that this is her version of a hug. The sensory room has given us a place where we focus on each other, undistracted by the rest of the classroom, and in here we have built a relationship that enhances our interactions in the classroom and elsewhere.

Learning to reach

We did not have a sensory room when Oscar was with us, in a shared classroom we used in a children's centre, so we put up a dark den. We had not seen any visual responses from Oscar, and we were not really succeeding in getting him to reach out to toys. This together with his posture when listening suggested that he may not be able to see very much. We were also aware that as we had a very mixed ability group, many of our toys that were just right for the other children weren't easily accessible to Oscar who had little movement. His mum came to the group with him, and it seemed that his needs set her apart from the mums of the more active children who moved around the room to their favourite toys and activities.

We wanted Oscar's mum to feel welcome as well as Oscar, and to have an area that was absolutely accessible and appropriate to her son. We set up a dark den, and kitted it out in a varied way that gave them both the opportunity for what we hoped would be an "ooh, what's in here?" feeling, but that was also inviting for the other children. Working in there, we noticed that his eyes were drawn to our bubble tube, and he seemed to be relaxed and happy in there watching it. We tried small light-up toys from our collection of cheap gimmicky bargain shop purchases, too. He liked the spiky light-up balls and was happy to feel them on his hands and arms, and he became motivated to reach his hand out a little. We needed something interesting to touch that would glow for longer so that it did not disappear before he could get it. Noisy mechanical toys scared him, so we tried our UV light with UV slinky springs, UV balls and homemade boards with textured UV items stuck on: fur, pompoms, springy plastic, feathers and pieces of fabric bought in various pound shops. Oscar seemed to look consistently towards them. When his mum helped him stretch out his hand to the boards, he moved his fingers to explore them. This lovely mum made her own boards at home as well and experiencing success, Oscar became much more motivated to reach for the tactile toys. His arm movements increased, and he now was able to pick out the textured pieces even without the UV light, and developed this further to use light-up toys, high-contrast toys like the slinky springs and switches in the classroom. With better use of his vision and more movements he could begin to enjoy toys and to experience his own ability to have an effect on his world, and he became an active member of our group, especially during the sensory stories. His lovely mum emerged as a wonderful support to other mums and a creative developer of her own resources for him at home, including her homemade tactile boards, and a sensory bedroom that he loved.

Learning to look

The bubble tube has been a great tool with our children who have very little sight. When Lucas joined us, his parents had been told that he could not see anything, not even light or dark. We felt that maybe he had some awareness of light as his initial reaction to the darker sensory room was anxious. He was comforted by the sound of the bubble tube, and was content to sit by it. We watched his gaze. After a few visits he would always put his hands on it, and we debated whether he was seeing it, or just enjoying sounds and slight vibrations. We observed that although his gaze drifted away from it, he turned back to it whenever the colour changed to red. Several weeks on, we were sure that we were seeing his eyes tracking bubbles upwards, that he gazed at it steadily, and showed excitement when it turned red. His mum invited other family members to come to form their own opinion about whether he could be see, and we all sat sharing his, by then unmistakable, pleasure in the changing colours. It was a great privilege and very moving to see his father and grandmother's joy as they saw for themselves his visual response to the lights. He pulled himself to standing using the tube, and held on tightly, with his face right up close. It was the start of his interaction with objects, and it gave his family hope that he could see a little and could learn to play. He soon graduated to locating a switch to turn it on, feeling around for it, then to following and grabbing light-up balls, reaching accurately to pick them up, and throwing them again.

Ready, steady, go!

We have a small group of very mobile children who all have difficulties with social communication, and who really enjoy our sensory room with its tiny ball pool area and a crawl under space with ceiling lights. The room provides them with a space for proprioceptive and vestibular stimulation that is always available to them. It also provides an engaging environment for the parents to be playful with their child, away from any disappointment about their child's interaction with the more overtly educational toys in the classroom. This feels like play, so in here we notice that a number of parents relax and have fun, engaging with their child without any preconceptions of what their child should be able to do. The room is inviting and it entices them to go in, and being in here feels like a break from the serious stuff, although in fact we often get to observe the best examples of parent-child interactions in this space. There are so many moments of shared fun, shared looks, watching each other, and parents following the child's lead in the way that parent and child play together in here. It is also a great space for our "ready, steady, go!" games, that are so effective in developing those anticipation, waiting, sharing and early language skills.

One little boy loves to bury himself under the balls, wait for me to say "ready, steady . . ." then to bust out, saying "go!" This was one of his first interactions with us, his early discovery that we could be fun and one of his first words. Another child likes to jump from the platform into the ball pit, waiting, balancing on his tip toes on the edge, waiting for "ready, steady, go!" before jumping. He has learned to wait for "go," and to watch me as I say it, enabling us together to ensure there is a safe landing for him. He laughs with delight as he jumps, looking to me to share his enjoyment, as he climbs out to do it again. It has been the beginning of him sharing pleasure with me, becoming aware that I can help with a hand to get out of the ball pit, and also, as he has learned to stop, and go in response to my words, he has begun to understand other directions, too.

A boy, new to our group, discovered the mirror-lined walls and lit-up low ceiling of the den. An adult can sit in there and our smaller children can just about stand, and they learn a lot about moving their bodies in this space. It challenges his body awareness as he figures out how to move in this interesting space, slowing him down, rewarding more carefully considered movements. We have seen a more settled, less distracted side to him in this small space, and he has been much more accepting of our presence, enabling us to play with him. He watched with interest as I gathered up a dozen or so balls that were on the floor, said the usual "ready, steady, go!" and threw them so that they bounced gently off the walls and low ceiling, the effect magnified by the mirrors all around. Sensing his interest, I repeated the action, and this time he laughed. After a couple more goes, he was looking at me expectantly to do it again, giggling a little as I said "ready" and squealing excitedly when I said "go!"

We have not always had a sensory room, and we did, at one time, find ourselves sharing a classroom with another group who did not want a dark den in the classroom for their sessions. The lunchtime gap between our session and theirs did not give us enough time to assemble our dark den, so we made one from a hoop and some fairly close-weave black fabric, a tent that could be hung from a ribbon looped over a hook in the ceiling, and put up and down very quickly. We were then able to use it for switch work or reaching other aims with our two children with low vision, using, at different times, a switch-operated portable bubble tube or simple toddler light-up toys, or we hung a balloon with a light, with grains of rice inside that made a rewarding noise when bashed.

Barry's story (Hirstwood and Smith 1995, pp. 86–88)

Barry is fifteen and large for his age. Although fully ambulant, he has spent most of his time in school within a special care group. The majority of his time has consisted of teachers attempting to get him to sit down instead of part walking, part stumbling around the classroom. No toys or equipment or other environmental artefacts have ever kept his interest on other than a perfunctory level and the attempts to direct his activities both educationally and simply to keep him safe have often led to violent outbursts resulting in various forms of control.

When the school installed a multisensory room the special care class was one of the first groups targeted and was taken in as a full group. Barry was quickly excluded from this session as he spent his time in the multisensory room still stumbling about especially on the soft play floor, falling onto children and equipment. The risk of injury to himself and other children was too great given the supervision that could be provided for a full group. After a while the group's session was reduced as it became clear that the full class did not benefit from a complete hour and the remainder of the session was utilised by giving Barry time alone in the room with his teacher. The first thing the teacher did was to lift the soft play up from the floor and stand it against the wall. This meant that because Barry was no longer walking on soft play he did not have as great mobility difficulties and it had a further advantage. When the room was dark he had difficulty assessing the limits of the room and frequently walked into the wall, and the soft play positioned against the wall now cushioned the impact.

In his first sessions all the equipment, bubble tube, fibre optics, projector and music were put on at the same time. It became obvious that Barry was attracted to the light as he moved continuously around the room from one effect to another but pausing for some moments at each lighting effect. The teacher then decided to put just one effect on at a time and see how he responded. Barry's movement continued, albeit at a much reduced level but what was noticeable was the increasing amount of time he was actually spending with one effect. A further modification was made to the room in that the soft play mats leaning against the wall were turned around. The white mats, whilst not reversible, had a black rubberised base, which reduced the amount of reflected light elsewhere in the room and emphasised the effect of the light source being used.

Barry seemed to prefer the bubble tube as this was the first effect with which he actually sat down at and spent increasingly longer periods of time. After several sessions Barry started to sit down directly in front of the bubble tube as soon it was switched on. His teacher sat with him talking gently to him but making no demands. However, if Barry looked or turned to another effect she switched off the one he had been looking at and immediately went and switched on the one that he had turned to. The result of this experimentation being that Barry was much calmer in these sessions and stopped his rather frantic stumbling about.

It became clear to Barry's teacher that for whatever reason the room provided an environment that for Barry was calming, comforting and safe and one in which he began to show the first evidence of interest in his environment. It was also one in which barriers that had been long established could be broken down on both sides. Because of his challenging behaviour his teacher was regularly faced with negative situations in which she always felt that she was getting nowhere with Barry. Because of the dangerous conflicts that arose Barry had been disliked by the majority of staff who had worked with him and in fact some had actually refused to work with him. Now, however, as a result of his calmer behaviour in the room his teacher actually began to view him in a positive light, and she was more than happy to work with him alone in a one-on-one situation in the room.

The culmination of these changes was that a far greater degree of positive interaction occurred within the multisensory room than had previously happened in any other setting. Whilst it was very difficult at the outset for his teacher to put to one side the notion that she should be proactive, always initiating developments, she realised that in this atmosphere Barry himself had begun to show positive initiations. He started to look for the other pieces of equipment in the darkness of the room, clearly indicating that he was remembering where they were instead of just happening upon objects as he had always done in the classroom. When he obviously began to look for other pieces of equipment the teacher responded by switching off the effect that he was at and putting on the next. Soon Barry was looking with intent at whatever piece of equipment he wanted switched on.

For the first time in his eleven years within the school, staff perceived Barry as a communicator. This change in Barry's behaviour had to a great extent occurred as a result of a combination of the power of the equipment to present a relaxing environment but possibly more importantly because of the way in which staff had interacted with him whilst in the room. Similar results have been found in many other establishments working with children and adults with challenging behaviour and there has also been significant success in helping children and adults with autism who displayed the same forms of behaviour. The whole process is not simply one of "laissez faire" and there are obvious dangers in simply using the rooms as a "super" time-out room.

OVERVIEW

These stories are all very different, from a group activity with many people accessing a story, to a highly focused one-on-one interaction, from people in times of stress or experiencing pain, to children keen to explore and families seeking fresh insight into the needs of their children. What they all have in common is a fabulous, responsive facilitator, a relationship between people. The equipment has been used as a tool to enhance the relationship or to target stimulation to the needs of a particular person. In some situations the equipment was critical, for example the swing for James and the light for Hugh. In others it was useful as a topic of conversation but the particular qualities of it were less essential, for instance, the sensory story and the conversation between Barry and his teacher. But in each case one feels that had that particular piece of equipment not been there, the facilitator would have found a way to achieve the same with what they had. The relationship between people in the multisensory room, not the equipment in the multisensory room, has been the foundation of all the transformations that we have heard about.

F.I.S.H.

What would your positive story about being in a multisensory room be, and what is at its heart?

Who are your role models when you think about sharing sensory experiences, connecting with sensation and with people?

What about the people?

ORIENTATION

Perhaps instead of pondering over the perceived failings of others we should instead be focusing on those whose example shines like a beacon. I want to draw you portraits of a few people I think are exceptional and use these to ask whether those who get it share a set of common qualities or whether each person has their own way of getting it.

Flo

My first example is Flo Longhorn, a woman who I regularly describe as one of my inclusion heroes. Her work in the late 1970s and early 1980s paved the way, along with many other heroes working at that time, for the meaningful education of people with profound disabilities. Children and adults once disregarded by society were held up as special by Flo and treated as such. The respect and creativity in her practice has rippled through the decades. When I first stepped into a special school in my first week of term, I was handed a great collection of Flo's books and told: "Read these, you will need to know what is inside." I cannot do justice to all she has achieved in this short paragraph, but I am relieved to know that I do not need to; if you are reading this book, you likely already know about Flo!

When I first began The Sensory Projects, Flo was one of my backers. And as the projects grew and Flo neared retirement, I was privileged to get to work alongside her, running training days together. It was an extraordinary chance for me to learn not only what she taught during those days but all the extra information I could glean around the edges. Beyond the inspiring advice and information she gave, I became increasingly aware of the manner in which she was giving that advice. She clearly knew more than did everyone in the room, but in speaking to people, she celebrated what they did over telling them what she could do.

Her positivity seemed endless; even over breakfast early in the morning before a busy hour setting up a room ready to receive delegates, that positivity did not slip. It was not a mask worn but a way of life. Initially you take it on face value: here is a woman who loves what she does and gets to do it. But it is not so simple. This type of work involves the hearing of a great many stories. You get to share in a great many disappointments, you become increasingly aware of how people let other people down, and you witness the deaths of many a brilliant young person and the grief of their families. How, in the face of so much awfulness, do you smile and say everything is jolly and bright?

To do so is a choice, one I knew Flo had made but could not work out how or why. It is so tempting to get angry in the face of injustice; why was she always so cheerful? And then in conversation she mentioned something that stuck in my mind and seemed to be of particular significance. "I was a twin," she explained, "and my twin died in childhood, and when she died I knew I had to live life for us both." I looked at her and considered the life that she has lived, and continues to live. She most certainly has lived enough life for two.

When Flo she speaks of life, it is of *life* that she speaks. The value she sees in life goes deeper than that which is normally recognised. Let me explain: consider for example when we ask people "What do you want to do with your life?" Although the topic of that sentence is life, the answer we expect is not life, it is a job or travelling or some such thing. We do not focus on the living, but the doing. When Flo's twin died it must have been exceptionally clear to her that what she had was LIFE, and that that life was exceptionally valuable. It makes sense that someone who places such inherent value on life would respect it in others. If it is about the living, not the doing, then those who live are *the ones*, regardless of whether they do or not. Flo recognises life, recognises the person and joyfully celebrates every aspect of that life, whosever it is, however short, however hampered, however burdened it may be.

Her refusal to indulge in the negative is, I can only imagine, a measure of priority. What time have we for all the grotty stuff when there is life to be lived?

Mo

My next example is a woman called Mo who used to work in the school where I taught. Unlike Flo you are unlikely to have heard of Mo, but there are plenty of Mos around. Mo's ability to connect with the young people in our school was second to none. Her affinity with them and involvement in their lives was extraordinarily intimate. They trusted her like they trusted their parents. Mo could connect with children who others could not.

She herself was very quiet, and appeared shy and lacking in confidence, often submissive and apologetic; she seemed to think little of herself. She certainly would not think of herself as standing out in any way. Sometimes she seemed to almost lose herself in the children; their will became so entangled with her own that she was almost their puppet, reaching to get them the biscuits that they wanted but she knew they were not allowed, or assisting them to escape from some academic task and sneak off and play.

She was especially noticeable on playground duty, that moment in the fresh air when the children are free to roam and the adults can take a breath, drink tea (from safety-lidded mugs) and complete a whole sentence without interruption. Mo was never anywhere to be found, no cup of tea in her hand. She would be part of a game, always chosen to be played with, never removing herself from play, never wanting to, caught up in their imaginary games almost completely. I might choose to play, I might willingly involve myself, but I was never lost to it. Mo, however, was completely absorbed in them.

I have asked her what it was, but she says very little: "I just liked to be alongside them." That word "alongside" is a perfect description, as she was always with them, never the adult above them or the director, just perfectly with them.

She was a godsend to my classroom and in moments between the busyness I would wonder what made her tick. It is always a privilege to get to know someone's private life, however little of it they let show. Over time I learned that Mo had been in an abusive relationship with a man who struggled with alcoholism. The only time I ever heard her say anything with any bite in her tone was once when she reflected that it had been "twenty-four wasted years."

And through that time her voice was not heard. The "voices" of the children were so loud to her. Louder than my protests that now was not the time to eat biscuits, louder than the world, louder even than her own voice. Mo had an exceptional capacity to hear people.

In our weakness we find our strength

I can think of others. One in particular springs to mind who has struggled with their mental health for years, another with a long-term health complaint. With these people I wonder whether their understanding of their own vulnerability gives them a greater insight into how deep vulnerability can go. Whilst I might know myself to be vulnerable to injury, to sadness, to illness, and I have experienced all of these, and can recognise the inherent vulnerability in someone who has a disability, and respect that and see the person through it, my insight goes only so deep. How much deeper would my insight be if my experience of suffering had been greater?

You might think I am only presenting those people who always look on the bright side of life, whose positivity can be so great as to seem overly sweet, nauseating. Recently I have had the pleasure of long conversations with someone who very clearly "gets it" but does not bother to window dress this in pleasant terms. Instead they rant and rail at the failings of the systems they see supporting people with complex disabilities and at the same time they design new ways of doing things, solving the problems that so annoy them. "If I do not do it, who else is going to?" The sense of responsibility they feel is enormous and the result of all their frustration and rage has been some amazing pieces of innovation that are set to change the lives of many people with complex disabilities.

Mo appeared to be someone lacking confidence – one of the problems identified in the "get it" question – but her lack of confidence did not mean she did not get it. Flo has experienced plenty of hardship in life, but she hasn't become insensitive because of it, and she hasn't toughened up.

I cannot provide evidence for it, but I can state it to be challenged or considered: everyone has their own way of "getting it," their own life experiences and capabilities that can, in the right context, make them exceptional. Finding the aspects of the people you work with that are the key to their brilliance and putting them in a position where that brilliance can shine would create an environment staffed by people who feel themselves to be living purposeful lives.

Getting it is not a case of having certain innate qualities or having had certain life experiences. Getting it is an expression of who you currently are, and there are ways for that expression to come out, like the two sides of a coin: one version equates to a person who gets it, the other to one who does not.

Use according to strengths

One of my interviewees described a practice that used to go on in her old school, the upshot of which was that people who might have been grouped as getting it and not getting it were enabled to operate together in the best interests of their students:

> I do think that some people are just too embarrassed to play. They function at a very linguistic level, "head/cerebral" level but cannot relate that to body level. . . . Cannot "get at" their sensory level . . . maybe due to society's expectations, upbringing, whatever. They tend to be uptight. Maybe they can see the benefits of it, but just cannot let themselves go and tap into their instinct.

It is really hard to get them to accept that it's the process, the experiencing and the repetition that supports real learning. Our excellent (now retired) head teacher used to take one off lessons every so often with a group of sensory learners mainly to help teach teaching assistants and new teachers about the process. He was outstanding at doing this. He'd do a sensory story or similar with virtually one to one staffing (very unusual) but he'd offer each stimulus and very clearly tell the staff exactly what he was looking for e.g. offer this to their right side, do not speak or move but watch . . . did any muscle move? Did Dylan's mouth twitch? Did Sarah open her eyes a bit wider? Did Sam's foot wriggle? etc. Now offer it to the left. Did you get the same reaction or a different one . . . say their name, how do they respond?

Very obvious things, but the TAs and new teachers were always amazed at what they learned to look for. It really improved their practice. Once the staff got the idea of what to look for, he'd organise the group so that they were in a circle starting with the lowest ability up to the most able. His comments were similar, but he'd add things like "wow, you've learned to X Sammy." That's the next step to look for after Y.

They were very simple lessons, and very effective. If he was teaching the children only, with experienced staff who got it, he would not verbalise much at all, but would expect them to be able to report the steps and learning very clearly at the end of the lesson. (Or make notes on the child's record sheet in developmental terms.) They were not allowed to take a child into the multisensory room to do individual or small group work until he was satisfied they could look for the steps he wanted teaching. It was a sort of badge of competence if he allowed a TA to use the multisensory room. It was rarely abused on his watch!

The approach did not help the sense of fun, but it did allow the uptight people to channel their up-tightness into careful, detailed observation, which went quite a long way towards them at least appreciating the why. And it was a very useful starting point. Perhaps it enabled the two different types of people to work cooperatively . . . a kind of "you watch for tiny reactions and next steps whilst I roll around the room in sparkly tights and throw some glitter" type thing.

F.I.S.H.

Who are you? How do you relate to the people you support and the people you work alongside?

What are your strengths?

What are your weaknesses?

How can you make use of both your strengths and weaknesses?

Discussion

There is a sense that in trying to work out how to fish together, we have come full circle. The original proponents of multisensory rooms were at pains to point out that their approach was not about the room but about the people. They rejoiced over the moments of connection, the awakening of people to be better known and understood. They urged us to celebrate people for who they are, to value them for their own particular skills and abilities, not view them as overwhelming bundles of deficits.

The commercialisation of multisensory spaces inevitably made it about the rooms and not the approach. Even with the very best of intentions, companies selling a product, however much they tell people it is not about the product, contribute to a view that describes the value of the rooms in terms of physical things: pieces of the kit, types of space.

Recently I was having a conversation with a parent of a 16-year-old girl with profound disabilities. We were talking about a completely different topic but this work was in the back of my mind, as it has been for the years that I have been working on this research. I noticed that the home environment that was the backdrop to our Skype call was indicative of a family that did not struggle for money. I presumed there would be a multisensory room, so I enquired after it. "Yes we have one, but we do not use it anymore," came the reply. This was particularly interesting because in larger settings a room that has fallen out of use may have done so for many reasons: the design suited a population of people who have been and gone, the room has been damaged by use, trained individuals have left the staff team and so on. But a room in someone's house, built for a particular person, bespoke to their needs, and in a situation where there are few barriers to it being updated is likely to be the ideal room.

"How come you do not use it anymore?" I asked.

"We recognised the benefits she was getting from it were relational, and she can relate to people in other environments, so we felt it was important that she get out and meet as many people as possible, rather than she be always in that room."

Other people I have spoken to over the course of this work have indicated reasons why the multisensory rooms they have access to might not be ideal environments for interaction. The "controlled" nature of the spaces puts someone in control and when you feel yourself to be in charge of a person and their situation, you do not so much feel yourself to be *with* that person. Les Staves (2018) points out that being in control can impair our abilities to play and be playful "whilst feeling free to react and reflect are basic to playfulness, being required to control, observe and record can surely inhibit it."

The controlled and fixed nature of the rooms, the amount of stuff in them, makes them difficult places to be playful. This is not because one cannot play with lights or the responsiveness of the equipment, but because their unique nature causes them to become a fixed point in people's minds, both for facilitators in the room and experiencers of the room. This is the place where we do X. This fixedness was what inspired the focus people spoke of as a strength, but the flip side to that strength is this weakness.

The amount of stuff in the rooms makes them difficult to animate. You can cast different coloured lights or pictures, play different sounds, but the experience always has greater sameness to it than difference, like sitting in a cinema. No matter how different the film, the feeling is of being at the cinema and we behave accordingly. The set space indicates a set way to behave. This combined with the known benefits of repetition of activities when supporting people with profound disabilities sucks the playfulness out of the rooms.

The process of controlling the environment can detract from playful interactions. And the presence of extraordinary pieces of the kit can mask the importance of tiny moments of connection. Les Staves (2018) explains:

> Another important point for staff to understand is the value of small actions, and where they lead. For example for staff to appreciate the value of the moments they might share with a child sensing an object or stimulus. Moments like looking and touching an apple, or a book page, or a simple photo on a tablet, together maybe taken for granted. They are moments of serve and return that develop the brain's functional awareness and communicative ability. In contrast staff may focus great efforts on turning on programmed effects or bubble tubes without recognising the contribution of their own responses.

Design elements contribute to the rooms being unpleasant spaces, practical things like lack of ventilation led them to being smelly. One of my interviewees said "I hate the smell of the room, it is too stuffy, dark, depressing. It is daytime, we want to be in the light, not locked away in some dark cupboard." Access issues like padded floors, which are difficult for people with mobility issues to walk upon, the inability to bring hoists into the room due to size constraints and the position of equipment further limit who can get into the room and use it in an unencumbered manner.

In some rooms the very things sold as being sensory were the things limiting access: four-dimensional immersive rooms with multi-walled projection are great for people whose eyesight can pick out the detail in those images and whose minds leap into the imaginative landscape. But for people still experiencing the early developmental stages of their sensory capacities, someone, for example, who might struggle to focus on an object in the day-to-day environment as their eyesight is not acute enough to pick it out from a jumbled backdrop of other shapes, the rooms are disabling, not enabling. The amount of backlight thrown off from a multi-walled projection is enough to effectively render many visually impaired people blind. Even if they can handle the amount of light, what you have created is a space where it is harder for them to access visual experience, not one where the visual experience is likely to be more engaging.

It is true that there are benefits to the responsiveness of the environments and the wow factor they create, but these are nothing in comparison to the potential of the environments. The realisation of these and nothing else is what leaves us all feeling so underwhelmed. With the exception of three of my interviewees, everyone I spoke to in the course of this research expressed the feeling that their room was underutilised and that they had somehow failed to unlock its potential.

Creating the wow space and having that wowness be a catalyst for behaviour change in those supporting the experiences has value, but that value is instantly neutralized if the space itself is not fully accessible, physically, sensorially and cognitively, to the person for whom it is intended to benefit.

The responsiveness of the environments is sold as being one of their main assets, but the potential value here is undermined, this time by a lack of understanding as to how that responsiveness should progress. People spoke of it being an area of reciprocal confusion, and of echo chambers, or feedback loops where people agreed with each other that it was a great thing but got nowhere with establishing why. This was reflected in my interviews where people spoke of the ability to control the stimulation in the room as being a positive, but then did not speak about using this within their interactions in the room; there was that initial statement of it being a good thing, but then little evidence of that being true.

Consider a situation where the illumination of the bubble tube causes a previously unresponsive person to look towards the light. We celebrate: "He looked towards the light!" Wonderful, what we need is another light. We get another light. He looks towards the light. We celebrate again. We are making progress here. Let us get him another light. What is the end goal? Whilst it has value that he is engaged, that he sees the light, the many, many lights, each one gently colour shifting through red, blue, green and yellow as so much sensory equipment does, this is a tiny fraction of the value we hoped to gain for this person.

One interviewee reflected:

> What is measurable? If they laugh and they are happy surely that is measurable. We went in to relax and they gave sounds and gave feedback. The stuff in multisensory rooms can be a bit of The Emperor's New Clothes I think a lot of the time. People just want the ooo response from everyone. They forget the children have

brains. When they get the ooo response they do not think what next they think their job is done. My daughter will look at a pretty light just like you would, but she needs to be pushed.

Likewise we have people trained to press switches. She presses the switch and sees that she controls an aspect of the environment. She feels the power in her action and her self-esteem is bolstered. She comes to understand that she is an entity that can have an effect on the world around her. So we fetch another switch and another item to control, and another switch, and another gadget. And it only goes so far.

The constant re-updating of the rooms with new pieces of equipment, with the next best thing, the thing seen in someone else's setting or at a roadshow, is just a bigger version of that same feedback loop: "this works, we want more of this." Not "this works, we want what is next."

The scar on our interactions left by behaviourism goes deep and mostly unnoticed, and whilst the logic of consistent repeated controlled environments is clear and does yield fruit, what is becoming clearer by the day is that the defiance of that structure, the embrace of playfulness, the letting down of boundaries, as unreasonable and unpredictable as it may be, is actually far more effective. Play research found neural pathways formed quicker through play than through repetition. Simmons (2019a) remarks on the speed of skill acquisition for a child with profound and multiple learning disabilities, contrasting a high-structured environment where there were multiple opportunities for consistent repetition and practice of a skill to a more chaotic and playful environment where communication and interaction was higgledy-piggledy. The child learned more swiftly amidst the hubbub and play than they did amidst the carefully maintained communication environment.

Bleming (2018b) calls into question the use of progression as a measure of value, arguing that for some "experience is equal to progression," not that it is the same thing, but that it has the same value. Bleming (2018b) goes on to say that "sensing never occurs without meaning. The senses are the beginning and the end of human knowledge." Bleming argues that for users of multisensory rooms who have profound cognitive impairments, "the experience has to be worth it in itself if you cannot stack memories or build learning." In my research I placed value on multisensory room experiences that had a lasting effect. To want a measurable outcome like this is typical of someone from an education background, and I am a teacher. Should we be measuring experiences in multisensory rooms by what was learned or by what was felt?

It is clear that the rooms have value, but the relationships have the most value. Gurney (2019) questioned why we use the rooms at all, asking, "why put something in the way of what is at the heart of this; a person is more responsive than a room will ever be." Many of my interviewees reported using the rooms as spaces to do other activities within, and all of these activities were relational. The features my interviewees valued most about the rooms were their darkness and their quietness. They used their rooms as a canvas for experience, not as an experience in itself. If you are supporting someone who cannot pick your face out of the multitude of shapes and patches of light around them in daily life, but within a darkened, quiet room can see your face illuminated by torchlight, then the room becomes a doorway through which you can access that connection and communication.

We need to stop thinking about multisensory rooms in terms of space and pieces of equipment and start thinking about them as being about people and the relationships between people. Speaking about his experience in small sensory spaces in the late 1970s, Les Staves (2018) said "we did not start from the point of view of having a piece of equipment to use, but rather from thinking about what the child needed to learn." Our question should not be about multisensory rooms at all, but about the people we support. What do they need? Where would they like to be? What can they do? What could they do? What would be fun for them? Perhaps a multisensory room will feature in our answers to some of these questions, and perhaps it will not.

The lack of the person in our questions about multisensory rooms is indicative of the problem faced. As I have written this book many people have gotten in touch with me to ask questions about their multisensory room, and I have become increasingly alert to these questions being asked online. The following was posted in a teaching forum online and is typical of the questions I have seen: "Does anyone have any pictures of good sensory room equipment? We are thinking of updating our room." This particular questioner was asking a group of several hundred educators. Missing from the question are the people who will use the room. How could any of us make a suggestion as to what would be suitable for that room without knowing who will use it? Yet all too often, the people are not even there in the question. We are asking the wrong thing.

The multisensory rooms of the future will enable greater access to life, not through the door of the room itself but through the door of the pre-existing abilities of the person interacting within the room. They will recognise that they are secondary to relationships. They will not present us with more and more exciting things we can affect, and they will give us the capacity to create a sensorially blank canvas upon which we can draw our interactions and form our relationships. They will become less noticeable, not more so.

The access points for the room, the control devices, switches, eye gaze and so forth will spill out of the room and into all areas of the room user's life. The stimulation within the room will provide content to enrich our connection with one another and our relationships. Imagine the perfect intensive interaction conversation where I am wholly present and the person I am sharing that conversation with is wholly present, and we each see each other, recognise and respond to each other. Once we have introduced ourselves for a while, expressed ourselves for a while, what is there to talk about? Have you ever witnessed a beautiful sunset and wished there were someone next to you to share it with? There is great value in sharing experience.

For a Sensory Being we do this at a sensory level, and a sensory room could provide that context.

With this in mind, we need the experiences within the room to be worth having in and of themselves, without looking to justify them by outcomes such as skills learned. The experience should be its own justification. They will be playful, and we will recognise the ridiculousness of asking "what is this for?" Play is its own answer. Ask a person at play what they are doing it for and they will look at you blankly, for your question does not make sense in relation to play. If we can create experiences like this, then we can ensure that the multisensory rooms of the future truly are spaces worthy of the time of the people we choose to take to them. If you are someone who senses but cannot apportion meaning, where does meaning come into things for you? There is no such thing as passive experience; sensation itself is active. The sensation in a multisensory room is its own meaning (Bleming 2019a).

The rooms of the future will be recognised as perfect environments for assessing people's thresholds for perception; we will be able to finely tune the stimulation so that we learn just how bright one needs something to be in order to see it, precisely what frequency sound needs to be to resonate with them, and we will use this information in the room a little, but in the world a lot. Similarly, we will watch their reactions and responses in the room and use them to empower their self-advocacy. Through exposure to a range of experiences within the rooms, we will be able to begin to understand how they express yes/no, like/dislike, and then ensure that these expressions are powerfully recognised in all areas of their life. The effect will go beyond the room not because they get better at expressing themselves – no doubt they are skilled enough at that already – but because we get better at listening to them with all of our senses.

The tech within the rooms will not be about turning the heads of staff or visitors to invite them to think about the users of those rooms in a different way, because that work will already be done. The future will be a quieter, calmer era, not about boasting or showing off or claiming that "our room is better than yours." We will come into the rooms to meet each other. The tech will be there to enhance that communication. Maybe it will enable us to notice a response we could not pick up with our own limited senses or concentration span. It will give people who currently have limited scope to convey their responses to us more avenues for doing that. These things are being designed as I type. We will come full circle and once again clearly state that it is not about the room; it is about how we relate to all of the extraordinary, bright, brilliant, different people around us, and the rooms may enable us to include more people in that, but the rooms will be a by-product of our intention to do that and our desire to connect with others.

Conclusion

A person can have any number of chisels and lathes and a wonderful workshop, and yet not be a carpenter. A collection of scalpels and needles and a state-of-the-art operating theatre does not make someone a surgeon. Likewise a bubble tube and fibre optic spray in a state-of-the-art multisensory room does not make someone a skilled multisensory room facilitator. With all of these roles it is the underpinning skills that are the essential component; the tools of the trade are sometimes necessary, sometimes niceties, but they alone do not shape the wood, heal the wound or create the magic in a multisensory room.

Paying for elaborate equipment does not make the equipment worth the money that you paid for it. That something costs a certain amount is not a measure of its worth; it is a measure of how much the seller of that item believes they can sell it for. The fundamental skill involved in generating the magic that occurs in multisensory rooms is a human one. If we want to see the greatest impact from our investments it is into the development of humans that we should pour our money.

Our primary goal should be for the people in multisensory rooms to meet, and regard each other, as they are. As for the facilitators in the space, this involves understanding who they are and how they learn, and developing them as respected individuals. With regards to the people experiencing the space, this involves appreciating and respecting them as they are now, and connecting with them as they are now. Lay aside notions that people with learning disabilities have lost the inherent ability to learn that is common to all people. Also lay aside the idea that learning should always be our main aim (counterintuitively, you may well find that more learning occurs when you follow their lead and play).

When we stop striving to change people and focus on meeting them in the present, we do something wonderful for them and for us: we foster connection.

In people with profound and multiple learning disabilities we get to meet a reflection of raw humanity, not an idealised notion of a Victorian invalid. They are an honest representation of a person. They are themselves, without artifice, without a front, communicating honestly and completely about how they feel. In an age where authenticity is respected as the highest form of morality, they offer a challenge to our dressed-up selves. In an age of anxiety when we all struggle to simply be in our own skin, they show us how to do it with supreme ease. We may assist them in better understanding the world, in orientating their sensory systems, developing motor skills and regulating emotional states. If this is a "done to" activity, it will be less effective and everyone involved will miss out. If we "do with," then the shared experience in the multisensory room, or in any space, is one where we stand to learn as much from them as they do from us. We are equals, and divides of physical ability or neurodiversity do not make us less so. They are divides of difference to be understood and accepted, not divides of a hierarchical nature to be solved or used to form the basis of prejudice.

Being invited to share in the state of being that I once called sensory-being (Grace 2017), a simple present-ness in a sensory moment, has value in, of and for itself. In that moment we are purely alive, and we share that experience of life with another as we connect with them. To simply *be* has value. And as we open our eyes and see someone different to us (as all people are) as they truly are, without thinking of how to change them, without placing judgement on their life, we are the embodiment of awareness and acceptance. The magic of multisensory rooms is that they have been, and can be, places where people previously separated by divides of prejudice inspired by neurological or physiological differences can, for the first time, see each other and connect.

Connection is the magic within, or without, a multisensory room. Fibre optics, multi-walled projections and the rest are wonderful, but they cannot cast the spell themselves. That has to be done by you.

References

Akbar, O. (2018) The quick Q&A: How to identify and tackle workplace bullying. *The Times Educational Supplement*. www.tes.com/news/quick-qa-how-identify-and-tackle-workplace-bullying

Ayer, S. (1998) Use of multi-sensory rooms for children with profound and multiple learning disabilities. *Journal of Intellectual Disabilities*, 2, 89–97.

Baker, R., Holloway, J., Holtkamp, C. C. M., Larsson, A., Hartman, L. C., Baker, R., Holloway, J., Holtkamp, C. C. M., Larsson, A., Hartman, L. C., Pearce, R., Scherman, B., Johansson, S., Thomas, P. W., Wareing, L. A., Pearce, R., Scherman, B., Johansson, S., Thomas, P. W., Wareing, L. A., & Owens, M. (2003) Effects of multi-sensory stimulation for people with dementia. *Journal of Advanced Nursing*, 43(5), 465–477.

Barry, L., & Celiberti, D. (2009) Child (?) choice between competing recreational environments: Support for multi-sensory environments for children with disabilities. *Southeastern Teacher Education Journal*, 5(1), 67–76.

Blatt, B., & Kaplan, F. (1974) *Christmas in Purgatory. Disability History Museum* www.disabilitymuseum.org/dhm/lib/detail.html?id=1782&page=all

Birrell, I. (2019) Mendip house care home has been fined a derisory £4,000 after staff rode a resident with autism 'like a horse' and forced another to drink vomit. *i.news*. https://inews.co.uk/opinion/columnists/mendip-house-autism-abuse-failings/

Bleming, L. (2018a) Private correspondence, November 22, Sensory Guru.

Bleming, L. (2018b) Private correspondence, November 28, Sensory Guru

Bleming, L (2019a) Private correspondence, April 4.

Bleming, L. (2019b) Visit to Sensory Guru HQ, March 22.

Botts, B. H., Hershfeldt, P. A., Christen-Sandfort, R. J., & Snoezelen (2008) Empirical review of product representation. *Focus on Autism and Other Developmental Disabilities*, 23(3), 138–147.

Bozic, N. (1997) Constructing the room: Multi-sensory rooms in educational contexts. *European Journal of Special Needs Education*, 12(1), 54–70.

Challis, B. (2014) *Designing for Musical Play*. Manchester: Manchester Metropolitan University

Challis, B., Kang, A., Rimmer, R., & Hildred, M. (2017) Enabling active interaction with music and sound in multi sensory environments. *EAI Endorsed Transactions on Creative Technologies*, 4(11), 1–8.

Chivers, C. (2019) https://twitter.com/ChrisChivers2/status/1088008939839590400

Clements, P. (2014) *Workplace Bullying in the Health Care Setting*. Drexel University College of Nursing and Health Professionals. https://drexel.edu/cnhp/news/current/archive/2014/September/2014-09-11-Workplace-Bullying-in-the-Health-Care-Setting/

Colley, A. (2015) Mental health issues in young people with severe, profound and multiple learning difficulties – Development of a brief guide for teachers. *SLD Experience*, 72, 11–17.

Coley, R., Kuo, F. E., & Sullivan, W. C. (1997) Where does community grow? The social context created by nature in urban public housing. *Environment and Behavior*, 29(4), 468.

Cook, A. (2017) Bullying and harassment in the social care workplace. *Bettal Quality Consultancy*. www.bettal.co.uk/bullying-harassment-social-care-workplace/

Count us in (2002) *The report of the committee of enquiry into meeting the mental health needs of young people with learning disabilities*. The Foundation for People with Learning Disabilities and the Mental Health Foundation.

Crombie, R., Sullivan, L., WalKer, K., & Warnock, R. (2014) Unconscious and unnoticed professional practice within an outstanding school for children and young people with complex learning difficulties and disabilities. *Support for Learning*, 29(1), 7–23.

Cuvo, A. J., May, M. E., & Post, T. M. (2001) Effects of living room, Snoezelen room, and outdoor activity on stereotypic behaviour and engagement by adults with profound mental retardation. *Research in Developmental Disabilities*, 22, 183–204.

Davies, J., & Hogg, J. (2004) Count us in. *PMLD Link*, 16, 4–8.

Department for Education (DFE). (2015) Area guidelines for SEND and alternative provision: Including special schools, alternative provision, specially resourced provision and units. *Building Bulletin 104*. https://assets.publishing.service.gov.uk/government/uploads/system/uploads/attachment_data/file/485223/BB104.pdf

Doukas, T., Fergusson, A., Fullerton, M., & Grace, J. (2017) *Core and essential service standards for supporting people with profound and multiple learning disabilities*. Available online at www.TheSensoryProjects.co.uk/PMLD-service-standards and www.PMLDlink.org.uk/resources

Enser, M. (2017) How can schools use research to better inform teaching practice. *The Guardian Teacher Network*. Accessed online on December 28, 2018 at www.theguardian.com/teacher-network/2017/nov/23/how-can-we-make-research-work-harder-in-our-schools

Fava, L., & Strauss, K. (2010) Multi-sensory rooms: Comparing effects of the Snoezelen and the stimulus preference environment on the behaviour of adults with profound mental retardation. *Research in Developmental Disabilities*, 31, 160–171.

Finnema, E., Droes, R. M., Ribbe, M., & Van Tilburg, W. (2000) The effects of emotion-orientated approaches in the care for persons suffering from dementia: A review of the literature. *International Journal of Geriatric Psychiatry*, 15, 141–161.

Flaghouse (September 2011) Versatile sensory experiences for all ages: What is Snoezelen? *EP Magazine*, 48–50.

Flaghouse (November 2012) Flaghouse forum: Inside a snoezelen room. *EP Magazine*, 17.

Fowler, S. (2008) Multisensory rooms and environments. *Controlled Sensory Experiences for People with Profound and Multiple Disabilities*. London: JKP Resource Materials.

Gerhardt, S. (2004) *Why Love Matters: How Affection Shapes a Baby's Brain*. Abingdon: Routledge.

Ghaziuddin, E., Weidmer-Mikhail, E., & Ghaziuddin, N. (1998) Comorbidity of Asperger syndrome: A preliminary report. *Journal of Intellectual Disability Research*, 42, 279–283.

Goward, P., Grant, G., & Ramcharan, P. (2005) *Learning Disability: A Life Cycle Approach to Valuing People*. London: McGraw-Hill International.

Grace, J. (2014) *Sensory Stories for Children and Teens with Special Educational Needs*. London: Jessica Kingsley Publishers.

Grace, J. (2017) *Sensory-Being for Sensory Beings*. Abingdon: Routledge

Grace, J. (2018) Inclusion: for pity's sake? *TEDx* www.youtube.com/watch?v=_PbWFcVcaWQ&t=60s

Gray (1994) Multi-sensory rooms – The views continue. *Eye Contact*, 8, 17–18.

Gurney, J. (2019) Private correspondence, March 21, Us in a Bus.

Haggar, L. E., & Hutchinson, R. B. (1991) Snoezelen: An approach to the provision of a leisure resource for people with profound and multiple handicaps. *Journal of the British Institute of Mental Handicap (APEX)*, 19, 51–55.

Hall, S (2018) Private correspondence, November 11, Willows Sensory Service.

Haegele, J. A., & Porretta, D. L. (2014) Snoezelen multisensory environment: An overview of research and practical implications. *Palaestra*, 28(4), 29–33.

Hewett, D. (2007) Do touch: Physical contact and people who have severe, profound and multiple learning difficulties. *Support for Learning*, 22(3), 116–123.

Hill, L., Trusler, K., Furniss, F., & Lancioni, G. (2012) Effects of multi sensory environments on stereotyped behaviours assessed as maintained by automatic reinforcement. *Journal of Applied Research in Intellectual Disabilities*, 25, 509–521.

Hirstwood, R. (2015) *PMLD Link*, 27(1), 80.

Hirstwood, R. (2017) *The Multi-Sensory Room/Studio . . . How to Design*. Lancashire: Hirstwood Training.

Hirstwood, R., & Crabtree, J. (2018) *The Role of the Multi-Sensory Room Co-Ordinator*. Lancashire: Hirstwood Training.

Hirstwood, R., & Gray, M. (1995) *A Practical Guide to the Use of Multi-Sensory Rooms*. Worcestershire: Toys for the Handicapped.

Hirstwood, R., & Smith, C. (1995) Developing competencies in multi-sensory rooms. In Murdoch, H. & Bozic, N. (Eds.), *Learning Through Interaction*. London: David Fulton.

Hoehn, T. P., & Baumeister, A. A. (1994) A critique of the application of sensory integration therapy to children with learning disabilities. *Journal of Learning Disabilities*, 27, 338–350.

Hogg, J., Cavet, J., Lambe, L., & Smeddle, M. (2001) The use of 'Snoezelen' as multi sensory stimulation with people with intellectual disabilities: A review of the research. *Research in Developmental Disabilities*, 22, 353–372.

Hope, K. W. (1998) The effects of multisensory environments on older people with dementia. *Journal of Psychiatric and Mental Health Nursing*, 5, 377–385.

Hopkins, P., & Willett, D. (1993) 'And also . . .' *Eye Contact*, 6, 26.

Houghton, S., Douglas, G., Brigg, J., Langsford, S., Powell, L., West, J., Chapman, A., & Kellner, R. (1998) An empirical evaluation of an interactive multi-sensory environment for children with disability. *Journal of Intellectual and Developmental Disability*, 23(4), 267–227.

Hussein, H. (2010) Using the sensory garden as a tool to enhance the educational development and social interaction of children with special needs. *Support for Learning*, 25(1), 25–31.

Hulsegge, J., & Verheul, A. (1986) *Snoezelen Another World*. London: Rompa.

Imray, P., & Colley, A. (2017) *Inclusion is Dead, Long Live Inclusion*. New York and London: Routledge.

Jacobson, J., Foxx, R., & Mulick, J. (Eds.). (2005) *Controversial Therapies for Developmental Disabilities: Fad, Fashion, and Science in Professional Practice*. Mahwah, NJ: Lawrence Erlbaum.

Jacques, D. (2016) *An Analysis of the Role, Purpose and Constitution of the Multisensory Room in a Special Educational Needs School in England*. Birmingham University dissertation submission for a BA in education.

Kaplan, H., Clopton, M., Kaplan, M., Messbauer, L., & McPherson, K., (2006) Snoezelen multi-sensory environments: Task engagement and generalisation. *Research in Developmental Disabilities*, 27, 443–455.

Kettle, E. (2012) Time to face up to workplace bullying in schools. *Guardian*. www.theguardian.com/teacher-network/teacher-blog/2012/apr/24/teacher-bullying-schools

Kossyvaki, L. (2019) Why is research important? Reflections for professionals and parents. *PMLD Link*, 31(2), Issue 83, 19–20.

Lancioni, G. E., Cuvo, A. J., & O'Reilly, M. F. (2002) Snoezelen: An overview of research with people with developmental disabilities and dementia. *Disability and Rehabilitation*, 24(4), 175–184.

Lewer, A., & Harding, C. (2013a) From 'What do you do?' to 'A Leap of Faith': Developing more effective indirect intervention for adults with learning disabilities. *Tizard Learning Disability Journal*, 18(2), 74–84.

Lewer, A., & Harding, C. (2013b) Communication is the key: Improving outcomes for people with learning disabilities. *Tizard Learning Disability Journal*, 18(3), 132–141.

Longhorn, F. (1988) *A Sensory Curriculum for Very Special People*. London: Souvenir Press

Longhorn, F. (2011) A short history of shout, glow, jump, taste, smell, touch and wobble: Multi sensory education (part2) *PMLD Link*, 23, 1, (68), 29–31.

Longhorn, F. (2018) Private email correspondence, November 9.

Lotan, M., & Gold, C. (2009) Meta-analysis of the effectiveness of individual intervention in the controlled multisensory environment (Snoezelen) for individuals with intellectual disability. *Journal of Intellectual and Developmental Disability*, 34(3), 207–215.

Louv, R. (2005) *Last Child in the Woods*. London: Atlantic Books

Lyddon, B (2019) Private email correspondence, February 25, Sensory Spectacle.

Making us count (2005) *Identifying and Improving Mental Health Support for Young People with Learning Disabilities: A Research Report*. Bristol: University of Bristol

Madden, R. (2010) *Being Ethnographic. A Guide to the Theory and Practice of Ethnography*. London: Routledge.

Martin, N. T., Gaffan, E. A., & Williams, T. (1998) Behavioural effects of long-term multi-sensory stimulation. *British Journal of Clinical Psychology*, Pt 1, 69–82.

McCormack, B. (2003) Snoezelen: A mother's story. *The Exceptional Parent*, 33(10), 38–41.

McKee, S. A., Harris, G. T., Rice, M. E., & Silk, L. (2007) Effects of a Snoezelen room on the behaviour of three autistic clients. *Research in Developmental Disabilities*, 28, 304–316.

Messbauer, L. (2012) A Snoezelen MSE approach to challenging behaviours: Flaghouse forum. *EP Magazine*, 10–13

Mitchell, R., & Popham, F. (2008) Effect of exposure to natural environment on health inequalities: An observational population study. *The Lancet*, 372(9650), 1655–1660.

Mount, H., & Cavet, J. (1995) Multi-sensory environments: An exploration of their potential for young people with profound and multiple learning disabilities. *British Journal of Special Education*, 22(2), 52–55.

Murray, J. S. (2009) Workplace bullying in nursing: A problem that can't be ignored. *MED-SURG Nursing*, 18(5), 273–276.

Nicodemus, T. (September/October 1999) Snoezelen: A magical place at camp. *Camping* 18–19

Noel, J. P., Pfeiffer, C., Blanke, O., & Serino, A. (2015) Peripersonal space as the space of the bodily self. *Cognition*, 144, 49–57

O'Brien, J. (2016) *Don't Send Him in Tomorrow. Shining a Light on the Marginalised, Disenfranchised and Forgotten Children of Today's Schools*. Carmarthen: Independent Thinking Press.

Orr, R. (1993) Life beyond the room? *Eye Contact*, Summer, 25–26.

Pagliano, P. (2001) *Using a Multi Sensory Environment – A Practical Guide for Teachers*. London: David Fulton Publishers

Pagliano, P. (2008) *Multi-Sensory Environments; Helping the Brain to Compensate in Positive Ways*. Townsville, Queensland: James Cook University.

Palmer, S (2006) *Toxic Childhood*. London: Orion

Park (1997) Loitering within tent. *SLD Experience*, 18, 24.

Park (1998) *Loitering within tent T(w)o SLD Experience*, 20, 5–6

Pavlik, J. V. (2017) Experiential media and disabilities in education: Enabling learning through immersive, interactive, customisable, and multi-sensorial digital platforms. *Ubiquitous Learning: An International Journal*, 10(1), 15–22.

Potter, J., & Wetherell, M. (1987). *Discourse and Social Psychology: Beyond Attitudes and Behaviour*. London: Sage.

Randell, E., McNamara, R., Delport, S., Busse, M., Hastings, R., Gillespie, D., Williams-Thomas, R., Brookes-Howell, L., Romeo, R., Boadu, J., Ahuja, A., McKigney, A., Knapp, M., Smith, K., Thornton, J., & Warren, G. (2019) Sensory integration therapy versus usual care for sensory processing difficulties in autism spectrum disorder in children: Study protocol for a pragmatic randomised controlled trial. *Trails*, 20, 113.

Ryan, J. K. (2018) Resources for multi sensory environments. *EP Magazine*, 66–70.

SeeAbility (2016) *Special School Sight Testing*. Accessed online on March 31, 2019 at www.seeability.org/special-schools.

Seguin, E. (1866) *Idiocy and Its Treatment by the Physiological Method*. New York: William Woods and Co.

Simmons, B. (2011) The "PMLD ambiguity": Articulating the lifeworlds of children with profound and multiple learning difficulties, paper presented at the Nordic Network on Disability Research (NNDR) 11th Annual Conference, Reykjavík, Iceland. Accessed online on May 28.

Simmons, B. (2019a) From living to lived and being-with: Exploring the interaction styles of children and staff towards a child with profound and multiple learning disabilities. *International Journal of Inclusive Education*, doi:10.1080/13603116.2019.156973

Simmons, B (2019b) Twitter conversation, April 5.

Singh, N. N., Lancioni, G. E., Winton, A. S. W., Molina, E. J., Sage, M., Brown, S., & Groeneweg, J. (2004) Effects of snoezelen room, activities of daily living skills training, and vocational skills training on aggression and self-injury by adults with mental retardation and mental illness. *Research in Developmental Disabilities*, 25, 285–293.

Smith, A. M., & Grzywacz, J. G. (2014) Health and well-being in midlife parents of children with special health needs. *Families, Systems & Health: The Journal of Collaborative Family Healthcare*, 32(3), 303–312, doi:10.1037/fsh0000049

Stamatakis, E. (2011) Screen-based entertainment time, all-cause mortality, and cardiovascular events: Population-based study with ongoing mortality and hospital events follow-up. *Journal of the American College of Cardiology*, 57(3), 292–299.

Staves, L. (2018) Personal correspondence FB, December 4.

Taylor, A., & Kuo, F. (2008) Children with attention deficits concentrate better after walk in the park. *Journal of Attention Disorders*, 12(5), 402–409.

US Department of Education (2016) *Guidance on Using Evidence to Strengthen Education Investments*. https://www2.ed.gov/policy/elsec/leg/essa/guidanceuseseinvestment.pdf

Verkaik, R., van Weert, J. C. M., & Francke, A. I. (2005) The effects of psychosocial methods on depressed, aggressive and apathetic behaviours of people with dementia: A systematic review. *International Journal of Geriatric Psychiatry*, 20, 3001–3310.

WAG (2006) *Routes for Learning: Assessment Materials for Learners With Profound Learning Difficulties and Additional Disabilities*. Cardiff: Welsh Assembly Government.

Ware, J. (1996/2003) *Creating a Responsive Environment*. London: David Fulton Publishers.

Williamson, M. (1992) *A Return to Love: Reflections on the Principles of "A Course in Miracles"*. New York: Harper Collins, 190/165.

Index

ability, developing 145–146
activity arches 82
ADHD 73
advertising: bias 68–70; taking place of
knowledge 64–67
affordability, of alternative sensory spaces
84
"almosts: a study of the feebleminded,
The" (MacMurchy) 15
alternative sensory spaces 3, 44,
75–87, 112, 114; activity arches 82;
affordability 84; association of space
with activity or atmosphere 78–79; big
spaces 76–81; blacked out spaces 78;
brollies/umbrellas 81; considerations
84–85; criteria for 75; gardens 77–78;
gazebos 80; Hula-Hoops and shower
curtains 83–84; hygge home 77;
multisensory rooms compared to 76;
Neilsen's Little Rooms 81–82; reasons
for entering 85; resources offered
in 86–87; sense assessment 84–85;
sequence strings 82–83; shadow theatre
79; small spaces 81–84; tents 76–77;
water worlds 80–81; withies 78
Alternative Sensory Spaces (Facebook photo
album) 76, 78–79, 81, 83–84, 114
Another World (Hulsegge and Verheul)
28, 33, 94
anti-research 48–49
association of space with activity or
atmosphere 78–79

@JeremyH09406687 14
@TheSensoryProjects: Alternative Sensory
Spaces (Facebook photo album) 76,
78–79, 81, 83–84, 114; Sensory-being
Project 85–86, 87, 96
attractive of multisensory rooms 44–45
awareness, generating 135–136
Ayer, S. 60–61, 64, 71

Baker, R. 43, 59
Barry's story 153–154
Baumeister, A. A. 67–68
behaviour 73–74
Bell, Sarah 48
Best Medicine, The 132
Bethany's Dad 14
bias 68–70
big alternative sensory spaces 76–81;
association of space with activity or
atmosphere 78–79; blacked out spaces
78; gardens 77–78; gazebos 80; hygge
home 77; shadow theatre 79; tents
76–77; water worlds 80–81; withies 78
Birrell, I. 12
blacked out spaces 78
Bleming, L. 41, 44, 95, 100, 137, 163
blue gyms 72–73
Botts, B. H. 45, 58, 61, 62, 67, 68
Bozic, N. 36, 37, 60
brain based visual impairment 147
British Education Index 49
broken items 100–101

brollies/umbrellas 81
Brooklands experiment 15
Bryan, J. 17
bubble tubes 15, 33–34, 50, 161

CanDoElla 22
Cavet, J. 40, 41, 43, 49, 53, 60, 64, 71
cerebral visual impairment 147
Challis, B. 48, 60, 61, 75, 95
Chapple, Elly 22
Christmas in Purgatory 25
cinemas 105–106
Clements, P. 120
Coley, R. 73
Colley, A. 18, 45, 55, 69, 72
compliance, forcing 11–13
confident facilitator 131–133
connections, making 149–150
containment zones 107–108
Contingency Sensitive Environment Project
    124, 133
continuing professional development
    (CPD) accreditation 122
control in multisensory rooms 110–111
Core and Essential Service Standards for
    Supporting People with Profound and
    Multiple Learning Disabilities 17
Crabtree, J. 101
Creating Responsive Environments
    (Ware) 133
Crombie, R. 116, 135

darkness of multisensory rooms 111
debating approaches 36–37
descriptive terms 17, 23
design of rooms, inaccessibility due to 95–96
directive approach 33, 37, 38, 90–91, 93, 109
disengagement of support staff 104–105
Down syndrome 16, 19, 20
dumping grounds 39, 43, 60, 97

Early Years Specialist Development Centre
    in Hertfordshire 149
Education Acts: 1970 15; 1981 16

Education Source 49
effectiveness of multisensory rooms 50–51,
    57–63; additional research needed 60–62;
    lack of evidence 60; mild findings 58–59;
    mixed results 58; negative findings 59;
    positive effects caused by other factors 58
efficacy of multisensory rooms 39–40
Emma Murphy blogs 146–148
empathetic facilitator 130–131
"ending up" doing a job 121–122
engagement by using multisensory rooms 93
Enser, M. 68
ERIC (Education Resources Information
    Centre) 49
Exeter University 48

facilitators: exceptional 155–157; strength
    of, rooms used according to 158–159;
    trigger-happy 98–100; weakness to find
    157–158
facilitators who do not "get it":
    characteristics of 119–122; "ending
    up" doing a job 121–122; ongoing
    support for 139–140; power 120–121;
    reflecting on the question 138–139;
    short thinking 122; those who "get it"
    distinguished from 117–118; toughened
    119–120; wheat from the chaff
    approach of identifying 118–119; see
    also strategies to enable someone who
    does not "get it" to "get it"
facilitators who "get it": characteristics
    of 123–133; confident 131–133;
    distinguished from those who don't
    117–118; empathetic 130–131; ongoing
    support for 139–140; personhood seen
    as separate from functionality 124–130;
    reflecting on the question 138–139;
    reflective 123–124; wheat from the
    chaff approach of identifying 118–119
Fava, L. 59, 60
feedback 133–134
fibre optics 15, 33–34, 39, 44, 50, 94, 101,
    144, 147, 153, 167

Finnema, E. 58, 61

F.I.S.H. (Find Idea Starters Here) 14, 24, 30–32, 38, 46, 52, 57, 63, 70–71, 75, 87, 98, 108–109, 114, 133, 140–142, 155, 159

Flaghouse 33, 40, 66–67

focus in multisensory rooms 112

forest bathing 72

4D immersive projections 33, 44

Fowler, S. 44, 59

functionality, personhood seen as separate from 124–130

funding 55–56

gardens 77–78

gazebos 80

Gold, C. 49, 61

Gray, M. 37, 40, 41, 42, 43, 49, 92, 136–137

Gurney, Janet 41, 55, 163

Haegele, J. A. 61, 74

Hall, S. 54

Hewett, D. 29

Hirstwood, R. 37, 39, 40, 41, 43, 49, 56, 81, 89, 92, 96, 101, 136–137

Hoehn, T. P. 67–68

Hogg, J. 43, 59, 73, 108

holding pens 39, 43, 60, 97

Hope, K. W. 42, 58, 59

Hope House Children's Hospices 42, 58, 59

Hopkins, P. 59

Houghton, S. 58, 61

Hugh learning to see 146–148

Hula-Hoops and shower curtains 83–84

Hulsegge, J. 25–30, 33, 36, 37, 39, 42, 43, 45, 47, 48–49, 53, 80, 94

Hussein, H. 72, 73

hygge home 77

Idiots Act 10, 11

improvised tents 77

Imray, P. 18, 45, 55, 69, 72

inaccessibility of rooms: due to design 95–96; due to usage 96–97

"Inclusion: for pity's sake?" (Grace) 21, 126

Inclusion is Dead: Long Live Inclusion (Imray and Colley) 72

independence, gaining 149–150

interviewees in research, overview of 88–89

Jacques, D. 98

journeys to the multisensory rooms, difficult 101–102

Kennedy, John F. 15

knowledge: advertising taking place of 64–67; foundations upon which multisensory room practice is based 47–63 (see also research)

Kossyvaki 48, 57

labels 17, 18, 22–23

Lancioni, G. E. 44, 58, 61, 74

language 16–23; with 19–20; doing away with 17–18; labels 17, 18, 22–23; no need for words 18–19; person-first 19, 22; #flipthenarrative 22–23; profound and multiple learning disabilities 20–21; rightness of a term 22

learning to look 151

learning to reach 150–151

Les Staves, L. 45, 161, 164

limitations of research 109–110

limiting factors influencing mulltisensory rooms 98–108; broken items 100–101; cinemas 105–106; containment zones 107–108; difficult journeys to the multisensory rooms 101–102; disengagement of support staff 104–105; set up time 107; tech fears 106–107; timetabling 102–104; trigger-happy facilitators 98–100

Linguistic Beings 21

LittleMamaMurphy blog 146–148

Little Rooms, Neilsen's 36, 76, 81–82

"Loitering Within Tent" (Park) 76

"Loitering Within Tent T(w)o" (Park) 76–77

Longhorn, F. 19, 28–29, 36, 39, 76, 81, 145, 146, 155–156
long-lasting effects from using the rooms 92–93
look, learning to 151
Lotan, M. 49, 61
Lyddon, Becky 111, 135

MacMurchy, Helen 15
Magic Blackout 78
Mandela, N. 7
Mary Dendy Hospital 10
McCormack, B. 66–67
McKee, S. A. 42, 59, 62, 65, 73
Mencap 11–13
Mental Capacity Act 10
Messbauer, L. 65
Mo (exceptional facilitator) 157
Mount, H. 40, 41, 43, 49, 53, 60, 64, 71
multi-sensory environments (MSEs) 40, 61
multisensory rooms (MSRs): alternative sensory spaces compared to 76; attractive 44–45; beginning of 33–38; branding of 36; debating approaches 36–37; efficacy of 39–40; facilitators 115–159; forcing of compliance 11–13; growth of 38–43; institutions of the past 9–10; knowledge foundations upon which multisensory room practice is based 47–63; lack of research underpinning use of 45–46; mistakes of past repeated in new era of 67–68; misunderstandings, dangers from 42–43; personalised 91, 97, 103; proliferation 38–45; research on use of, within UK 88–114; structures of the past scaffold the present 13–14; see also Snoezelen
multi-walled projections 60, 67, 105, 161–162, 167
Murray, J. S. 120

National Association of Parents of Backward Children 11–13
National Multi- Sensory Storytelling Day 72, 80

National Star College 80
nature 30, 72–73
negative research findings 59
Neilsen, Lilli 29, 36, 76, 81–82
Nicodemus, T. 65
non-directive approach 33, 37, 90–91, 93, 94, 109
non-directive users of multisensory rooms 92–93
Nordic Network on Disability Research 69
numinous tent 78–79

Openfuturelearning.org 20

Pagliano, P. 33, 37, 40, 56
PAMIS (Promoting A More Inclusive Society) 77
parents, address to 4–5, 7–8
Park, K. 76–77, 100, 103
Pavlik, J. V. 67
person facilitating multisensory room see facilitators
person-first language 19, 22
personhood seen as separate from functionality 124–130; thought experiment 127–130
PMLD Ambiguity, The (Simmons) 69
Porretta, D. L. 61, 74
positive research findings 58, 110–114; control 110–111; darkness 111; focused 112; uninterrupted 111–112; wowness 112–114
#flipthenarrative 22–23
#Notspecialneeds 16, 22
#TeachUsToo campaign 17
powerful facilitator 120–121
practice from within multisensory rooms 142–154; Barry's story 153–154; developing sensory awareness and ability 145–146; finding rest 148; Hugh learning to see 146–148; learning to look 151; learning to reach 150–151; making connections and gaining independence 149–150; multisensory

room with preschool-aged children 149; proprioceptive and vestibular stimulation 151–153; sensory story 143–145

prejudice 16, 17, 20, 136, 167

preschool-aged children, multisensory room with 149

professionals, address to 5–8

profound and multiple barriers to learning (PMBL) 18

profound and multiple learning difficulties (PMLD) 18, 45, 55, 69, 123, 133

projection 33, 44, 60, 67, 79, 105, 161–162, 167

proprioceptive stimulation 151–153

questions prompted by research findings 93–95

reach, learning to 150–151

reflective facilitator 123–124

relaxation in multisensory rooms 93

research: advertising taking place of knowledge without 64–67; anti-research 48–49; on claims that multisensory rooms do no harm 55; on control groups 51; on current use of multisensory rooms 88–90; on effectiveness of multisensory rooms (see effectiveness of multisensory rooms); failures in 50–52 (see also stand-up routine of research fails); findings (see research findings); flaws (see research flaws); limitations of 109–110; on love of multisensory rooms 51; materials, lack of 49; misunderstandings from lack of 45; need for 60–62; reasons for lack of 47–48; on relationship between person in room and person facilitating experience 53–54; on relationships within the room 56–57; on settings 51–52; themes identified from interviews 92–93; vulnerability due to lack of 54

research findings 57–63, 110–114; on current use of multisensory rooms 90–91; evidence 60; mild results 58;

mind findings 58–59; mixed results 58; negative 59; positive (see positive research findings); questions prompted by 93–95; on room accessibility 95–98

research flaws 52–56; claims that multisensory rooms do no harm, validity of 55; dark humour, unpicking 53–54; funding is not available for other resources 55–56; vulnerabilities due to lack of research 54

research on use of multisensory rooms within UK 88–114; furthering engagement by using 93; inaccessibility of rooms due to design 95–96; inaccessibility of rooms due to usage 96–97; interviewees 88–89; limitations of research 109–110; limiting factors influencing mulltisensory rooms 98–108; long-lasting effects from using the rooms 92–93; positive findings 110–114; promoting relaxation by using 93; questions prompted by findings 93–95; results 90–91; themes identified from interviews 92–93; see also limiting factors influencing mulltisensory rooms; positive research findings

rest, finding 148

Robinson, L. 72

room accessibility see inaccessibility of rooms

Routes for Learning (WAG) 55

Ryan, J. K. 67

safe spaces 107–108

Sandlebridge Colony 10

Scoobies 81

Scopus 49

Scottish Sensory Centre 49

SeeAbility 84–85

Seguin, Edouard 13

Seismic Sensory Project 13–14

sense assessment 84–85

sensory approaches, other 71–74; behaviour 73–74; nature 30, 72–73; value of 74

sensory awareness, developing 145–146
Sensory-being Project 85–86, 87, 96
Sensory Beings 20–21, 22, 85
Sensory Curriculum For Very Special People, A (Longhorn) 145
Sensory Guru 41
sensory integration theory 67–68
sensory processing disorder (SPD) 135
Sensory Spectacle 111, 135
sensory story 143–145
Sensory Trust 27, 72
sequence strings 82–83
set up time 107
severe learning difficulties (SLD) 18, 45, 88
shadow theatre 79
Sherbourne, Veronica 29
shinrin-yoku 72
short thinking facilitator 122
shower curtains 83–84
Simmons, B. 69, 124–125, 163
Singh, N. N. 39, 58, 61
small alternative sensory spaces 81–84; activity arches 82; brollies/umbrellas 81; Hula-Hoops and shower curtains 83–84; Neilsen's Little Rooms 81–82; sequence strings 82–83
Smith, C. 39
Snoezelen: anti-research and 48–49; contact and 29; dawning of 24–32; defined 28–29; example of 25; misunderstandings 42; MSE (Multi-sensory Environment) industry and 40; ownership of 33–35; persuasive marketing strategies 64; philosophy of 33–35; proliferation of claims 66–67; reasons for creating 43; research findings, mixed 58–59, 61; trademarking of 26, 33, 38
Spastic Society 16
"Spaz" 16
special needs 16, 22, 40, 48, 66, 72
stand-up routine of research fails 50–52; control groups are not necessary 51; fibre optics and bubble tubes hold magical healing properties 50; love of multisensory rooms is universal and knows no bounds 51; magic vanishes at the door 51–52; person with additional need represents all people with that need 50; voice of staff is the voice of everyone 51
stereotypic behaviour 72
strategies to enable someone who does not "get it" to "get it" 133–138; develop their view of their role 136–137; feedback 133–134; generate awareness 135–136; teach in a way they learn 134–135; thinking points 140–142; wow space 137–138
Strauss, K. 59, 60

tech fears 106–107
TEDx 21, 126
tents 76–77; improvised 77; numinous 78–79; yurts 77
terms and conditions 15–23; labels 17, 18, 22–23; language 16–23; prejudice 16, 17, 20, 136, 167; understanding 15–16, 22, 23
TES SEN show 88
themes identified from interviews 92–93
thinking points 140–142
thought experiment 127–130
timetabling 102–104
Tingly Productions 138
toughened facilitator 119–120
trigger-happy facilitators 98–100
Turner, Esme 148

umbrellas/brollies 81
understanding 15–16, 22, 23
uninterruptedness of multisensory rooms 111–112
US Department of Education 45
use of multisensory rooms: inaccessibility of rooms due to 96–97; lack of research evidence to support 47–49; research on, within UK 88–114

Us in a Bus 41, 55
UV light 78, 81, 150–151

value of other sensory approaches 74
Verheul, A. 25–30, 33, 36, 37, 39, 42, 43,
    45, 47, 48–49, 53, 80, 94
Verkaik, R. 49, 58, 61
vestibular stimulation 151–153

Ware, J. 124, 133
Waterman, Christine 149–150
water worlds 80–81

wheat from the chaff approach 118–119
White, Katie 132–133
Willetts, D. 59
Williamson, M. 7
Willow's Sensory Services 54
Winterbourne View Scandal 14
withies 78
World Down Syndrome Day 16
wowness of multisensory rooms 112–114
wow space 137–138

yurts 77

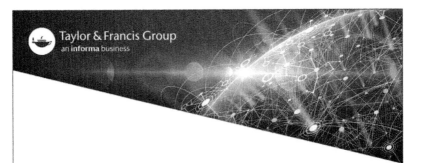